MARGARET DICKINSON AND SARAH STREET

CINEMA AND STATE

The Film Industry and the Government 1927–84

BFI Publishing

First published in 1985 by the British Film Institute
127 Charing Cross Road
London WC2H 0EA

British Library Cataloguing in Publication Data

Dickinson, Margaret
   Cinema and State: Film Industry and
   the Government 1927–84.
   1. Moving-picture industry—government policy—
   Great Britain—History
   I. Title   II. Street, Sarah
   384'.8'0941   PN1993.5.G7

ISBN 0 85170 160 4
ISBN 0 85170 161 2 Pbk

Cover design: John Gibbs

Printed in Great Britain by Centurion Print Ltd of Hertford

Contents

Acknowledgments

We would like to acknowledge the following for invaluable help, information and advice during the preparation of this book: Ed Buscombe, George Elvin, D. J. Wenden, David Wilson, Lord Wilson of Rievaulx, the staffs of the BFI Library Services, the Public Record Office and John Keyworth at the Bank of England's archive. Special thanks to Simon Hartog for his crucial role in the early stages of this project and subsequent interest and encouragement. The cartoon by Sir David Low on p. 185 is reproduced by kind permission of *The Standard*. Acknowledgment is made to Syndication International, IPC, for the cartoons which originally appeared in *Kinematograph Weekly*; to Vicky Publications for the cartoons which originally appeared in *World Film News*; and to Patricia Perilli for permission to reproduce extracts from her 'Statistical Survey of the British Cinema Industry' which appeared in *British Cinema History*, edited by James Curran and Vincent Porter (Weidenfeld and Nicolson, 1983).

Introduction

The cinematograph film is today one of the most widely used means for the amusement of the public at large. It is also undoubtedly a most important factor in the education of all classes of the community, in the spread of national culture and in presenting ideas and customs to the world. Its potentialities moreover in shaping the ideas of the very large numbers to whom it appeals are almost unlimited. The propaganda value of the film cannot be over-emphasised.[1]

The British Film Business is Big Business. Every week over twenty million admission tickets are sold in British cinemas, enabling the American renters, who control the bulk of the films shown, to send back to their parent company in the United States between six and eight million pounds every year.[2]

During the first half of the twentieth century the cinema in Britain enjoyed an unrivalled place in popular entertainment. In 1934 there were 963 million admissions to 4,305 cinemas.[3] It is hardly surprising that this success was accompanied by political controversy. In the 1920s a sharp division of opinion became apparent between those who stressed the potential influence of the cinema over its vast audience, arguing that the development of such a medium required public supervision, and those who held that it should be regarded primarily as a business, and that there were no special grounds for official intervention. The issue was complicated by the fact that the overwhelming majority of films screened in Britain were made in Hollywood, a state of affairs that had both cultural and commercial implications.

Official interest in the cinema took several different forms, including that of indirect influence over the censorship process. The area of policy explored in this book, however, relates to the economic management and control of the film business. Government attention was initially drawn to the film trade by the effects of Hollywood competition on British producers, and the response was to introduce commercial protection.

The first step towards intervention along these lines was the passage of the Cinematograph Films Act in 1927. This obliged renters (distributors) to acquire and exhibitors to show minimum quotas, or percentages, of

1

British films. The Act was not considered satisfactory in practice because renters were able to exploit loopholes in the regulations in order to fulfil the letter of the law while flouting the spirit. A second Act was passed in 1938 with some modifications, but war broke out before the impact of the changes could be assessed. Soon after the war, film production entered a new phase of crisis that suggested protection alone would not lead to stability. New legislation was passed establishing a specialised finance corporation to provide risk capital for film production. Arrangement was also made for the payment of a form of trade subsidy, known as the Eady Levy, to producers of British films, and this was extended on a statutory basis in 1957. Since then the basic elements of state assistance for the film industry have been the quota, the National Film Finance Corporation and the Levy. The quota was suspended in 1983. The other two forms of aid remain in force at the time of writing, although a government White Paper published in July 1984 proposes that they should be discontinued.

The films legislation was clearly conceived of within the framework of commercial policy. Film production was protected and later subsidised as an industry. The government department responsible for drafting and administering the Acts was the Board of Trade – but government was not entirely consistent in its approach. Protection was introduced at a time when Britain was pursuing a policy of free trade, and to some extent a special case had to be made for assistance to the film industry. Economic arguments were not persuasive since the sector to benefit, film production, played a minor role in the national economy and employed only a few thousand people based in the relatively prosperous South-East. Cultural arguments were therefore invoked to justify the quota, and a few remarks about the cultural importance of film became an almost obligatory element in any preamble to a statement on policy. Since this policy was one of providing indiscriminate assistance to producers of all films defined as 'British', there was great emphasis in the rhetoric on the cultural significance of nationality. Yet the criteria chosen for determining whether a film was 'British' had relatively little to do with cultural characteristics: the main factor was the proportion of labour costs paid to British nationals. The creative team could in fact be American as long as a sufficiently large British labour force was employed on a production.

In practice, little account was taken of the claim that film was an 'educational and cultural medium'. The Board of Trade followed its tradition of seeking advice primarily from within the business and showed no interest in extending its area of influence. There was, however, a series of unsuccessful attempts to persuade the government to set up a more interventionist structure. The Departmental Committee formed in 1936 to examine the workings of the first Films Act strongly recommended the establishment of an independent authority with powers of 'initiative and control'. Since this report the case for a supervisory body of the kind proposed, a Films Commission or a Films Authority, has been frequently restated. Almost every independent report on the film industry has advised that some powers should be exercised by persons from outside the trade.

The case for public control was sometimes formulated in terms of industrial or commercial policy: intervention was needed because the trade was too divided to pursue its own long-term commercial interests, or because it represented American rather than British interests. However, particularly consistent support came from those who thought that a films policy should have some cultural objectives as well. Similarly, state aid was discussed in relation to both industrial and cultural aims, and the character of aid proposed varied with the context – automatic subsidy and commercial loans being appropriate for industry; discriminatory subsidy and grants or non-commercial loans being appropriate for culture.

At the time when the first quota Act was being discussed, film production stood little chance of gaining assistance except as an industry. Interest in the artistic potential of film developed very late in Britain. But even if the cinema had been acclaimed early on as an art form, as it was in Russia and, to some extent, in France, it would not automatically have become eligible for any other form of aid. With the exception of municipal support for art galleries and museums public funding for the arts was minimal in the 1920s. The position was very different twenty years later. During World War Two the principle of subsidising the performing and visual arts gained ground, and the creation of the Arts Council in 1946 provided a formal framework for the provision of state support for the arts. The development of sound broadcasting had also set new precedents for the management of a popular medium. A public corporation, the BBC, had been granted a monopoly in the field of programme-making and, under the guidance of John Reith, its policy was strongly influenced by a concept of public service. As Asa Briggs observed:

> The BBC did not interpret its task as the provision of entertainment alone: to supply entertainment by itself was thought of as the betrayal of a trust. 'Education' in the broadest sense was thought of as an equally important objective. 'I think it will be admitted by all,' Reith wrote in 1924, 'that to have exploited so great a scientific invention for the pursuit of entertainment alone would have been the prostitution of its powers and an insult to the character and intelligence of the people.' There was a sharp divergence at this point with the history of the cinema.[4]

In the 1940s, therefore, the question of whether the cinema should be regarded primarily as culture or as commerce ceased to be academic.

3

The state had evolved structures for dealing with both aspects, and they were quite distinct. Both the Arts Council and the BBC were held up as offering useful models for the development of films policy. The trade, however, organised vigorous opposition to the introduction of any fundamental changes in the nature of industry-government relations, and the government proved unwilling to precipitate a confrontation. The Board of Trade retained responsibility for the cinema, and commercial interests continued to exercise a preponderant influence over the process of decision-making.

The argument about films policy rumbled on for the next forty years, but political interest in the issue diminished after the cinema's popularity was eclipsed by that of television. The public service concept remained a strong influence on broadcasting policy even after the introduction of commercial television, and political debate about the media came to focus on the interpretation of this concept. The position of the film industry seemed of limited relevance to the general public.

The context, however, is again changing. It is arguable whether broadcast television as it now exists will, in the future, retain its special hold over the popular audience. Competition from video, satellite and, above all, cable television may change the pattern of viewing. Current plans for the exploitation of the new media technology envisage a commercial service subject to a relatively weak form of public control. The resulting structures could have more in common with those of the film industry than with those of broadcast television. Thus the history of films policy, as much as that of broadcasting, forms the background to current questions about public policy and the audio-visual media.

Appropriately, there has been a certain revival of interest in political and economic aspects of film history. The work of Rachael Low has made an important contribution by opening up the area of the politics of the film trade, and by stressing the importance of the industry's economic history.[5] James Curran and Vincent Porter have edited a collection of essays dealing with such questions.[6] And in America Tino Balio's work on United Artists shows what can be done when access to the business records of film companies can be obtained.[7]

This study is based on unpublished official documents, concentrating on the years 1925–51, although the Board of Trade's files on the 1927 Films Act were destroyed. We have not attempted to explore the question of how the economics and the power structure of the film industry has affected the character of the films produced: this would be difficult to assess and requires a different approach. Here the emphasis is on policy, in an attempt to explain why and how the legislation came into being and how it influenced the character of the industry at a time when the cinema played an important role in the lives of a very large part of the population.

1   A Quota for the Film Industry?

By 1925 the depressed state of the British industry was causing general concern. Apart from the purely industrial aspect of the matter it was felt that from the point of view of British culture and ideals it was unwise to allow the United States to dominate the cinemas of this country.

R. D. Fennelly, of the Board of Trade's Film Department, minutes of evidence, Committee on Cinematograph Films, 1936.

The Cinematograph Films Act (1927) was the first case of the government intervening to protect the commercial film industry. Its intention was to foster production so that a larger percentage of screen time would be devoted to the exhibition of British films. It did not do this by providing a subsidy for producers, or by ensuring that they received a larger share of box-office receipts, or by levying a high import duty on foreign films, but instead imposed a statutory obligation on renters and exhibitors to acquire and show a minimum 'quota' of British films out of the total number they handled, British and foreign. Up to 1927 the majority of films exhibited in Britain had been American – one estimate calculated that the proportion was as high as 85–90 per cent. In 1914 some 25 per cent of the films shown were British, but by 1923 this percentage had dropped to 10 per cent and by 1925 it was only 5 per cent. In 1924 the total number of British films 'trade shown' (films shown to exhibitors before hiring) was fifty-six. In 1925 only forty-five were shown, and in 1926 the figure had slumped to thirty-seven.[1] It was this state of affairs that the first Films Act aimed to rectify.

The Act provided that in the first year the renters' quota should be 7½ per cent, and the exhibitors' 5 per cent. The renters' quota was higher because exhibitors wanted to be offered an adequate selection of films. Both quotas were to increase by stages to 20 per cent in 1936, and remain at that level until 1938 when the Act expired. A British film was defined

5

as one made by a British subject or company. The definition did not specify that control had to be in British hands, but only that the company had to be constituted in the British Empire and that the majority of the company directors should be British. All studio scenes had to be shot in the Empire, and not less than 75 per cent of the labour costs incurred in a film production, excluding payments for copyright and to one foreign actor, actress or producer, had to be paid to British subjects, or to persons domiciled in the Empire. The 'scenario' – a term never clearly defined, so that the provision became a dead letter – had to be written by a British subject. The Act also regulated booking practices in an attempt to open up more of the home market to British films. The Board of Trade, whose Industries and Manufactures Department was responsible for the film industry, was to register the films, and to consult with an Advisory Committee consisting of trade and independent members.

The Films Act was passed before Britain adopted a major programme of general protective industrial tariffs in 1931. In the late 19th and early 20th centuries a policy of free trade was pursued, even though Britain's share of the world export trade in manufactured goods fell from 35.8 per cent in 1890 to 28.4 per cent by 1900, and in 1921–5 was only 23.8 per cent.[2] The rise of competing industrial economies had meant that Britain gradually lost its traditional role as the 'workshop of the world' to Germany and the United States, who protected their newly developed industries and began to supply markets, especially in the British Empire, previously dominated by British goods. Britain's trade deficit widened as its major export became capital, much of which was not invested in Britain's staple industries or in new technology but exported to Australia, Canada and Latin America. By 1929 the leading export trades were suffering high levels of unemployment, and it was not until the 1930s that the newer growth industries began to expand. Before the First World War manufacturers began to question the free trade policy, but the economic orthodoxy of the Liberal Party and of some sections of the Conservative Party was difficult to challenge.

During the First World War trade was controlled, and afterwards, as foreign competition grew more intense, the pressures increased for a more protectionist policy. Politicians like Neville Chamberlain, Sir Philip Cunliffe-Lister and Leo Amery were all interested in developing Imperial Preference and instituting a general tariff to arrest Britain's industrial decline. The McKenna Duties, introduced in 1915, imposed duties on 'luxury' items, including cinematograph films. Duties on film imports were 1s 3d on blank film, 1d on positive film and 5d on negative film. These rates were not high enough to perturb foreign importers, and in 1923 the Conservative MP Sir Arthur Holbrook suggested a 33⅓ per cent import duty on American films. Like other demands for higher duties in the 1920s it failed, largely because British exhibitors opposed any discouragement of American films since they depended on them to fill their halls and argued that higher duties would increase the price but reduce the number of films offered for hire. In February 1925 a group of producers agreed to press the government for an inquiry into the film industry and suggested a 33⅓ per cent *ad valorem* duty.

The 1919 Finance Act introduced the principle of Imperial Preference for some Empire goods. The first real peacetime protectionist measure was passed in 1920, restricting the importation of dyestuffs, to be followed by the Safeguarding of Industries Act in 1921. This Act protected 'key industries' with a 33⅓ per cent *ad valorem* tariff for goods such as dyestuffs, glassware, scientific instruments and optical goods. In 1925 the Act was extended to include cutlery and lace, and duties were imposed on silk and hops.

The Conservatives lost the 1923 General Election over the protection issue. Philip Snowden, Chancellor of the Exchequer in the first Labour government, refused to renew the McKenna Duties, but once the Conservatives were back in power in 1924 Winston Churchill reimposed them. Therefore, although some precedents had been set for a break with free trade in the 1920s, most imports paid little or no duties: in 1930 protective duties affected only 2–3 per cent of imports. Although the Safeguarding of Industries Act was supposed to protect 'key industries', it did not cover crucial industries such as iron and steel. It is in this context of gradual but limited pressures for protection that the Films Act should be seen. It was a modest form of protection, imposing quotas but not duties. As will be shown later, the Act was linked with the desire of some politicians to abandon free trade; and the interest of Sir Philip Cunliffe-Lister, the President of the Board of Trade, who piloted the Bill through Parliament, and of the Federation of British Industries, the manufacturers' body which had a Film Manufacturers' Committee in 1925 and set up a Film Producers' Group in 1926 to agitate for protection for the film industry, can be explained with reference to these debates on tariff policy.

STATE INTERVENTION IN THE FILM INDUSTRY BEFORE THE QUOTA

The state had previously been involved in regulating the commercial film industry only for reasons of safety, censorship and taxation. The 1909 Cinematograph Films Act was designed to protect audiences from fire hazards. All cinemas exhibiting inflammable films to the public had to acquire a licence from their local authorities. Conditions could be attached, and authorities began to impose regulations on films considered 'unsuitable' on moral grounds. The trade was afraid that hopeless confusion would result if some authorities banned a film while others allowed it to be shown. To resolve this problem, the trade established the British Board of Film Censors (BBFC) in 1912. The Board provided a uniform censorship system, and encouraged local authorities to accept its rulings. In 1920 the Cinematograph Exhibitors' Association (CEA) decided that members could only show films which had obtained a BBFC certificate. The system reduced the number of experimental projects, and encouraged producers to make films acceptable to the censor, or which at least evaded the rules in subtle ways.[3] In theory the BBFC was an autonomous body, but in practice it was susceptible to government interference because its President had to be approved by the Home Office. This gave the government an opportunity to exercise a subtle form of content control, and some films deemed 'controversial', especially for political reasons, were banned. Lord Tyrrell, President of the BBFC, announced to the CEA in 1937: 'We may take pride in observing that there is not a single film showing in London today which deals with any of the burning questions of the day.'[4]

The imprecision of the 1909 Act meant that local authorities, by issuing cinema licences for only six days, could prohibit Sunday opening. Despite rulings that Sunday opening was permitted, provided that the profits went to charity, in 1915 the courts ruled against it. The 1909 Act was deemed to have much wider scope than audience safety, and local authorities could legitimately restrict Sunday opening if they so wished.

Apart from the McKenna Duties, another tax, the Entertainments Tax, affected the cinema. When imposed in 1916, it was bitterly resented by exhibitors, being additional to normal admission prices. The exhibitors formed an Entertainments Tax Abolition League, and conducted many campaigns, with partial success, to have the tax reduced or abolished. Table I opposite shows how remission was granted in 1920 and 1924.[5]

The total yield from the tax was considerable. In 1917 the figure was £3 million. In 1921 it was £11.7 million, and in 1925 £10.2 million. In 1926, after the remission had taken effect, the tax yielded £5.7 million, and by 1928 the amount taken from cinemas averaged £3 million pounds a year or half the total.[6] For the Exchequer, film business was becoming big business.

HOLLYWOOD EXPORTS AND THE 'AMERICANISATION OF THE WORLD'

The 1927 Films Act owed much to a concern about American domination of the cinema screens. Most of the films shown in Britain and the Empire were American, while British production lurched from one crisis to another. The reasons for this were mainly economic.

Before the First World War London, as the centre of international trade, was the world's clearing house for films. Wartime disruptions and the imposition of the McKenna Duties altered this, and Britain never regained its dominance. Negative films, instead of being exported to London for the making and distribution of positive prints, were retained in New York and exported direct to each market. For the first two years

TABLE 1
Entertainments Tax 1916–1924

Year	Seat prices up to	Tax
1916	2d	½d
	2d – 6d	1d
	6d – 2s 6d	2d
	2s 6d – 5s	3d
1920	2d	no tax
	2d – 2½d	½d
	2½d – 4d	1d
	4d – 7d	2d
1924	6d	no tax
	1s 3d	reductions

of the war British production fared quite well, but long-term factors – shortage of capital, poor scripts and rising costs – undermined the industry's ability to withstand American competition. As Rachael Low commented: 'British inferiority, both commercial and artistic, was openly recognised some years before the war, and the myth that the British led the world until 1914 and lost their lead through no fault of their own must be recognised as a convenient excuse.'[7] One crucial factor was the dramatic increase in United States film exports to South America. In 1910 most of Argentina's film imports came from Europe, but by 1917 it was buying 6.5 million metres of American film. In 1915 Argentina imported 1.8 million feet of British films, but in the first six months of 1917 the figure was a mere 181,843 feet:[8] Thereafter South America and Britain became America's most important overseas markets, and both were major targets for the aggressive export strategies of the leading American film companies.

The advantages possessed by the Americans were considerable. Before and during the First World War the structure of the industry was changing. Particularly after the disintegration of the Motion Picture Patents Company in 1918, there was a shift towards vertical integration, as distributors and exhibitors acquired production units. By the late 1920s the five 'majors' were established – MGM, Paramount, Warners, Fox and RKO. These companies amalgamated the three sections of the industry – production, distribution and exhibition – into single concerns. The rationale for this form of economic concentration was simple: the distributors and exhibitors did not have to worry about searching for product, and conversely the producers could be certain that their films were marketed well, would reach the cinemas promptly, and would enable them to accrue profits to finance their next pictures. This encouraged financiers like Kuhn Loeb, Dillon Read and J. P. Morgan to back the 'majors' because the vertically integrated structure reduced the high risk normally associated with film finance.

The implications of the development of the 'majors' in America were serious for Britain. Since these companies were assured of success in their home market, exports were considered a vital and customary source of revenue – films sent abroad were 'dollar-earners'. As Sidney Kent, general manager of the Paramount-Famous-Lasky Corporation, put it in 1927: 'Out of every dollar received, about seventy-five cents still comes out of America and only twenty-five cents out of all the foreign countries combined. . . . Of course, the profit in these pictures is in that last twenty-five per cent.'[9] In the mid-1920s, 65 per cent of America's revenue from exports came from Europe. Table II illustrates the growth of American film exports.[10]

TABLE II

Total t·s film exports (negative and positive) 1913–1926

Year	Total (million feet)				
1913	32m				
1914	32m				
1915	36m				
1916	158m				
1917	128m				
1918	84m				
1919	97m				
1920	188m				
1921	140m				
1922	133m				
1923	146m		*1913*	*1924*	*1925*	*1926*
1924	178m				
1925	235m	*UK*	16m	26m	36m	14m*
1926	223m	*In July 1925 the McKenna Duties were reimposed.			

The Americans possessed a much larger home market than the British. In 1925 there were 20,000 cinemas in the United States, whereas in Britain there were 4,000. Writing in *Kinematograph Weekly*, Simon Rowson calculated that in 1925 twenty million people a week went to the cinema in Britain; by 1929 weekly attendances in America had risen to eighty million. In 1926, 1½ billion dollars (£308 million at the 1926 rate of $4.86 to the pound) was invested in the American film industry, and thirty-five million pounds in the British industry – largely in exhibition, the most profitable sector of the trade. Distributors made profits too, but the producers did not fare so well: of the £35 million, less than £500,000 was invested in production.[11] American producers, because finance was easier to obtain than in Britain, made costly, lavish films. The average return per film in America was £100,000–£120,000 in 1928, but in Britain it was only £7–10,000. These figures say enough about the disparity in economic advantages.[12]

The Americans established renting companies in Britain to ensure their films were distributed effectively. Vitagraph registered a British company as early as 1912, Fox in 1916, and the Famous-Lasky (Paramount) Service in 1919. The leading renters in Britain were American, but before the quota hardly any of them distributed British films. In 1920 Famous-Lasky offered eighty-nine films for hire, only three of them British. The native firms, Stoll and Butchers, offered between them forty-five films for hire that year, and of these thirty-one were British. In 1926 Famous-Lasky offered sixty-four films – none of them British. Stoll and Butchers acquired forty-nine films, but because British production was so weak only seven of the forty-nine were British.[13]

Booking practices exacerbated the situation for British producers. Blind, block and advance booking kept British films off the screens. Renters would seldom offer films for hire singly, but in blocks. To obtain one popular film, an exhibitor would invariably have to accept other films, often of a low standard. These other films had usually not been seen by the exhibitor, and the transaction would be completed months in advance with the result that the cinemas would be fully booked. British producers often had to wait for months to have their films shown after they had been offered for hire. Many went out of business because finance for a subsequent production would seldom be available if the previous film had not yet shown a profit. Exhibitors accepted these practices because they were dependent on American films. In 1926, 625 feature films were released in Britain, and of these 577 were American, twenty-five from Continental Europe and only twenty-three were British.[14] Another American booking practice that encouraged exhibitors to book American rather than British films was 'underselling'. American films could be hired as cheaply as thirty-six shillings a time, whereas the economic rent for a British film in 1927 was about twelve pounds.[15] This excluded British films; and it is clear that producers suffered most from the American stranglehold over the distribution sector.

The defence of overseas markets was taken very seriously by the US film companies. It was undertaken by the Foreign Department of the Motion Picture Producers and Distributors of America (MPPDA), or the Hays Office as it was popularly known. The latter was formed in 1922 after a wave of Hollywood scandals prompted a call for a trade organisation to censor films. The Chairman was Will H. Hays, a Republican who later became Postmaster General in the Harding administration. The Foreign Department, under Major Frederick L. Herron, a former US Military Attaché, was formed to assist the 'majors' secure fair treatment in distributing American films abroad. This organisation had contacts in the US State Department and in the US Department of Commerce. The industry was also well served in its quest for foreign outlets by the Motion Picture Division of the Bureau of Foreign and Domestic Commerce, formed in 1926. This agency claimed that each foot of film exported and exhibited abroad yielded one dollar in foreign purchases of American goods. The work of the Hays Office was instrumental in maintaining Hollywood's dominance abroad, as Will Hays later declared:

> Among most of America's industrial enterprises the 'foreign' or export side is a comparatively minor factor in relation to gross income . . . but not so with motion pictures. Aside from the fact that from 35 to 40 per cent of the industry's income is normally derived from foreign sources, the global ramifications of the screen make foreign relations a vital and integral part of the business.[16]

In 1923 Hays visited Britain, and was reported to have said that the aim of the American film industry was to 'Americanise the world'. In Britain the film industry was in no position to counter the challenge.

THE BRITISH FILM TRADE BEFORE THE QUOTA

Talented British producers and directors – like Michael Balcon, Graham Cutts, Anthony Asquith, H. Bruce Woolfe and Alfred Hitchcock – were few; and before the Films Act, as Table III shows,[17] the production industry was in a state of crisis from 1922 onwards. In the early years of the decade the most important producers were Hepworth, Welsh-Pearson, Stoll and Ideal (the latter two had originally been renting companies, but had soon expanded into production). The structure of the industry was changing, and a trend towards vertical integration, which was to be accelerated by the quota, could be discerned in the mid-1920s with the expansion of circuits. The output of Stoll and Ideal fell, and Hepworth went bankrupt in 1923. Newer firms began to take the place of the older companies – British Instructional, Gaumont, Gainsborough, Wilcox and British International Pictures. Michael Balcon and Graham Cutts established Gainsborough in 1924, and the company went public in 1928 when Gaumont-British, the giant that emerged as a fully integrated company after its reorganisation in 1927, acquired a large holding. The other combine, the Associated British Picture Corporation (ABPC), was evolving in the late 1920s, and John Maxwell's British International Pictures provided the production link (see p. 35).

British producers were represented by several organisations. The Kinematograph Manufacturers' Association (KMA) had been formed in

1906, but the two bodies involved in the quota debates were the British Association of Film Directors (BAFD), formed in 1922, and the Film Producers' Group of the Federation of British Industries (FBI). The latter organisation received most attention from the government, probably because the FBI was an influential association. Before 1933, when the Association of Cine-Technicians (ACT) was formed, labour in the film industry was represented mainly by the National Association of Theatrical Employees (NATE) and the Electrical Trades Union (ETU).

TABLE III
British feature films trade shown in the 1920s

1919	103	1924	56
1920	145	1925	45
1921	136	1926	37
1922	95	1927	45
1923	75	1928	72

The biggest change in the industry during the 1920s was in exhibition. Circuits expanded, and from the middle of the decade there was a cinema-building boom. It was the need to rationalise the sector, and to improve booking terms, which encouraged the formation of circuits. Table IV illustrates their growth in the ten years up to 1926.[18] By 1927, up to £50 million was invested in exhibition. The largest circuit was Provincial Cinematograph Theatres, which was later to be absorbed into the Gaumont-British combine.

TABLE IV
Growth of circuits

Year	Circuits in the UK	No. cinemas in circuits
1917	90	429
1920	157	787
1926	139	856

The exhibitors were represented by the Cinematograph Exhibitors' Association (CEA), formed in 1912. It was a large and powerful body, with many regional branches and a membership by 1928 of 2,882. The CEA conducted vigorous campaigns against Entertainments Tax, which gave it an experience in lobbying MPs that was put to use during the debates on quota. The organisation's other main aim was to reduce rental charges while maintaining the level of film supply. This led to frequent clashes with the Kinematograph Renters' Society (KRS), the other major trade organisation, which had been formed in 1915 and whose membership, numbering forty-eight in 1923, included American as well as British renters. The KRS was by now a powerful body.

By 1925, many people were convinced of the need to revive British production. The problem was how. As the *Kinematograph Weekly* commented in February: 'One and all believe that the British film needs protection, but as to the nature and degree of that protection there are still almost as many opinions as persons.'[19] Debates about methods of rescuing British production were not new. As early as 1917 Sidney Morgan, a film producer, suggested an exhibitors' quota; and in November 1924 he argued for a higher import duty on films. The British National Film League was formed in 1921 to 'encourage the production and exhibition of British made films, to eliminate blind and block booking, to shorten the interval between the trade show of a film and its release and to develop an effective publicity service'.[20] The League was headed by A. C. Bromhead of the Gaumont Company, and F. W. Baker, a renter and leading member of the KRS. In 1924 it arranged a series of 'British film weeks', but these failed dismally. The 'weeks' had originally been planned for 1922, but booking problems and the waning enthusiasm of the exhibitors forced their postponement. The films were poor. Paul Rotha later described the campaign as untimely and

> the worst thing that could have happened. . . . For months the Press told the public how good the British films then in the making were going to be. After all this publicity, with the public hypnotised into readiness to applaud the worst picture in the world because it was British.[21]

The industry began to hope for aid from the government, or at least for an inquiry or Royal Commission to establish the facts. The Conservatives were back in office in November 1924, with Stanley Baldwin as Prime Minister. Protection was a sensitive issue. In his election address Baldwin pledged not to introduce a general tariff, but stated his party's determination 'to safeguard the employment and standard of living of our people in any efficient industry in which they are imperilled by unfair foreign competition, by applying the principle of the Safeguarding of Industries Act or by analogous measures'.[22] In February 1925 the trade press speculated on whether the film industry qualified for protection under the Safeguarding of Industries legislation. The *Morning Post*'s film correspondent wrote a number of articles calling for protective measures, and a meeting of the British Association of Film Directors called for an inquiry. This was reported in the *Morning Post*, a paper read by many Conservative MPs, including Baldwin. However, an investigation was unlikely: a report had just been approved which stipulated that an industry had to be of 'national importance' for the Board of Trade to initiate an inquiry into whether it required 'safeguarding'. And in December 1925 the Chancellor, Winston Churchill, persuaded his

The Westminster Pilgrims

State protection for the film industry? The producers look to Westminster. (*Kinematograph Weekly*, 19 March 1925.)

government colleagues that iron and steel should not be granted an inquiry because this would conflict with Baldwin's election pledge.

Lord Newton raised the question in the House of Lords, asking the government to appoint a Departmental Committee to inquire into the causes of the depression in the film production-industry, and 'to make recommendations as to the best means of re-establishing this industry, having regard to the industrial, commercial, educational and Imperial interests involved'.[23] Newton stressed that the cinema was important for commercial and propaganda purposes; and these two aspects pervaded the subsequent debates. The tenet 'trade follows the film' was frequently mentioned, and it was claimed that audiences watching American films were hypnotised into purchasing items they had seen on the screen. British trade commissioners and American spokesmen provided evidence for this argument – evidence quoted by the British at the Imperial Conference in 1926 and during the Parliamentary debates on the film question. Dr Julius Klein, director of the US Bureau of Foreign and Domestic Commerce, had stressed the importance of film for American exports in a statement to a Congressional Committee in 1926. He said that the increased demand in South America for American clothing 'might be traced directly to the influence of the motion-picture film'.[24] The FBI and the Board of Trade agreed and linked the films question with a 'Buy British' campaign. In September 1926 Sir Philip Cunliffe-Lister, President of the Board of Trade, visited Warrington for a 'Civic Empire' exhibition and a 'shopping week', and declared that he wanted to see every means of propaganda used to increase British trade. A report in *The Times* commented: 'That was one of the reasons why he was so keen to get British films established.'[25]

Newton stated that 90 per cent of the films screened in the Colonies were foreign, mostly of American origin. This was considered a 'denationalising' influence, and the propaganda value of film was recognised: 'Imagine what the effect must be upon millions of our coloured fellow citizens in remote parts of the world who perpetually have American films thrust upon them which frequently present the white man under the most unfavourable conditions.'[26] In this context film was seen as a bond of Empire, and the objection was to American 'cultural invasion'. There was no objection to propaganda in itself, as long as it was the right type. As Lord Newton stated:

> The Colonial market, especially in Australia, is completely domi-nated by American films so that it is almost impossible to show a British film at all. I am told that even when Lord Jellicoe was Governor of New Zealand it was only with the utmost difficulty – I am not even sure that they succeeded – that the Jutland film could be shown. Then there was the film called 'Armageddon', which was produced for the purpose of showing what the Australians had done in the war. I believe it was impossible to find a cinema in Australia which would produce that film because they were all booked up with American films.[27]

As early as 1923 representatives from the Colonies commented on the alarming decline of British production. At the Imperial Educational Conference the Director of Education for Victoria feared that 'the cinematograph . . . might be made the means of the most insidious propaganda. . . . People were being familiarised with ways of thinking and acting and speaking that were not British ways'.[28] The Conservative Party was the first to use film for party political purposes, and the mobile cinema vans, introduced in August 1925, showed Empire and Colonial films from the Dominion offices.[29]

Lord Gainford, speaking for the FBI in the Lords debate, asked for a postponement of any inquiry, since the organisation was studying the films question and had 'not yet come to a definite opinion as to the character of the evidence which they ought, on behalf of the industry, to place before an Inquiry'.[30] Lord Peel, who replied for the government, asked Newton to wait for the results of 'searching investigations' being undertaken by the Board of Trade. These were something of a mystery, and the data Newton quoted in the May debate came from another source. He said there were 4,000 cinemas in Britain, attended by twenty million people a week. Total takings were estimated at thirty million pounds a year, and the yield from Entertainments Tax at about three million pounds a year. These figures were the same as those revealed in a paper given by Simon Rowson in July 1925 at a round-table conference of producers, renters and exhibitors. Rowson was the co-founder of Ideal Films, and became renowned for his statistical work on the cinema. He was later to advise the Board of Trade on films policy, but on this occasion he was not involved, as his comments to the trade press revealed: 'I have the greatest possible admiration for the skill and capacity and efficiency of the officials at the Board of Trade, but not even that great department can be expected to reach definite conclusions on so complex an issue without consultation or conference with members of the trade.'[31] Newton was disappointed with Peel's negative reply, and the debate was concluded.

The FBI had indeed been studying the question. On 6 May it held a conference on British film production, and among those present were Lord Newton, F. Vernon Willey (the FBI's President), Charles Tennyson (the FBI's Deputy Director) and William Borradaile. According to Tennyson it was Borradaile, a former exhibitor who had become the FBI's expert on contracts and company law, who persuaded the FBI to arrange the conference. Tennyson recalled in his autobiography: 'Mr Borradaile came to see me in a more than usual gloomy mood, and said that the time had really come when something must be done to save British film production, and that the FBI must take the lead.'[32] As well as FBI personnel, the conference included educational and Imperial interests, among them the Society of Authors, the Stage Guild, the British Drama League, the National Union of Teachers, the Headmasters' Association, the League of Empire and the Royal Colonial Institute. It was decided to establish a committee to work out a scheme, and on 28 May Tennyson sent a memorandum to Austin Earl at the War Office summarising the position. Trade and Imperial considerations were uppermost:

> At the present moment, cinema audiences in this country and the Dominions are being shown almost entirely American films, depicting American life and ideas. This is actually having a reaction upon the demand for goods in favour of American styles.[33]

Several remedies were discussed, including duties on imports and a Films Bank to extend subsidies to British producers. The FBI later dropped this latter provision, but the memorandum suggested that 'the State might readily undertake this responsibility'. The German

Kontingent method was examined as a possible basis for a British quota scheme. The German model was the most frequently cited example of protection for a film industry at this time, although German production was much stronger to begin with because there had been no great influx of American films during the First World War, and the major companies had much more financial backing than their counterparts in Britain. In 1921 the German film import law stipulated that the maximum scale of film imports should be 15 per cent of the number of German films produced. In 1924 this system was revised; and from January 1925 renters had to handle one German feature for each imported one of equal length – a high renters' quota. The FBI memorandum was doubtful whether the *Kontingent* model should be applied to Britain as it 'might put a fictitious value upon any British film that could be produced, no matter how low a standard'. It was well known that in Germany the Americans financed or acquired cheap films so that they could continue to import their films. In 1928 the Germans abandoned this system, and an import permit was substituted.

One variation considered by the FBI was that for every film imported one British film would have to be exported. The danger here was that it would encourage the Americans to finance British films and effectively put the British industry in American hands. At any event the Films Bank plan was the FBI's main policy recommendation.

Why did the FBI concern itself with the film issue? It had been established in 1916, and received formal recognition as a central organisation for industrialists in 1923. In the 1920s it was dominated by representatives of the staple industries – iron and steel, shipbuilding and engineering – all suffering from intense foreign competition. The FBI's aim was to increase trade, and its interest in film sprang from the medium's power to advertise goods. In 1924 the Gaumont Company distributed a series of FBI-sponsored films, shown among other places at the British Empire exhibition. For the FBI, trade did follow the film: the organisation had a Film Manufacturers' Committee in 1925, and a year later the Film Producers' Group was established on a more formal basis. Charles Tennyson was its first Chairman; other members included Cecil Hepworth, George Pearson, H. Bruce Woolfe and A. C. Bromhead. When the Empire Film Institute was established in 1926, the Vice-President of the FBI, Lord Askwith, was a founder member. He was, as Paul Swann has commented, 'typical of a class that was forced to take an interest in the cinema, the most vulgar of the mass media, on account of the threat posed to their commercial interests by American feature films.'[34]

In the meantime, Churchill had announced that the McKenna Duties were to be reimposed from July, and in June there had been speculation in the press about the likelihood of an inquiry. A letter calling for an inquiry, signed by such eminent patriots from the arts world as Edward

Elgar and Thomas Hardy and by Lord Burnham, who had taken part in the Lords debate, was published in the *Daily Telegraph*. Baldwin finally made a statement in the Commons during a debate on unemployment:

> I think the time has come when the position of that industry in this country should be examined with a view to seeing whether it be not possible, as it is desirable, on national grounds, to see that the larger proportion of the films exhibited in this country are British, having regard . . . to the enormous power which the film is developing for propaganda purposes, and the danger to which we in this country and our Empire subject ourselves if we allow that method of propaganda to be entirely in the hands of foreign countries.[35]

In June a wave of patriotic hysteria was unleashed when James V. Bryson, the agent of Universal's UK subsidiary, the European Motion Picture Company, duped a detachment of the Hampshire Heavy Artillery Territorials into providing a guard of honour, and a band to play 'The British Grenadiers', for a print of *The Phantom of the Opera* that was being transported from Southampton to Wardour Street. The incident was filmed, and in the House the Secretary of State for War, Sir Laming Worthington-Evans, had to explain the 'stunt', assuring members that the film of the event would not be released. Apparently the detachment had no knowledge of the stunt, and thought the film shot was to encourage recruitment:

> No mention was made to them of an American film to be met and escorted, and nothing was said to make them suspect the real purpose for which they were required. The officer commanding the brigade was the more easily persuaded to fall in with the proposal because he was engaged at the time in a recruiting campaign in Southampton, where the first part of the film was to be taken, and further he was informed that London territorials would take part in the march in London.[36]

The Foreign Office was informed, and asked whether it was possible to prevent the film of the incident from being exported. An official wrote of the difficulties:

> It is, of course, deplorable that the Army should have been trapped into making of itself a humorous advertisement for an American motion picture company, but in view of the amount of publicity the affair will already have got in America, the suppression of the film would be to some extent not only a case of shutting the door after the disappearance of the horse, but also of giving fresh advertisement to the American company and to American ingenuity. We should also run the risk of a controversy with Washington.[37]

19

The War Office asked Bryson if officials could see the film shot of the troops. When it was returned he told them to keep it, and later sent the negative to Whitehall to save further embarrassment. The CEA resolved that members should not show *The Phantom of the Opera*, and Carl Laemmle, head of Universal, apologised. The CEA's ban was not lifted until November 1928, in response to a special request from Laemmle. But the incident had provided more fuel for anti-American sentiment.

At the end of July 1925 a deputation representing the FBI and other national organisations saw Philip Cunliffe-Lister, a fierce advocate of protection who had become President of the Board of Trade in 1922, after working on the publicity sub-committee of the Supply and Transport Committee, an organisation whose tasks included strike-breaking. He was also involved in the Safeguarding of Industries Act and the reimposition of the McKenna Duties, and had hopes for a general tariff to arrest Britain's industrial decline. But he was constrained by Baldwin's election pledge. Tennyson said later that his hopes were not high for a Bill for the film industry:

> For Baldwin had only two years before sent the Conservative Party out of office by his unexpected declaration for tariff reform which was now regarded as political dynamite. The result showed how wise we had been to base our claim on cultural grounds, for Sir Philip Cunliffe-Lister seized this point at once and showed himself strongly sympathetic.[38]

This was one of the reasons why the FBI and the Board of Trade stressed the 'prestige' value of the film, although their main concern was with trade. Later Cunliffe-Lister claimed the Films Bill as his personal crusade, but he relied heavily on the trade's advice and the Bill was based on proposals from the FBI and the CEA. At first he wanted the trade to devise a voluntary scheme, and his views on the decision that the Board of Trade should be responsible for the film industry are illuminating:

> British industry was the business of the Board of Trade, and though in the Board of Trade none of us knew much about the film industry, I thought it was up to us to do something about it. . . . Though I had always been what is now called a 'film fan', I knew little about the structure of the industry.[39]

He was convinced that Britain could only regain its place as the most important industrial nation by adopting a general tariff and Imperial Preference. The Board of Trade's basic perspective was that legislation for the film industry, despite all the rhetoric to the contrary, was primarily a commercial matter. In practice, therefore, little attention was paid to cultural objectives, and the Industries and Manufactures Department treated the industry like any other under its authority. Cunliffe-Lister saw the Films Bill as being in the same mould as the Safeguarding of Industries legislation, and was frustrated that he could not go further: 'We reached the paradoxical position that, while we could protect industries of moderate size, the largest industries, even though they were still more in need of protection, must not benefit.'[40] In 1937, when the second Films Bill was being considered, Cunliffe-Lister again admitted, at the CEA Annual Conference, that his main interest in 1927 had been commercial: 'I was the President of the Board of Trade, and it is his job to aid British trade.'[41]

The *Kinematograph Weekly* leaked the full text of the FBI's latest memorandum.[42] An exhibitors' quota, based on showing a certain percentage of British films in relation to the number of foreign films shown, was added to the Films Bank provision. The percentage recommended was one British film in eight for one year, and three in eight for a further three years. The maximum quota was to be 37½ per cent, and topical news films were to be excluded from quota. The Bank was to finance a studio under the Trade Facilities Act by means of a guarantee. It was felt that a 'British Hollywood' was essential to reduce producers' overheads. This would involve establishing a central unit with stocks of scenery, advanced lighting installations and adequate floor space; and would create a nucleus for the exchange of talent and ideas. E. Beddington Behrens, a financier who devised a scheme for Brighton, argued:

> Only by creating a centre, a home for the industrial art of the cinema, will it be possible by study and experiment to try out the economic, aesthetic and technical issues and the social, political and moral values implicit in them. . . . To place the industry on a footing of equality with its foreign competitors we must contribute something of our own. . . . There can be no national tradition of the film until there is an ideological nucleus.[43]

Meanwhile the CEA had also seen Cunliffe-Lister, and in September announced its policy for release-reform. This was that all films should be trade-shown at recognised trade centres, that block-booking should be declared illegal, and that a central studio should be built. A meeting was held representing the whole trade, and Behrens' central studio scheme was formally adopted. It was agreed that the government should be asked to provide a guarantee. Behrens suggested Brighton as the location for the studio after Wembley was rejected on the grounds that foggy weather would make filming difficult. In January 1926 Behrens appeared before the General Purposes Committee of the Brighton Corporation, and was informed that the Council was favourably disposed to his idea, provided the government would assist. At first Cunliffe-Lister was sympathetic, and despite reports in the press early in 1926 that there were no funds available to support the scheme, the government was prepared to assist provided private capital was also forthcoming and that an application for aid was made under the Trade Facilities Act. Later, there were other schemes for a central studio (Ralph Pugh, of British Incorporated Pictures, wanted one established at Wembley in 1927, but could not raise the capital). But for now the idea was not carried through, and the debate began to focus more narrowly on the issues of the quota and release-reform.

The exhibitors' concern about reform of the release system was linked to the 'key theatres' problem. American renters tried to control first-run cinemas in London's West End and in the major cities. Exhibitors could only retaliate by boycotting American films. Early in 1927 the CEA General Council recommended a boycott against the Famous-Lasky Film Service because of its intended purchase of two 'key theatres' in Birmingham. The boycott did not last long, and in the end the Americans were not prevented from acquiring the cinemas. When the affair was settled, J. C. Graham, managing director of Famous-Lasky, agreed that one of the cinemas would be operated by a British exhibitor, while the other was to be used as a 'shop window' rather than as a hall competing with other exhibitors.

A Joint Trade Committee was formed, which appointed a sub-committee to produce a quota scheme, since Cunliffe-Lister wanted to avoid legislation if reform from within was possible. Its report, published in November 1925, suggested a quota of 10 per cent for renters and exhibitors, rising to 25 per cent in three years. The report had originally included a provision that 'If any British film offered is of a low standard of production and entertainment value it can be disallowed for quota purposes'.[44] This was to be decided by an authority, set up by the Board of Trade, including renters' and exhibitors' representatives. Before publication the report was revised, and this provision was altered so that films disqualified for quota because they were poor could be resubmitted to the Board of Trade. If the films had cost a 'reasonable' sum to produce, quota registration would be possible. The report did not expand this suggestion, but it does seem that even with the weaker 'quality clause' some safeguards were considered to avoid possible quota abuses – abuses that became all too frequent after the Act was passed. The *Kinematograph Weekly* drew attention to the fact that the amended report provided a much weaker 'quality clause' than the original: 'It knocks the bottom out of the pretence that there will be any guarantee whatsoever that the films which the British exhibitor will get under the quota will be any better than those which he has received in the past.'[45] Here the 'quickie' was anticipated – cheap, low quality films made or acquired by renters solely for purposes of quota registration.

The trade report, named the 'Ormiston Plan' after the CEA President, provided the safeguard (a similar provision was included in the Act) that exhibitors could be excused from fulfilling the quota system if renters exploited the scarcity value of British films by increasing rentals. This could be avoided by allowing renters to stand out of the system if British films were in short supply or were too expensive. A 'British' film was defined more narrowly than in the eventual Act. The scheme stipulated that the producing company had to be British-controlled and the film shot in a British studio, except for location scenes, and that 75 per cent of salaries and wages (what was later known as 'Form C' in the Films Act), excluding fees paid to the producer and one principal artist, had to be paid to persons living in Britain. The block-booking provisions and central studio plan of the CEA's earlier report were included in the Ormiston Plan.

The CEA General Council approved the report by twenty-two votes to ten. The renters were also said to have supported it, although only a minority of the KRS were present when the report was discussed. Ormiston saw Cunliffe-Lister, who by now had put his faith in a trade-devised scheme, and told his members that Cunliffe-Lister

> explained to me that all his colleagues in the Cabinet are keenly interested in stimulating the production and exhibition of British films, and he hopes the trade will reach agreement amongst themselves upon a scheme. Failing such agreement he will be compelled to take definite action on his own lines.[46]

With each ballot paper sent to CEA members Ormiston included a covering letter stressing this point, but also implying that Cunliffe-Lister would use the FBI's scheme as his draft Bill if the CEA rejected the Ormiston Plan. In a 50 per cent poll the plan was rejected by 679 votes to 609. The *Kinematograph Weekly* blamed the CEA General Council for refusing to allow the plan to be amended a second time. It was decided that the whole problem should be reconsidered, and the FBI resolved to ask Cunliffe-Lister to accept its draft Bill. The trade's failure to produce a plan at the end of 1925 had profound consequences. The interests of the three sections could not be reconciled, and subsequent attempts to reach agreement were unsuccessful.

Early in 1926 the reconstituted Joint Trade Committee tried to agree on a scheme, but yet again this proved impossible. The exhibitors rejected a quota, and the renters would not accept release-reform, even though the London County Council had adopted a report from its Music Hall and Theatre Committee recommending the abolition of block-booking. All that was left was the central studio plan; but the government was unwilling to provide production subsidies, and the trade decided it would only participate financially if there was a quota.

In February the FBI saw Cunliffe-Lister and presented him with another memorandum – an expanded version of its earlier one – again recommending a 12½ per cent quota, but this time excluding the Films Bank plan.

Cunliffe-Lister submitted a memorandum to the Cabinet outlining the options.[47] He was influenced by Lord Ashfield, Chairman of the largest cinema circuit, PCT. Ashfield did not want a statutory quota, and tried to shift attention back to the national studio idea, coupled with a voluntary trade solution to the production problem. It was agreed that Cunliffe-Lister should announce that the trade was to be given a year to decide on a plan, and he assured the Cabinet that 'Lord Ashfield had promised to do what he can to bring the exhibitors into line'. If the trade failed to produce a scheme, the government would legislate. A subsidy for producers was rejected, but the government agreed to legislate against block-booking if the trade could suggest a suitable formula for a Bill. Cunliffe-Lister made his announcement in March. Soon after yet another Joint Trade Committee was formed, which authorised a sub-committee to try to obtain the release-reform legislation; in the meantime the quota was to be reconsidered. It was also agreed that 'reciprocity' talks with the Americans should be opened, in an attempt to persuade them to distribute more British films in the United States. Simon Rowson was especially keen on this idea, and the *Kinematograph Weekly* explained optimistically:

> American concerns have already shown many signs of realising that . . . the distribution of British films in America may be very good business. . . . American distributors are dependent on British exhibitors for the larger proportion of their whole overseas sales. If the British exhibitor puts into practice a policy of dealing preferentially with those American concerns which handle British films in America, it will not be long before every . . . American firm is in that category.[48]

When the talks with the representatives of the American renters in Britain began in April 1926, the Hays Office sent an observer, Colonel Lowry. A detailed plan was formulated, which included the provisions that every American renting firm should take at least one British feature film a year for every twenty-five American films offered for hire in Britain, and that British producers should receive a third of the gross rental receipts from the exhibition of the films in the US and Canada.[49] On the British side there were fears that the Americans would demand too much control over 'British' production in exchange for distribution in America. A discussion of the scheme ended with a resolution reflecting these doubts:

That the Joint Committee recognises that the reciprocity plan submitted by the sub-committee is based on principles that would develop a considerable initial output of good British films, but feels that further consideration should be given to expressed fears and apprehensions in order to discover whether these cannot be removed.[50]

Simon Rowson, on behalf of the Joint Trade Committee, corresponded with the Board of Trade on the subject of 'reciprocity'. Cunliffe-Lister's view was that the main aim of the Committee should be to devise a scheme to ensure that more British films were shown in the home market, but even so he was prepared to consider a plan 'to combine the acquisition and exhibition by American interests of films produced by British producers in this country with American production in this country of films which may be considered British films'.[51] The plan was sent to America for examination, but since there was no formal reply the talks ground to a halt. In July the Committee resolved that 'in the absence of any message from America . . . giving approval in principle to the reciprocity proposals . . . no useful purpose would be served by giving detailed consideration to them at the present time'.[52]

Back in August 1925 Will Hays had shown some enthusiasm for 'reciprocity', at least if it would avert a quota. There had been no real progress, however, and by the end of the year the Bureau of Foreign and Domestic Commerce was more concerned about 'anti-American' outbursts in the British press, especially in the *Daily Mail*. In January 1926 Hugh Butler, the Acting Commercial Attaché, informed Washington that one American expert had assured him a British quota might not, in the end, be wholly disadvantageous to the Americans:

> The American industry, having before it the precedent of the German quota system and its outcome in the past year – namely – the purchase of the control of Ufa by American interests, feels it is most likely that the British situation would develop along similar lines in case a quota was established, in which case the American producers have nothing to fear in as much as they could eventually control British production.[53]

In 1924–5 Ufa, the large German film conglomerate, was in financial difficulties despite the *Kontingent* legislation. It was offered, and accepted, a loan of four million dollars by Paramount and MGM, but the price demanded by the Americans was that Ufa had to put its *Kontingent* certificates and many of its cinemas at their disposal. As the American trade paper *Variety* explained: 'The Deutsche Bank has tired of a yearly deficit and demanded the Ufa be made self-supporting. And so the capitulation to America.'[54]

The Hays Office seems to have miscalculated about the British quota legislation. In April 1927, just after the Films Bill was introduced, C. J. North, head of the newly formed Motion Picture Division of the Bureau of Foreign and Domestic Commerce, wrote to George Canty, a US trade commissioner in Paris:

> The Hays people came in for a certain amount of underground criticism that their representative abroad should have returned to this country just about the time that the film bill was introduced. Of course Herron laughs it off by saying after all there is nothing further which can be done as the situation is out of hand . . . the said representative did not believe that there would be a quota.[55]

The Americans shared in the general confusion over whether there would be a quota in 1926, and so did not intervene directly as they did in 1937–8 just before the renewal of the first Films Act (see p. 94).

During the summer the trade talks had floundered. For a second time, the trade had not been able to agree on a scheme. The Joint Trade Committee produced a report in August announcing its failure. This outlined all the solutions that had been considered, giving reasons for their rejection. No agreement was possible on the quota – the exhibitors were worried about the quality of the films and feared the overall supply might be reduced. The 'reciprocity' scheme failed because the Americans had not replied, and in any case the British had reservations. Plans involving import duties were rejected on the grounds that they would conflict with international trade treaties. Oswald Stoll had consistently argued for a 'reel tax' of one shilling per day for all films shown, to finance British production, but the Committee felt it would fall unfairly on small, less profitable cinemas. The Committee concluded that the trade had not been able to agree on a protective method 'to remove the apprehensions of the . . . exhibitors'.[56]

Cunliffe-Lister stated that no government action would be taken until after the Imperial Conference. Even on the issue of block and blind booking trade agreement was impossible – once the deadlock was announced it had been hoped that the trade might agree on a plan for release-reform. Simon Rowson hoped this would encourage reciprocity because it would increase the exhibitors' bargaining power over the American renters. In July 1926 the CEA held a ballot, and 1,704 members declared they were in favour of, and only 198 opposed, the abolition of blind booking. By September a draft Bill was ready for presentation to the KRS by the CEA, and the latter expected in turn to receive the KRS draft scheme being prepared at the same time. This was based on the idea that voluntary rules were enough to bind all sections of the trade, whereas the CEA wanted its scheme to be a blueprint for legislation. The CEA rejected the KRS plan, declaring it was 'not workable, as neither your society nor this association has effective machinery available in the absence of legislation to make it effective'.[57] In other words, the trade could not trust itself to come to an agreement without statutory force to make it effective. The CEA decided to present its scheme to Cunliffe-Lister anyway, and the FBI produced a draft Bill to be presented to the Imperial Conference. It also issued a 'manifesto' on marketing British films in the Dominions, proposing the formation of a central distribution company, coupled with a quota scheme. As soon as the FBI's draft Bill was published, W. R. Fuller, General Secretary of the CEA, announced that the FBI's 12½ per cent quota was impossible, and that renters should bear the brunt of the quota. Attention then shifted from the trade's internal wranglings to the Imperial Conference.

On 8 April the FBI's Overseas Committee passed a resolution calling on Cunliffe-Lister to put the films question on the agenda of the Imperial Conference due to meet in November:

> The Committee view with great alarm the practical monopoly which has been obtained by foreign film production concerns of the kinema programmes of the British Empire. They consider that this must have a most detrimental effect on British prestige and must be seriously prejudicial to the best interests of the Empire, especially in those parts of the overseas Dominions which contain large coloured populations.[58]

THE EMPIRE MARKETING BOARD

Linked with the heightened awareness ·of the trade and propaganda value of the film expressed by the Conservative Party, the Board of Trade and the FBI was the foundation of the Empire Marketing Board (EMB) in May 1926 'to further the marketing in the UK of Empire products, including home agricultural produce'.[59] There were also more specific political reasons for the Board's foundation. In 1923 Cunliffe-Lister had been chairman of the Imperial Economic Conference, at which it was agreed that some new duties would be introduced as well as preferences on articles already paying tariffs. In all, the programme would have meant a considerable increase in Imperial preferences, but after Baldwin's 1924 election pledge the Conservatives could not implement it in full, as Leo Amery, the Colonial Secretary, remembered:

> When we came into office we were confronted by some loose remarks made by Baldwin in one of his election speeches which were held, by the Cabinet, to preclude even the most modest additional preferences on anything that was edible or potable. I protested as best I could against the idea that a formal agreement between Governments should have to be repudiated simply because of a stray and really

ambiguous phrase in a speech. But the panic complex left by the unlucky 1923 election was still too strong.[60]

As a compromise, reluctantly accepted by Amery, Cunliffe-Lister suggested that one million pounds, the amount of revenue raised by the new duties, should be set aside each year to promote 'the better marketing of Empire produce in this country'.[61] Amery then established the Empire Marketing Board. Under the direction of Stephen Tallents, the Board encouraged scientific research to improve the quality of Empire goods, investigated market conditions, and publicised Empire produce. In the latter field the Board was particularly innovative, especially in its use of film. Tallents recruited Walter Creighton as film officer, and John Grierson to prepare memoranda on film propaganda. Cunliffe-Lister was impressed by his reports, but when it came to the question of the Board producing its own films the Treasury was obstructive. Cunliffe-Lister, despite his part in its foundation, was later ambiguous in his attitude to the EMB. He did little to support its survival when it was threatened by Churchill's Treasury cuts.[62] When Grierson's first film venture for the EMB, *Drifters*, was considered in 1928, its subject – the herring industry – was deliberately chosen by Tallents because the Financial Secretary to the Treasury, Arthur Michael Samuel, had written a book on the topic. Amery recalled: 'At the decisive interview at my office his weighty official objections to the whole fantastic idea of our film project were successfully countered by the judicious suggestion that his personal expert knowledge might be invaluable to us for the particular film.'[63]

With Grierson at its head, the EMB Film Unit attracted talented people: J. D. Davidson, Edgar Anstey, Arthur Elton, Basil Wright and, for a time, Paul Rotha and John Taylor. The American documentary film-maker Robert Flaherty was brought in to shoot *Industrial Britain*. A film library was established in 1931, and by the autumn of 1933 it was distributing 800 films to schools and institutes. Costs rose, however: in 1926 film absorbed £1,217 out of the EMB's total expenditure of £134,804; by 1929 the figure had risen to £17,748 out of £222,361.[64] The films did not do well in commercial cinemas, and the Unit was not able to convert to sound until 1933, when Ideal Films agreed to buy six films to which a soundtrack was added. A report of the Imperial Committee on Economic Consultation and Co-operation recommended that the EMB should be dissolved in 1933 – not because of the performance of the Film Unit, but because of the generally unfavourable economic climate in the early 1930s. Sir Stephen Tallents was appointed as Public Relations Officer of the General Post Office; and when the EMB was disbanded, its Film Unit was transferred to the GPO.

Although a Colonial Film Unit was not established until 1939, there were experiments earlier in the 1930s in the use of film for educational and propaganda purposes in the colonies, for example the Bantu Educational Kinema Experiment which produced films from 1935 to 1937.[65] The Colonial Office also helped produce the influential report that led to the foundation of the British Film Institute (see p. 48). These developments were clearly central to the debates on the protection of the British film industry, whose revival the Colonial Office depended on to counter the 'denationalising' and harmful commercial influences of the American cinema.

(see p. 48)

THE IMPERIAL CONFERENCE, 1926

An Imperial Conference had taken place at irregular intervals three times since 1911. It gave the British government and the Dominions an opportunity to discuss Imperial relations, and the 1926 Conference was held in London. An Economic Sub-Committee was appointed to prepare reports on various problems, including the film issue, for submission to the main gathering in November. The Board of Trade supplied the data and a secret draft quota Bill recommending a $7\frac{1}{2}$ per cent renters' quota, rising to 25 per cent by 1933, and steps to curb booking abuses.

The Economic Sub-Committee's report made no mention of the secret draft Bill, but showed that few British films were exhibited in the Empire. Although many Dominions gave British films tariff concessions or, like Australia and New Zealand, allowed them free entry, this did nothing to increase the number of films exhibited. In Britain the proportion of Empire-produced films to the total imported was 8 per cent in 1925. The figure was 10 per cent in New Zealand; 8 per cent in Australia, and a mere 1 per cent in Canada. The report commented: 'It is a matter of most serious concern that the films shown . . . should be to such an overwhelming extent the product of foreign countries, and that the arrangements for the distribution of such Empire films as are produced should be far from adequate.'[66]

The possible solutions were duly surveyed. A tax on foreign films was rejected because it would conflict with the provisions of many commercial treaties. A reduction in Entertainments Tax for cinemas that showed a minimum number of British films was thought likely to create a demand for similar concessions for other forms of entertainment. One idea was that the specific duty on imported films should be replaced by an *ad valorem* duty levied on the purchase price or rental value of the film. However, most films were not bought by importers and there were difficulties in estimating how much a film would earn. An increase in the existing duty on film imports was rejected because exhibitors were opposed to any measure that might threaten the film supply. The quota was mentioned, but the report did not recommend a definite solution, warning that if a quota was adopted it would have to be ensured that the films would be 'of real and competitive exhibition value'.

After considering the Economic Sub-Committee's report the Imperial Conference agreed that British production had to be revived, but left the lead in protective legislation to be taken by Britain. After much rhetoric and little action it was resolved that:

> The Imperial Conference, recognising that it is of the greatest importance that a larger and increasing proportion of the films exhibited throughout the Empire should be of Empire production, commends the matter and the remedial measures proposed to the consideration of the governments of the various parts of the Empire with a view to such early and effective action to deal with the serious situation as they may severally find possible.[67]

THE FILMS BILL IN PARLIAMENT

In January 1927, Cunliffe-Lister informed the Cabinet that the trade had failed to produce a formula. He had further talks with the trade, and the FBI submitted a final memorandum reiterating its demands. A. C. Bromhead proposed the creation of a private Film Bank, and the press took sides on the quota. *The Times* was generally against it, while the *Daily Telegraph* welcomed the prospect. The *Daily Express* had been full of stories warning of the dangers of 'Americanisation': 'We have several million people, mostly women, who, to all intent and purpose, are temporary American citizens.'[68] However, in 1927 Lord Beaverbrook was against a quota, probably because of his cinema interests in the PCT circuit, and the paper opposed the Bill.

The government's Bill had its first reading in the Commons on 10 March. The quota percentages were 7½ per cent for exhibitors and renters, rising to 25 per cent by 1935–6. Otherwise the Bill was much the same as the FBI's draft Bill and the CEA's proposals to abolish blind and block booking. All films were to be trade shown and delivered within six months of the rental agreement. To qualify as a 'British' film, the film 'maker' had to be a British subject (in the terms of the Bill, 'maker' referred to 'the person by whom the arrangements necessary for the production of the film are undertaken', i.e. what is known today as the 'producer'. The 'producer', in the Bill's terms, was 'the person responsible for the organisation of the scenes to be depicted on the film', i.e. what we now refer to as the 'director'). The company had to be British 'controlled', which was defined as 'a company constituted under the law of some part of the British Empire the majority of the voting power of which is in the hands of persons who are British subjects'. The studio scenes had to be photographed in a studio in the British Empire, and the author of the scenario, or of the original work on which it was based, had to be British. Not less than 75 per cent of the labour costs, exclusive of copyright costs and of the salary of one actor, actress or the producer, had to be paid to British subjects or persons living in the Empire. The Advisory Committee was to be trade-dominated: it was to have eight members from the trade (two film-makers, two renters and four exhibitors) and three independent members, including the chairman. The Act was to be administered by the Board of Trade, a provision welcomed by the exhibitors, who felt it would serve their interests best.

In Parliament the Labour Party opposed the Bill, tending to support the exhibitors' case. One of its MPs, Colonel Harry Day, was himself an exhibitor and argued that the Bill would not improve the quality of British films. The Liberals, as a free trade party, were mostly opposed to the Bill. But with a Conservative majority in the House it was unlikely that the Bill would be defeated. At times the debates were lively. In the debate on the Bill's Second Reading, Ramsay MacDonald for the Labour Party favoured protection for the film industry, but not by the quota method. He was opposed to an Advisory Committee dominated by the trade, and warned that, 'In a Committee like this it is not the interests that you want represented, it is the people who are interested in the cinema industry not merely from the production point of view but from its social and artistic point of view'.[69]

In a letter to the trade press after the debate, MacDonald clarified his views and advocated a subsidy for production coupled with a BBC-type film Commission:

1) The assistance should only be for a time, sufficient to enable British film production to root itself.
2) It should be of a kind to bring pressure to bear upon the producers to give us quality both in subject and technique.
3) The Committee or commission which must be set up under any form of assistance to watch the working of the system must not be one of financial interests mainly, but of what – for want of a better expression – I would call film policy, and must be capable of viewing production from a large national, artistic and entertainment point of view.[70]

It is not clear who advised MacDonald, but his views were similar to those expressed by *The Times*, which argued against a quota and defined the problem in national, rather than trade terms:

There is little prospect of reaching a right solution . . . so long as it is considered wholly or principally from the point of view of those whose object is to multiply the length of British film annually exhibited . . . the enforcing of a quota would not only fail to raise but would actually debase the standard . . . the doubtful advantage to the manufacturing section of the trade would be no compensation whatever for the resultant damage to the public interest.[71]

'The Try-out. How will she go as an Act?' (*Kinematograph Weekly*, 17 March 1927.)

Philip Snowden, for Labour, pointed out other flaws in the Bill. He argued that the provision that 75 per cent of the labour costs must be paid to British subjects did not guarantee that the film would look British, a point also made in *The Times*: 'A foreign star may be engaged at a salary which will be larger than all the other costs of production. 25 per cent of the other expenses may be paid to foreigners.'[72] Another Labour MP, Lt. Com. Kenworthy, thought the Bill failed to get to the root of the problem – lack of finance. Other members accused Cunliffe-Lister of being a tool of the FBI, and of using the film industry legislation as another step towards his goal of a general tariff. Despite these criticisms the Bill was passed on Second Reading by 243 votes to 135.

The Committee stage of the Bill had to deal with over 250 amendments. The main changes involved the quotas, the definition of a British film, and the composition of the Advisory Committee. In the Act as passed, the exhibitors' quota was reduced from 7½ per cent to 5 per cent, and by 1936 both quotas were to be 20 per cent instead of 25 per cent. Exhibitors had pressed for these reductions, arguing that a margin between the exhibitors' and the renters' quota would enable them to exercise an element of choice. Cunliffe-Lister broadened the definition of a British film by dropping the stipulation that the production company had to be British-controlled, proposing instead that the majority of the company's directors had to be British – a disastrous move in the light of subsequent developments. One amendment, which failed, intended to make it statutory for the producer (i.e. the director) to be British as well as the scenario author. The Act was to remain in force for ten years, rather than for twelve years as the amended Bill had proposed; and the 'independent' members of the Advisory Committee were increased to five, one of whom had to be a woman.

The Films Act was given Royal Assent on 1 January 1928. The question now, as a cartoon in *Kinematograph Weekly* pertinently asked, was 'How will she go as an Act?' There had been enough indications in the debates that problems would arise, but little had been done to provide safeguards. Although the Films Act was formulated in a context of heightened official awareness of and concern about the propaganda value of film and its general importance in national life, the mechanism adopted to combat the 'Hollywood invasion' was not really appropriate as a means of establishing a flourishing British film industry which would be independent of American economic and cultural influence. The 1927 Films Act was the cornerstone of the Board of Trade's films policy, but important questions had not been answered. How can a film industry be encouraged to serve the national interest from the perspective of production? What kinds of film reflect the national image?

2 Adjusting to Protection

> Governments, banks, insurance companies, electrical cartels
> and other holders of big capital guide the destiny of the
> motion picture medium rather than the creative artists who
> seek to use it as an outlet for their ideas and imagination.
>
> Paul Rotha, *The Film Till Now*

THE REORGANISED BRITISH FILM INDUSTRY

In the 1920s the outstanding development in the structure of the film
industry was the growth of the circuits. The optimism created by the
prospect of quota legislation accelerated the trend towards vertical
integration. By 1933, two combines dominated the scene. The Gaumont-
British Picture Corporation (GBPC) controlled 287 cinemas, and the
Associated British Picture Corporation (ABPC) had 147 cinemas.[1]

The Gaumont Company was founded in 1898 by A. C. and
R. C. Bromhead as a distribution subsidiary of the French firm Léon
Gaumont. During the First World War, A. C. Bromhead was sent to
Russia by the War Propaganda Bureau to supervise the distribution by
Gaumont-British of propaganda films, such as *Britain Prepared*, which
were shown to troops and civilians. By 1917 Bromhead was in charge of a
special film bureau, which was wound up after the Bolshevik
Revolution.[2] The Bromheads bought out the French interest in the
company in 1922, and started to produce films themselves. In March
1927, when the Films Bill was presented to Parliament, Gaumont-
British was reorganised as a public company with a capital of
£2,500,000. The new company was an amalgamation of concerns,
including the renting firms Ideal and the W. & F. Film Service. It was
backed by Maurice and Isidore Ostrer, financiers who had bought the
Biocolour circuit in 1926, and who had helped finance the Bromhead
brothers' purchase of Gaumont in 1922. The Biocolour circuit added
about twenty-four 'first-run' cinemas to the Gaumont chain, and in 1928
the Denman Picture House and the General Theatre Corporation halls
were acquired. The jewel in the Gaumont crown, however, was the
purchase of the PCT circuit in December 1928. Lord Beaverbrook had
formed the Standard Film Company as a holding company for PCT and
First-National Pathé. Isidore Ostrer paid Beaverbrook two million

pounds for PCT – a huge amount given that Beaverbrook had invested only £400,000 in the company. Another 100 cinemas were added to the growing circuit, making a total of just under 300. GBPC dominated the first-run outlets in London's West End, where it had five 'key theatres', the remainder being controlled by American interests. The production side was strengthened when GBPC bought a substantial interest in Gainsborough, the company founded in 1924 by Michael Balcon.

The other major combine, ABPC, was formed by John Maxwell, a Scottish solicitor. Maxwell entered the film business in 1912 as an exhibitor, and expanded into renting when he became chairman of Wardour Films in 1923. In March 1927 the private company he had formed in 1926, British International Pictures, was refloated as a public company with a capital of one million pounds, taking over the studio and plant of British National Pictures. In November, British International Pictures made a public issue of £350,000, and Wardour Films amalgamated with the new organisation. Maxwell also acquired the distribution company First-National Pathé from Lord Beaverbrook, just after the battle for the control of the PCT circuit had been lost to GBPC. The role of the quota legislation in these mergers was acknowledged by the shrewd and ambitious Maxwell in January 1928:

> Financial support can be secured in a way that was impossible a very few months ago. The City is certainly more inclined to look kindly on the film trade than ever before, and thus a considerable weight that had handicapped us in the past is removed.[3]

In November 1928, Maxwell registered his company, Associated British Cinemas (ABC), as a public concern, with a capital of one million pounds. The new company took control of British International Pictures, and absorbed the Scottish Cinema and Variety Theatres chains. In 1933 the ABPC was formed as a holding company, taking over the entire capital of British International Pictures, British Instructional Films, Wardour Films, Pathé Pictures and ABC.

Vertical integration had not developed before 1927 because British production was not strong enough to supply a large cinema-circuit. As the 1952 PEP report noted, 'There was no British production company with a sufficiently large and stable output to constitute the production end of an integrated group.'[4] PCT had started production in 1913, and as early as 1909 Electric Theatres had tried to create a combine. But these were isolated attempts, and before 1927 there were no British 'majors' in the American sense. A major combine in Britain would probably only have been possible if the production end had been American.

Cinema-building accelerated during the early years of the quota (see Table V). Between 1927 and 1932, 715 new cinemas were built, providing 921,228 seats.[5]

TABLE V
New cinemas in Britain 1927–32

Year	Number of new cinemas	Seats added
1927	100	95,000
1928	70	90,000
1929	171	200,000
1930	195	292,000
1931	100	142,919
1932	79	101,309
TOTAL	715	921,228

In 1930 large, luxurious 'super'-cinemas were built, but in the following years cinemas with a seating capacity of 1,450–2,500 were considered the most successful. Smaller exhibitors suffered from this expansion. The combines were able to obtain the best British films and circumvent the blind and block booking restrictions of the Films Act, because of the close link between the renting and exhibiting sectors in a combine. Also, once sound films became popular double feature programming was introduced to use up supplies of silent films. Percentage terms, instead of the flat-rate rental, were introduced. These changes made exhibitors more dependent on renters to maintain film supply.

Exhibitors feared for a long time that American companies would seek exhibition outlets in Britain. The Americans did not attempt to penetrate that sector before the quota legislation because their domination of the renting sphere ensured that they monopolised the British market. Once the Films Act was passed and the two major British combines began to form, it became more important for the Americans to try to control cinemas. As an American report commented in 1930: 'It is obvious that the only sure way of stabilising American film interests in Great Britain is by the continuance of the acquisition or construction of cinemas, and direct control over the distribution and exhibition of the American films.'[6]

The Fox Film Corporation tried, in 1929, to ensure that its films were properly exhibited in Britain. GBPC needed money to equip its cinemas for sound, and so the Ostrers offered a substantial amount of shares for sale. The purchase of PCT had been costly, and the company was badly in need of extra working capital. Fox, one of the largest of the American 'majors', offered twenty million dollars for the shares. The aim was to secure control of GBPC and its huge chain of cinemas. Gaumont earned less than $500,000 a year; but William Fox, founder and head of the American company, calculated that if he bought the shares the income from Fox films in Britain would increase to about five million dollars a year.[7] As an American report put it:

A quality picture represents a substantial investment in a rapidly wasting asset and the production of such pictures cannot be safely undertaken without a fairly well-assured market. When there are numerous individual theatres or a number of circuits competing for the best product, the producer can be fairly confident of the marketability of first-class pictures, but a monopoly of the exhibition of pictures, which is legally possible in Great Britain, could result in a ruinous boycott against any producer.[8]

Indeed later, in 1936, Fox Films refused to sell the shares to Maxwell, who had bought the Ostrers' 'B' (non-voting) shares in the Metropolis and Bradford Trust Company, the holding company controlling Gaumont-British. The reason was that such a monopoly held by Maxwell would have kept American films out of the Gaumont cinemas. In the long term, though, the Americans need not have worried since the Rank Organisation certainly did not object to showing American films in its cinemas because of its links with the American company, Universal, and because the exhibition end of the business continued to be by far the most lucrative.

Fox wanted to buy into GBPC for another reason. Isidore Ostrer had refused a bid by Western Electric, a subsidiary of the American Telephone and Telegraphic Company, the chief supplier of 'talkie' equipment, to wire the Gaumont cinemas for sound. Fox owed Western Electric fifteen million dollars, and just before the GBPC deal he consulted John E. Otterson, a representative of the Western Electric Company. If the Fox/GB deal went through, Fox promised to make sure the Gaumont cinemas were equipped with Western Electric equipment. This was an attractive proposition for the Telephone Company because their sets cost $25,000 each, and if all the Gaumont cinemas were equipped the sum involved would be about $7,500,000. Upton Sinclair described Fox's meeting with Otterson:

> Otterson said that it was all right, the Telephone Company was behind him; if necessary, the note for $15 million would be renewed. . . . So William Fox bought the Gaumont theatres, paying $6 million, due in six months. Immediately the Telephone Company got its contract to install sound equipment in these theatres, and so everybody was happy.[9]

In the summer of 1929 the press announced that Fox had bought GBPC, and that the Bromhead brothers had resigned. A condition of their resignation was the insertion of a clause into the Gaumont-British Articles disenfranchising every shareholder who was not of British nationality. In effect, although Fox had a majority shareholding in the company, he did not have control, which stayed with the private company controlled by the Ostrers, the Metropolis and Bradford Trust (MBT). This vehicle was recapitalised with 10,000 voting 'A' shares, and one million non-voting 'B' shares in preparation for the Fox/GB deal. In the end the Fox Film Corporation and the Ostrers each had 4,950 'A' shares, and Lord Lee of Fareham held one hundred. Lord Lee was an independent arbitrator between Fox and the Ostrers; his wife was the daughter of the chairman of the Chase National Bank, the group that was trying to wrest the Fox Corporation from William Fox. It was Lord Lee who later decided that control should reside with the Ostrers. Fox held the majority of the 'B' shares, but since these shares held no voting rights the deal was thought to be worthless. As the American report commented later:

> The Fox pictures never got the best playing dates, unreasonably large numbers of its pictures were never played at all . . . they were discriminated against. . . . Practically all, if not all, of the money was advanced by the Fox Film Corporation to the Ostrers, and the Ostrers . . . secured for themselves a position which has enabled them to control GB.[10]

By 1930 Fox's investment in MBT was about nineteen million dollars. When William Fox lost control of his company, a series of lawsuits was instigated by the new chiefs of the Fox Corporation in an attempt to gain control of the British company.

On 22 May 1931, the President of the Board of Trade received a letter from Isidore Ostrer's solicitors informing him that 'Mr Ostrer has . . . come to the conclusion that the danger of a control prejudicial to the public weal could be permanently avoided either by a gift to the Nation of the Ostrer voting shares . . . or by the creation of a special voting trust.'[11] The position was that if either party wanted to sell their 'A' shares the other had to be given first refusal. If the Ostrers did not want the Fox shares they could be offered elsewhere, but the Ostrers could only sell to a buyer approved by the Fox Corporation, provided the latter still held at least 2,451 'A' shares. The only way Isidore Ostrer could dispose of his shares without consulting Fox was by giving them to the state, or to a new trust approved by the state. The Board of Trade rejected this offer on 29 May 1931. An official was suspicious of Ostrer's motives, and confirmed the government's stance on intervention: 'It would be extremely embarrassing for the Government to have, or appear to have, control of the policy of the big cinematograph concerns, and all the more so in view of the Cinematograph Films Act.'[12]

The Fox Film Corporation never gained control of GBPC, and in 1933 Lord Lee's shares passed to the Ostrers. Three years later there was talk of a deal whereby Fox and MGM would buy the Ostrers' shares, but this was never completed. In October 1936 Maxwell bought some of the

Ostrers' shares, but he did not obtain the Fox holding or control of the company. Gaumont-British embarked on an unsuccessful series of 'international' pictures in the 1930s, and after 1936 it distributed through General Film Distributors, before being absorbed into the Rank Empire in 1941.

THE EARLY YEARS OF THE QUOTA

The quota legislation did attract capital to the industry. Many new companies were formed (see Table vi[13]), and by the end of the 1920s the major companies were established: Gaumont-British; British International Pictures; British Instructional; ABC; British Lion; Gainsborough; British and Dominion; and Associated Talking Pictures.

TABLE VI
Film companies formed in UK, 1925–32

Year	Production*	Renting	Exhibition	Miscellaneous**	TOTAL
1925	15	25	110	26	176
1926	21	25	138	26	210
1927	26	17	143	29	215
1928	37	16	94	25	172
1929	59	3	150	58	270
1930	36	4	176	48	264
1931	55	5	174	49	283
1932	46	7	212	38	303
TOTAL	295	102	1,197	299	1,893

*includes a small number of renter-producers
**including equipment

In July 1928, the *Economist* published the results of an investigation into public issues by eleven companies (excluding Gaumont-British and PCT) since March 1927. The capital involved was £2,408,000, of which £1,936,750 was subscribed in cash. Most of this money, the survey revealed, was wasted on untried, speculative ventures whose directors tricked the public into buying their shares during a stock market boom. The study compared par and present values of shares held by the public and by the vendors on 6 July 1928. The public made a loss of £436,365, whereas the vendors made a total profit of £388,897.[14] A similar study, published in April 1929, showed that the situation had worsened. This time the loss to the public was £784,627.[15] The blame was placed squarely on the Films Act:

The late Government cannot evade a share of moral responsibility for the consequences of the flotation of £2,322,200 worth of new securities which are now valued in the market at £613,255. The business of producing films is, by its very nature, speculative, complex and specialised. Unfortunately the Films Act deluded the public into thinking that British films had only to be made, irrespective of quality, to bring in money.[16]

Many of these companies had collapsed by 1931 – in 1930 alone fifty corporations were liquidated. For example, Whitehall Films, formed in November 1927 with support from some Conservative MPs, collapsed in 1929. A combination of factors sealed the fate of such companies: the costs required to buy sound recording and reproducing equipment; general mismanagement and inexperience; and the emergence of the major combines. Even then, the *Economist* was doubtful about the quality of British films:

> Most of the 'bubble' promotions have disappeared or no longer count – the advent of the 'talkies' gave them their *coup de grâce* – and the few survivors, together with the pre-Act companies, namely Gaumont-British and BIP and a few fleeting private enterprises, are now beginning to show results of quality, even if the quality of British films has not yet reached the level of the best American productions.[17]

Much of the early debate on the Films Act was concerned with the omission of a quality clause – the major issue to be discussed by the Moyne Committee in 1936 (see pp. 66–69). It was claimed that because a film did not have to reach a minimum standard of cost or quality to obtain quota registration, American renters made or acquired poor, cheap British films, 'quota quickies', to comply with the law. When American renters showed films to the trade for hire, hardly any British films were offered as first features.

A Liberal MP, Geoffrey le Mander, tried unsuccessfully to introduce an amending Bill in 1930. He wanted the quota to be raised in stages to 50 per cent by 1934, and a minimum cost test for quota films of £12,000 to be introduced. He also proposed that not less than 75 per cent of a film should be produced wholly in Britain, but that the clause in the Act stipulating that 75 per cent of the labour costs must be paid to British personnel be dropped because 'If that requirement were in force in the US, it would destroy and ruin the American film industry. It so happens that many of the great stars who have to be employed in order to make big successes are not by any means all British.'[18] 'Quota quickies' hardly enhanced the reputation of British films, but many British directors and technicians gained valuable experience working on them (Korda, Balcon and Brunel, for example). Brunel produced 'quickies' for Fox-British, and wrote later that the cost of production was as low as £1 a foot, but:

For most British film-makers it was this or nothing. Many experienced and promising directors, cameramen, editors and artists fell by the way, and were relegated to obscurity or went out of the industry. . . . Gradually there was evolved a technique of production which avoided finesse, risky experiment and subtle touches; treatments were straightforward and simplified; many technicians and artists got continuity of employment for the first time and became expert performers in their various fields, a number of them graduating into big production.[19]

Even so, Brunel realised the limitations of this type of production when he described the making of *The Prison Breaker*, a bad 'quickie' that gave James Mason his first major role:

The so-called finished film was full of those blemishes which a patient editor can whittle out. . . . In our case our editor was additionally handicapped by our contract, as for every foot cut out that brought the total footage below the guaranteed total of 6,000′, £1 was charged against us. To have cut from the film, say five minutes, might have made it an acceptable little film of 64 minutes running time, instead of a rather terrible film lasting 69 minutes – but such a cut would have eliminated most of the producer's profits. This was one of the worst features of quickie contracts.[20]

Total British film production, including 'quickies', increased considerably. The Board of Trade figures show that whereas in 1929 128 long British films were registered for renters' quota, by 1935 the figure had risen to 189. The British share of the home market increased, as shown by the American reports on the European film industries (see Table VII), at a time when the US industry was hit by the Depression and the effects of the changeover to sound.[21]

The major producers maintained the highest output, especially British International Pictures. The American report for 1932 stated: 'The trade in Great Britain continued to make rapid strides; its production rose to a point within reach of the world leaders, while local conditions probably surpassed those of any other country.'[22] Exhibitors consistently exceeded their quota requirements, despite protestations to the Moyne Committee that their percentages should be reduced. When the statutory exhibitors' quota was 7½ per cent in 1929, the percentage actually shown was 17.8 per cent, and when the quota was 15 per cent in 1935 exhibitors showed 25.5 per cent.[23] Even so, there is no doubt that the large circuits with production affiliates inflated these figures, and many independent exhibitors found it hard to obtain British films other than 'quickies'. Local release conditions were also crucial, as was revealed in the evidence given to the Moyne Committee (see p. 68). Not

TABLE VII
US and UK share of British domestic film market

Year	Total features shown in UK	No. US films shown	US % of market	UK % of market
1926	742	620	83.5	4.8
1927	892	723	81.0	4.4
1928	778	558	71.7	12.2
1929	663	495	74.6	13.1
1930	747	519	69.5	19.0
1931	647	470	72.6	21.5
1932	641	449	70.0	24.0

all British films were bad in the early years of the quota, but most of the 'quickies' were best forgotten.

THE 'TALKIES'

It is clear that some of the 'quota companies' went under because of the coming of sound. The average cost of a silent film production was £5–12,000, whereas a 'talkie' cost £12–20,000. Hitchcock's *Blackmail* cost £24,000 to make, and many of the new companies did not have the capital to produce on that scale. On top of that the sound recording equipment was expensive, as was the apparatus required to wire cinemas for sound. The quota helped the larger companies adjust to sound, but could not save the 'bubble' promotions mentioned earlier. Britain was the first European country to convert its cinemas: 22 per cent of UK exhibitors had wired by 1929, and by 1930 the figure had risen to 63 per cent.[24] 980 cinemas had converted in 1929, but by the end of 1930 as many as 3,151 were wired.[25] Table VIII illustrates how quickly the 'talkies' superseded silent films at the end of the 1920s.[26] The proportion of British films to the total number of films registered rose from 14.7 per cent in 1930 to 16.7 per cent in 1931. The average weekly length of silent films registered in 1931 showed a sharp decrease compared with the 1930 figures, while the proportion of 'talkies' rose considerably.

Table IX on page 44 illustrates how the major towns wired first, and how the cinema building boom was concentrated in the south and in the major northern towns.[27]

Although the American film industry was hit by the Depression, this did not prevent two American companies, Western Electric and the Radio Corporation of America (RCA), from supplying most British cinemas and studios with sound apparatus. There were British manufacturers of sound systems (for example, British Acoustic, De Forest Phonofilm and British-Thompson-Houston), but at an early stage the Americans more or less cornered the market. Both British

TABLE VIII

Average weekly length of films registered in the UK, 1928-31

| Year | SILENT | | | SYNCHRONISED | | | TOTAL | | |
	Weekly average total (feet)	% British to total		Total (feet)	% British to total		Total	% British to total	
1928	112,532	13.6		nil	nil		112,532	13.6	
1929	72,065	14.9		61,482	7.5		133,547	11.5	
1930	44,752	15.0		96,074	14.5		140,826	14.7	
1931	7,701	15.3		97,084	16.8		104,785	16.7	

TABLE IX
Regional divisions: Number of cinemas wired and silent: New houses built 1930

Region	Wired	Silent	New cinemas, 1930
Nth. Scotland	145	195	8
Sth. Scotland	172	183	17
Newcastle	242	157	14
Leeds	345	173	13
Manchester	298	174	8
Liverpool	226	124	18
Nottingham	179	105	8
Birmingham	206	124	20
Wales	206	128	6
West England	163	149	21
London and suburbs	385	98	26
Outer London counties	465	247	34
Ireland	119	158	2
TOTAL	3,151	2,015	195

International Pictures (BIP) and ABC used the RCA Photophone process, and Oswald Stoll equipped his cinemas with Western Electric apparatus. British Sound Film Productions, a subsidiary of British Talking Pictures, used the De Forest Phonofilm system; but although Gaumont-British had developed the British Acoustic apparatus, it also used Western Electric. An American report noted: 'This has led to an outcry against American companies as it is feared that they will get a stranglehold on all of the best cinema theatres in England before the British talking film industry can develop to a point where it can compete.'[28]

American firms insisted that their films must be used only in conjunction with Western Electric apparatus, claiming that this gave the best reproduction. There were questions in Parliament in 1929 about the American monopoly over sound equipment, but the Board of Trade did nothing to ensure that more British systems were developed and used. In the spring of 1929 the CEA and the FBI protested, and asked Western Electric to agree that 'films produced under your licence may be projected and reproduced upon apparatus other than that supplied by your company'.[29] On 24 April representatives of the CEA and the FBI attended two performances of the same film, one using American equipment, the other British. There was no appreciable difference in the quality of reproduction, and it was pointed out that British sets were much cheaper. It cost £5,000 for a single American installation, whereas the British set cost only £1,000–1,500. On the other hand, the Americans claimed their sets were popular because the initial agreement usually included servicing, unlike the British systems. In June, United Artists,

MGM and Paramount agreed to the running of their sound films on British 'talkie' equipment, and this forced Western Electric to drop its prices.[30] However, the exhibitors pointed out that in their anxiety to acquire apparatus they had been exploited by the Americans:

> The best talking set that we had the opportunity of securing was the Western Electric and the RCA. . . . The British sets were then indifferent. . . . When the talking phase took place there was a rush on the part of the exhibitor to get a talking set, and many of us signed these documents without thinking or realising what we were signing. . . . A service charge which we regard as excessive is still being imposed upon us.[31]

By mid-1929 American apparatus accounted for over half the installations.[32] In December 1931 about 4,000 cinemas in Britain were wired for sound, and the five main installation companies – RCA, Western Electric, British-Thompson-Houston, British Talking Pictures and British Acoustic – supplied 3,103 of them. The two American systems accounted for 48 per cent of the total installations. The British companies did recover ground in 1932. 233 cinemas were wired, of which about forty used American equipment, the rest being supplied mainly by British Acoustic, Morrison's and British Talking Pictures.[33]

At that time the only European country to develop sound equipment that seriously rivalled the American apparatus was Germany. The cartel Tobis-Klangfilm (TK), established in 1929, claimed the sole right to sound patents in Germany. The American companies retaliated by boycotting the German market, but this move failed when TK obtained a court injunction against the use of American equipment and managed to get the support of the German government. TK often helped foreign countries wanting to use equipment that was not American, and in November 1929 a large sound-film company was formed – Associated Sound Film Industries – which amalgamated the patent interests of TK and British Talking Pictures. There was also a series of international agreements between the Americans and TK, but these led to numerous disputes and did not work effectively. Although TK supplied all German cinemas and studios with its equipment, even that bastion against American domination was not totally independent, since the American RCA had a holding in the company.

How far did the quota ease the adjustment to sound? The Americans thought it was the coming of sound, more than the quota, that rescued the British film industry. They thought particular types of film were more suited to British audiences, especially comedy-farces. One study in 1931 revealed that a higher proportion of farces and murder mysteries made by British companies were shown in Britain than similar American films. The report went on to say: 'The farces were among the most successful of British pictures, while most of the American were relatively unsuccessful. . . . Farce is a form of humor more appreciated on its native heath than elsewhere.'[34] American Westerns and dramas were still very popular, but clearly sound gave British producers the opportunity to develop certain types of film that audiences found more acceptable than has been supposed.[35]

The quota helped in the process of adjustment to sound because the influx of capital it encouraged enabled the larger companies, and even some of the new companies that survived, to equip their cinemas and studios for sound. This required a considerable capital outlay, and it is doubtful whether the industry, in its moribund state before the quota, could have attracted the finance necessary for the changeover.

The Board of Trade continued to shun the idea of a films policy in addition to the quota legislation. After the collapse of the 'bubble' promotions in 1929–30, the City was far less willing to invest in the film industry, although it is true that the existence of a quota enabled the larger companies to attract support. The Liberal MP Geoffrey le Mander saw the 'talkies' as 'a unique opportunity for building up on a permanent basis the multi-lingual film industry. . . . The Americans have to come to Europe now to get into close touch with the foreign artists whom they must have for speaking purposes. Paris is a possible centre, but London is a far better centre'.[36] In March 1930, the Board of Trade was asked by Sir Frederick Maurice, chairman of the Committee on Adult Education, to advise on whether the Lord Privy Seal should write a letter, which could be presented to potential financial backers, expressing his approval of the establishment in Britain of a centre for the production of International Talking Pictures. The scheme had been proposed by Sir Gordon Craig, of New Era Films, a company associated with the EMB's Film Unit, who had told Maurice that 'the City is generally prejudiced against the British film industry but the Midland Bank are prepared to underwrite the scheme if the Government would give the kind of encouragement involved.'[37] The idea was that an 'encouraging letter' would be written, not mentioning the specific scheme, but merely to serve as an inducement for the public to participate when the company issued an appeal for £2½ million. The Board of Trade's reply was negative, showing that it regarded film production as a risky business:

It may well be sound policy when making pictures for an English-speaking market, at the same time to make versions in other languages, and this course is being adopted by some of the established film production concerns in this country. But to set up a huge studio and embark upon the production of a large number of films annually in this country is quite another matter. Even leaving the US out of account, the English-speaking market is more important than any other. The enterprise could hardly be a success unless the English

46

versions succeeded in competing in the home market with American producers, and it is very much to be doubted whether the sudden throwing upon the market by a new organisation of a greatly increased number of British films would be good either for the new organisation or for the British industry in general. . . . In any case, the enterprise is bound to be a speculative one. Neither the trade nor the public have yet forgotten the heavy losses sustained by investment in various new film-production companies about the time of the passing of the Films Act, and the Government would expose themselves to criticism for which there might be a good deal of justification if they attempted to encourage the now less willing public to repeat the experiment.[38]

Thus one plan to replace a proportion of American with British and European films was dashed.

'THE FILM IN NATIONAL LIFE' AND THE BIRTH OF THE BRITISH FILM INSTITUTE

It soon became clear that the Board of Trade thought little of the educational and cultural significance of film, and when the British Film Institute was founded no direct part was played by the Board. The Films Act did nothing to improve quality. Short films could only obtain registration for quota if they could prove 'special exhibition value', and this was defined in purely commercial terms. 'Quickies' were widely criticised, and it was clear that the quota legislation needed amendment long before the Moyne Committee reviewed its progress in 1936.

There was a growing interest in the 'art of the film'. One of the most important groups to promote the intellectual respectability of film was the Film Society, formed in 1925. Its founders included Adrian Brunel and Ivor Montagu, and the group specialised in importing foreign films normally shunned by exhibitors as too 'highbrow'. Russian films like *Battleship Potemkin*, *Mother* and *End of St. Petersburg* were shown, as well as Erich von Stroheim's *Greed*, Murnau's *Nosferatu* and Grierson's *Drifters*.

Social surveys drew attention to the popularity of the cinema. The *New Survey of London Life and Labour* had a low opinion of most films of the time:

> The cultural and artistic value of the majority of them leaves much to be desired. . . . It is impossible to rest content with the present standard of achievement and it is to be hoped that the new invention of the 'talkie' will not divert attention from the film, as a branch of dramatic art and a means of healthy and rational amusement.[39]

There had been several inquiries into the cinema and education – for example, the Report of the National Council of Public Morals in 1917 –

and the subject had been discussed at the Imperial Conference in 1923. In 1930 the Colonial Films Committee, appointed by L. S. Amery, the Colonial Secretary, reported on the situation in the Dominions with special reference to questions of education, culture and censorship. Among its recommendations was a proposal that legislation should be introduced to increase the number of cultural films shown in the Empire. Hesketh Bell, the Governor of Mauritius, stressed the value of films in educationalist/Imperialist terms, claiming that they

> should aim at the gradual improvement of native character and customs and should especially show the progress that has been made by natives of Africa who have been transferred to other parts of the world, such as the West Indies and Mauritius, where they have been beneficially affected by contact with a higher race.[40]

It was another report, however, published in June 1932 and entitled *The Film in National-Life*, which recommended the establishment of a National Film Institute for Britain. This was the work of the Commission on Educational and Cultural Films, an unofficial body that included representatives from government departments, set up in December 1929 by John W. Brown, the secretary of the Institute of Adult Education, and R. S. Lambert, editor of the *Listener*. The Commission's report was largely the work of Alan Cameron, then Director of Education for the City of Oxford and later a member of the Moyne Committee. Its central recommendation was that a Film Institute should be established, financed in part by public funds and incorporated by Royal Charter.

> A National Film Institute could help to educate an informed public. An informed and critical public would applaud and encourage constructive British film production, and critical appreciation does more to stimulate healthy growth than the most elaborate quota legislation.[41]

The proposed Institute was to have a Board of seven Governors, appointed by the government. Their term of office was to be for five years and renewable, and the governing body was to set up an Advisory Council

> including representatives of learned and scientific societies, educational associations and educational authorities, and of the film industry, together with persons nominated by Government Departments, or individually co-opted, and representatives of the self-governing Dominions and of India appointed by the Governments concerned.[42]

Before the Report was published, the key questions were how the Institute was to be financed and which government department should administer the fund. R. S. Lambert claimed that he devised an ingenious solution to the financial question. At the time the government intended to permit cinema showings on Sundays, provided that a certain proportion of the takings went into a fund for charity. Lambert thought part of the money accumulated in the fund could be used to finance the Institute. When the Sunday Entertainments Bill had its second reading in the Commons, John Buchan, the author, who was director of the British Instructional Film Company and had been director of the wartime Department of Information, proposed that a small proportion of the profits from Sunday showings 'should go to the assistance and development of British films'.[43] Herbert Samuel, the Home Secretary, claimed to have made a similar proposal to Buchan in 1931 before the original Sunday Performances (Regulations) Bill had had to be dropped when the Labour government fell. In Parliament, Buchan outlined the proposed Institute's functions:

> A school for the study of technique and the interchange of ideas . . . help improve public taste . . . advise teachers and educational authorities about the educational possibilities of the film . . . advise Government departments as to the use of films . . . advise about the distribution of films throughout the Empire . . . it would do a great deal to secure the development of the great assets for film production which this country and the Empire possess.[44]

Oliver Stanley, then Under Secretary of State for the Home Office, approved; and it was decided that Buchan's proposal would be considered during the Committee stage of the Bill.

In June, Herbert Samuel wrote to the Lord President of the Council, Stanley Baldwin, about the financial question:

> It would be impossible for Parliament to promise this money to the proposed Film Institute before it is actually established and before the soundness of its policy can be ascertained. Moreover, it would be impossible to justify a subsidy to this one institute to the exclusion of other organisations which may be established to do similar work. . . . The best solution . . . lies in the direction of establishing a central fund under the control of some member of the Government who should have discretion to decide the manner in which the money is to be used.[45]

The question now was which 'member of the government'? Samuel rejected the Home Office because it was too associated in the public mind with censorship. He thought the Board of Education was too narrowly concerned with education and would not want to take responsibility for a body intended to have wider functions. The Board of Trade, because of its commercial associations, was not even mentioned. Instead, Samuel decided that the most appropriate administering body was the Privy Council Office, and Baldwin accepted this suggestion on 15 June 1932.

The Film in National Life report was published on 10 June, and received an enthusiastic reception from the *Daily Telegraph*, the *New Statesman and Nation*, the *Spectator* and *The Times*. The latter thought the Institute would 'provide a rallying point for the expression of that kind of opinion which believes in the yet unrealised possibilities of the film, and wishes to give confidence and backing to those who are trying to introduce a sense of responsibility and dignity into film programmes'.[46] The trade did not agree, especially the renters and exhibitors, although two members of the FBI's Film Group signed the report. The *Morning Post* and the *Evening Standard* were hostile, the latter providing an outlet for the views of the Reverend Sir James Marchant, who was connected with Visual Education Ltd, and was involved, together with Oswald Stoll, in a scheme to set up a 'People's Cinema University' in London. Marchant had been Chairman of the 1917 Commission of Enquiry set up by the National Council of Public Morals, and edited subsequent reports entitled *The Cinema in Education*. His plans for capturing the market for educational films included the formation of a 'Royal Institute' – a trade-supported body with an educational section to be headed by Simon Rowson.[47]

When Buchan's amendment was debated in Standing Committee, there was so much opposition, particularly from the exhibitors' representative, Tom Ormiston, that the clause had to be left to the decision of a free vote of the House during the Report stage of the Bill. It was carried after the debate by 186 votes to 168 on 29 June. In the Lords the Archbishop of Canterbury expressed doubts about the Institute, and had to be reassured that the money in the Fund would be sensibly used. There was a link between the Archbishop's scepticism and Marchant's opposition. At the first meeting of the BFI's Advisory Council in February 1934, Tom Ormiston revealed that Marchant had an application for a grant before the Privy Council in the name of an organisation called the 'Christian Cinema Council', which was said to be connected with the Archbishop of Canterbury.[48] In the end the clause was accepted, and the Sunday Entertainments Bill received Royal Assent on 13 July 1932.

Once the trade realised that the Film Institute was a *fait accompli*, it launched a campaign to make the organisation innocuous. Any body that threatened the trade's control over exhibition was resented, a factor taken into account later when the Moyne Committee suggested an independent Films Commission to regulate the industry.

In August 1932, Simon Rowson wrote a letter to *The Times* outlining the trade's new strategy. He accepted the need to make provision for the 'cultural film', but argued that an Institute must 'enlist a large measure of co-operation from the trade itself. Indeed, I think the best of all forms of organization is one which left the greater part of the control to the trade.'[49] John W. Brown and Alan Cameron responded for the Commission:

> The film Institute will have to be in a position of undisputable commercial disinterestedness. And we therefore believe that the film trade will show wisdom and foresight if it does not try to secure 'control' of the new organization, but rather takes the opportunity of putting its practical experience and technical skill at the service of the Institute.[50]

In the end Rowson's argument was successful. When the Institute's constitution was discussed, the trade managed to ensure that the original *Film in National Life* proposals were revised. By the summer of 1933 the negotiations with the Commission were over, and the BFI was founded in September to 'encourage the use and development of the cinematograph as a means of entertainment and instruction'. The Certificate of Incorporation was received from the Board of Trade under the Companies Act, 1929, and the Privy Council decided to grant £5,000 to the new organisation for its first year.

In January 1934 Walter Ashley, a journalist, published a book addressed to Stanley Baldwin, entitled *The Cinema and the Public*. Later Tom Ormiston claimed that James Marchant had written it, since it was a bitter indictment of the setting up of the BFI. Ashley probably was the author, particularly since the book was highly critical of the trade, although Marchant made a financial contribution towards its publication. Ashley lamented 'that so fine an opportunity of building up a really independent and representative organization, which might have proved of real value . . . has thus been completely missed.'[51] His book showed how the Commission's original proposals differed from the Institute's final constitution. There were, he argued, telling additions to make sure that the trade dominated the Institute: for example, 'The Institute shall neither seek to control nor attempt to interfere with purely trade matters in the film industry. . . . The Institute shall neither seek to control nor attempt to interfere with the censorship of films for public entertainment.'[52] The Commission had recommended seven Governors to be appointed by the government, but in the event the BFI was constituted as a private organisation with nine Governors and an independent Chairman. The trade appointed three Governors: Tom Ormiston of the CEA, Sam Eckman of MGM (later replaced by F. W. Baker) and C. M. Woolf (proposed by the FBI instead of H. Bruce Woolfe, who was thought to be too sympathetic to the Commission's original aims). These Governors could stay in office as long as the trade wished, unlike the three Governors representing the 'public interest', who had to retire annually. The Commission also made three nominations: Sir Charles Cleland, Alan Cameron and R. S. Lambert. The 'public interest' representatives were chosen by the other six Governors, and for the first year they were John Buchan, Lady Levita and John Lawson MP. The BFI's first Chairman was the Duke of Sutherland; J. W. Brown was appointed General Manager. Publication of the journal *Sight and Sound* was taken over by the Institute from the Institute of Adult Education, and the BFI's first *Monthly Film Bulletin* appeared in February 1934. A year later the National Film Library (later to be called the National Film Archive) was founded; and throughout the 1930s the Institute's links with film societies across the country were extended. By November 1936 the BFI's membership was 755.

From the beginning the trade had been in a position to influence matters, but the opportunity had been missed. As R. S. Lambert later commented, the BFI was 'debarred by its Constitution from touching questions of censorship, interfering with trade interests, or undertaking trade operations itself, nor had the funds to subsidise others to do so.'[53] Predictably, the Board of Trade's view of Ashley's book was dismissive:

Mr Ashley thinks that there ought to be a body looking after films which would exercise authority comparable to that of the BBC. How it would work and by what means it would obtain such power on an income of £5,000 a year . . . he does not explain. I do not think this book should be taken very seriously.[54]

In this instance the trade had aborted the idea of an independent regulatory body for the industry. The issue was not dead, however. The same controversies arose when the Moyne Committee – an independent Departmental Committee set up by the Board of Trade in 1936 – recommended a Films Commission with aims and functions similar to those envisaged for the Film Institute by the Commission on Educational and Cultural Films.

3 Reviewing the Films Act

> It is clear to us that any body which is not entirely
> independent of any trade connection would be quite
> unsatisfactory and that, accordingly, absolute independence
> from professional or any other pecuniary connection with
> any branch of the film industry is essential in all the members
> of the proposed Commission.
>
> Moyne Committee Report, 1936.

THE ORIGINS OF THE MOYNE COMMITTEE REPORT

The Moyne Committee was appointed by Walter Runciman, President
of the Board of Trade, in March 1936 'to consider the position of British
films, having in mind the approaching expiry of the Films Act, 1927, and
to advise whether any, and if so what, measures are still required in the
public interest to promote the production, renting and exhibition of such
films'.[1] The immediate cause of its appointment was the failure of a sub-
committee of the Cinematograph Films Advisory Committee to produce
a comprehensive set of proposals when asked to examine the workings of
the 1927 Act. The sub-committee reviewed the period April to December
1934, but could not reach unanimity, so a majority report was submitted
in October 1935 by Mrs H. A. L. Fisher, P. Guedalla, G. R. Hall
Caine, J. Hallsworth, E. Hewitson, S. W. Smith, E. Trounson and
C. M. Woolf, with separate recommendations by the dissenting
individuals, A. B. King, J. Maxwell, C. P. Metcalfe and F. W. Baker.

In 1933, the Board of Trade, despite the knowledge that many aspects
of the Act were unsatisfactory, would not consider amendment:

> The present Act works exceedingly well and under the protection
> afforded by it British production has made far more progress than the
> sponsors of the Act dared to expect. Where an Act is clearly fulfilling
> its main function and no overwhelming case has been made for
> amending it, there is everything to be said for leaving it untouched.[2]

The Board feared amendment would cause controversy within the trade
– it was alleged that American renters produced or acquired 'quickies' to
comply with the letter of the law – but the trade could not agree on a
remedy. The CEA favoured a 'quality test' based on viewing, whereas the
FBI wanted a test based on cost, assuming that if a film cost a statutory

minimum sum to produce, considerably more effort would be put into its production to avoid heavy losses. However, the exhibitors had constantly pressed the Board of Trade to lower their quota, and in November 1934 an official wrote in a memorandum:

> In view of the possibility of renewed pressure from the exhibitors and of the fairly short period for which the Act has yet to run, it is suggested that it would be useful to appoint an independent Departmental Committee to examine the working of the Act and to recommend a long-term policy for the industry.[3]

The 'independent Committee' was not set up for another one and a half years, but once the Advisory Committee's report was submitted it was clear that the trade, yet again, would fail to formulate constructive proposals upon which all sections could agree.

THE CINEMATOGRAPH FILMS ADVISORY COMMITTEE'S REPORT

This report reviewed two major problems: contraventions of the blind and advance booking provisions of the Films Act, and how to deal with 'quickies'. The major American renters were blamed for taking advantage of their control over distribution in Britain 'to induce exhibitors to take bookings of blocks of films in contravention of both the prohibition of blind booking, and the limitation of advance booking'.[4] Exhibitors, dependent on renters for supplies of films, accepted these practices. Illegal bookings were 'fixed' by 'gentlemen's agreements', formal contracts only being drawn up later so that in theory the law was not broken. The report explained:

> The difficulty of enforcing the statutory restrictions lies in the fact that no offence is committed until an agreement has been made and that evidence of the offence can normally be obtained only from one of the parties to the agreement. Naturally, neither is willing to confess. . . . In addition the exhibitor fears that, were he to give evidence against the renter he might have his supplies of films cut off, and find his livelihood endangered.[5]

The majority report recommended that these problems could be resolved by stipulating that each application for registration of a film should be accompanied by a statutory declaration on behalf of the renter and his associates that the film had not been booked in contravention of Part 1 of the Act. The penalties for offences, it was proposed, should be extended so that renters and exhibitors, after three convictions, should have their licences suspended or cancelled by the court. C. P. Metcalfe, an independent exhibitor, disagreed with the majority view, suggesting that all booking restrictions should be abolished. If they were retained, he wanted them only to apply to renters, and that all film hire contracts should be registered and inspected.

On the problem of the 'quickie', the majority report recommended a 'cost test', based on a suggestion by the FBI in 1930. The Committee's idea was that 'the conditions of eligibility for the registration of films as British should require that the cost of the production of such films should be not less than £2 a foot'.[6] Films of 'outstanding value' were to be allowed full quota if they failed the cost test but satisfied a tribunal that they merited registration. Metcalfe again disagreed, and recommended a quality test.

John Maxwell, Chairman of ABPC, wanted more foreign labour to be allowed to work on British films, because of his plans to invade overseas markets. To make films attractive to American audiences, he believed, more foreign stars and technicians had to be involved in the production. The majority disagreed, and instead proposed retaining the requirement that 75 per cent of the labour costs must be paid to British persons working on a quota film. The report recommended that the exhibitors' quota should be 15 per cent, but A. B. King, a small-circuit exhibitor, wanted one of only 10 per cent.

Out of this inconclusive and indecisive report was born the Moyne Committee. A Board of Trade official concluded that an independent inquiry was the only answer:

> It is clear that it will be very difficult, if not impossible, for the Board of Trade to frame satisfactory legislation based on a report such as this, in which certain recommendations are made by, *inter alia*, some individual members of the film industry whilst divergent recommendations were made by other members of the trade and none of those making the recommendations were apparently empowered to express views on behalf of their representative sections of the industry.[6]

Once the FBI heard about the inquiry it wrote to Runciman suggesting that a producers' representative should join the Committee to offer 'expert advice'. The Board of Trade, thinking Simon Rowson would be chosen, rejected this idea because of the influence he would undoubtedly bring to bear on the Committee.

THE MOYNE COMMITTEE REPORT, 1936

The Committee's Chairman, Lord Moyne, was a former Minister for Agriculture and Fisheries. He had been Chairman of the Departmental Committee on Housing in 1933, and of the Royal Commission on the University of Durham in 1934.[7] The other members of the Committee were A. C. Cameron, who had worked on *The Film in National Life* report, and was currently a Governor of the BFI; J. Stanley Holmes, MP for Harwich and an accountant and director of public companies; J. J. Mallon, Warden of Toynbee Hall and Honorary Secretary of the Trades Boards Advisory Council; and two independent members of the Cinematograph Films Advisory Council, Hon. Eleanor Plumer and Sir Arnold Wilson. Wilson was Conservative MP for Hitchin. He had entered Parliament in 1933 after being chairman of the Industrial Health Research Board since 1926. He was a retired army officer and colonial administrator, sympathetic towards Nazi Germany in the 1930s.[8]

The Moyne Committee received its minute of appointment on 25 March 1936, and heard evidence from May to July. The final report was presented to the Board of Trade in November 1936.

The report drew attention to the dangers of foreign control of the film industry:

> We have received evidence which suggests that, owing to the increased strength of the home industry, foreign interests are adopting means which are tending to prevent a further expansion of the output of British films and are, moreover, endeavouring to obtain a further measure of control of the producing and exhibiting as well as of the distributing sides of the industry.[9]

This 'evidence' led to the report's first recommendation:

> That the Government should keep a close watch on transfers of interests in British producing, renting and exhibiting units with a view to prevent control passing abroad.[10]

However, the published minutes of evidence to the Moyne Committee did not indicate that American companies had substantial interests in the British film industry, except in the renting sphere. R. D. Fennelly, who gave evidence for the Board of Trade, said that apart from the Fox holding in Gaumont-British there was little foreign capital invested in production.[11] Warners and Fox had studios at Teddington and Wembley, and the only recent financial deal between a British and an American company mentioned was Universal's decision to distribute its films in Britain through General Film Distributors (GFD). The Committee was worried about American penetration of the exhibition sector, but it was reported that only one company, Paramount, owned any cinemas, a small group of twelve which included several 'key theatres'.

The origins of the 'foreign control' recommendation lie in a confidential meeting in July 1936 between the Committee, Alexander

Korda, chairman and managing director of London Film Productions (LFP), and Sir Cunnop Guthrie, the City figure (later to become the head of the security division of the organisation that supervised British secret service work in America during the Second World War) who had persuaded the Prudential Assurance Company to become LFP's main financial backer in 1934, and who was also a director of Korda's company. Korda and Guthrie had been called in to give evidence on 'finance . . . and attempts at American control'.[12] This was to be kept secret because of LFP's links with United Artists (UA). UA distributed LFP's films, and in September 1935 Korda was made a partner of the American company. Obviously Korda did not want to jeopardise this useful connection, and he was anxious that it was not made public that he had given evidence against UA's interests. Sir Cunnop Guthrie commented that 'such knowledge might have severe repercussions on LFP'.

The Moyne Committee had obviously received its information about the threat to exhibition from the meeting. Sir Cunnop Guthrie said:

> The American industry is designing to sabotage the British film industry. Exhibitors in certain circuits are prepared to give up 50 per cent of their equity for a guaranteed programme supplied by UA and in ways such as this American interests are endeavouring to obtain what virtually amounts to control of the screens in a large number of cinemas in this country.[13]

He even claimed that the Americans wanted to buy up LFP, but that this would not happen if the government helped the industry by making it 'very clear to the American interests that they are not going to be allowed to control the British industry'. He also said that LFP employees were being offered high salaries to induce them to work in America. LFP had offered Robert Donat £6,000 to star in *The Ghost Goes West*. When the Americans suggested that if he went to work in Hollywood he would be paid £35,000, LFP had had to increase subsequent payments to £25,000 to retain Donat's services. Korda warned of the dangers of American control over British production:

> If American interests obtained control of British production companies they may make British pictures here but the pictures made would be just as American as those made in Hollywood. We are now on the verge of forming a British school of film making in this country.

So the Moyne Committee made the 'foreign control' recommendation largely on the basis of the fears expressed by Korda and Guthrie. The report made no specific proposals as to how control could be prevented from passing abroad, and the Committee did not seem to be aware that another study of the film industry was being undertaken by Stuart Legg, the documentary producer, and F. D. Klingender, a Marxist art historian. This was clear from an article in the periodical *World Film News*, published just before a book by Klingender and Legg, *Money Behind the Screen*, appeared in January 1937.[14] *World Film News*, which first appeared in April 1936, was unashamedly anti-American, as an editorial in November 1937 illustrates:

> The American drive to obliterate every vestige of a native British film industry is succeeding admirably. Cynics are comparing the situation with the Italian conquest of Abyssinia, and there are indeed certain resemblances. The Americans, with their impressive supply of Hollywood pictures, have the necessary tank power to put native exhibitors at their mercy. They are using it remorselessly. With their large financial powers, they have been able to set up their own American production units here. By giving all their orders for Quota films – not unnaturally – to their own units, they have turned the independent British producer into a humble applicant at their factory gate. . . . So far as films go, we are now a colonial people.

Whereas the Moyne Report failed to take adequate notice of recent tendencies in the industry, the Klingender and Legg study focused on alleged American intentions to gain a more dominant position in Britain.

The Moyne Report did not refer to UA's recent purchase of an interest in County Cinemas, and a half-interest in Odeon Cinemas in February 1935 for a nominal £50. Odeon was the third largest circuit in Britain with 150 houses, and Klingender and Legg cited this as evidence that American interests were intent on buying up the British film industry;[15] although they did not mention that a clause in Odeon's Articles of Association gave Oscar Deutsch, Odeon's owner, the 'casting vote' and control.[16]

The other recent changes, partially reported in the evidence to Moyne, concerned General Film Distributors (GFD), the company founded in 1935 by C. M. Woolf after he had resigned from Gaumont-British, and the American 'major', Universal. J. Arthur Rank, the industrialist and co-founder of Pinewood Studios, helped establish the General Cinema Finance Corporation (GCFC) in March 1936. This purchased control of GFD, and a 25 per cent interest in Universal after it was reorganised early in 1936. GFD was, therefore, the main distributor of Universal's films in Britain, and the growing Rank group hoped the link would mean that Universal would facilitate better exploitation of British films in America. In this case, Rank had taken advantage of Universal's financial weakness, and the deal was an example of a major British company buying into an American one, not vice-versa. However, the interlocking of American and British interests made Rank more

ISIDORE'S INTERNATIONAL RESTAURANT

THE SCHENCK'S

GAUMONT BRITISH

"*Will you please leave a slice for the poor English?*"

Cartoon by Vicky, *World Film News*. August 1936.

dependent on showing American films once he acquired the Odeon circuit in 1941. According to Klingender and Legg, the two 'Anglo-American alliances' – UA-Odeon-County Cinemas-LFP-British and Dominion, and Universal-GFD – were linked because UA distributed British and Dominion films, and the latter company was connected with GFD through C. M. Woolf. There were other links: A. H. Giannini, President and Chairman of UA, was on the reconstituted board of Universal.[17] These complex cross-relationships were part of the emerging Rank Empire – a development the Moyne Committee did not foresee, although in the evidence to the Committee there were fears expressed, especially by smaller exhibitors, about the growth of circuits and the power of the combines.

One Anglo-American deal that did not take place, and if it had would have caused a sensation, concerned Gaumont-British. In the summer of 1936 it was announced that Fox and MGM were to buy the Ostrers' shares in Gaumont-British. A price of £1,500,000 was mentioned, but the deal never took place. Even so, the very mention of the possibility was enough to increase doubts about how 'British' the film industry actually was, as a cartoon in *World Film News* in August 1936 illustrated. Later in the year Maxwell acquired the Ostrer holding of 250,000 'B' shares in the Metropolis and Bradford Trust Company for £620,000, plus an option on the Ostrers' 'A' shares. However, the latter could not be transferred without Fox's consent, and when this was refused Maxwell failed to gain control of Gaumont-British. Table x shows the links between British and American companies in 1936.[18]

TABLE X
The British Film Trade in 1936

Renter	American affiliation	British production affiliation	Exhibition affiliation
(A) AMERICAN RENTERS			
Metro-Goldwyn Mayer	Loew's Inc. (MGM)	Various quota producers	London pre-release hall
Radio Pictures	RKO Radio	Various quota producers	—
Warner & First National	Warner & FN	Own subsidiary with studio in Teddington	—
Fox Film Co.	20th Cent. Fox	Fox British, Wembley & New World Pict. Denham	—
Paramount Film Serv.	Paramount Inc.	British & Dominion, Boreham Wood studios and quota producers	14 super halls and tie-up with Union Circ. (250 halls)
Columbia	Columbia Pict. Corp.	Paul Soskin Prod. & others	—
(B) ANGLO-AMERICAN RENTERS			
United Artists	UA Corp.	London Film Prod., British & Dominion Films Ltd., Criterion Film, Brit. Cine Alliance, Bergner-Czinner Prod., Trafalgar F. Pr., V. Saville Pr., E. Pommer Pr., Garrett-Klement Pr., Atlantic Films, Pall Mall Pr., Denham, Worton Hall & Pinewood Studios	Participation in Odeon (about 150 halls) & County Circ. (about 50 halls)
General Film Distr.	Universal	Pinewood Studios, British & Dominion Films Ltd., H. Wilcox Prod., Capitol Prod., City Films, Universal-Wainwright, Brit. National Films, Cecil Films, Grafton Films, etc.	New circuit in process of formation

60

Renter	American affiliation	British production affiliation	Exhibition affiliation
(C) MAJOR BRITISH RENTERS			
Gaumont-Brit. Distr.	(20th C.-Fox).*	Gaumont-British Pict. Corp., Shepherds Bush, Gainsborough P. Corp. Islington	Gaumont-British Circuit, over 300 halls
Wardour F. & Pathe Pic.	Various occasional contracts	BIP, Elstree and Welwyn and other indep. units	ABC Circuit, about 290 halls
(D) OTHER BRITISH RENTERS			
Ass. Brit. Film Distr.	Grand Nat. Films Inc.	Ass. Talking Pict., Ealing studio, and indep. prods.	None
Twickenham F. Distr. (incl. PDC).	Various	Twickenham F. Stud., New Ideal P., Hammersmith, J. H. Prod., Boreham Wood	None
British Lion Film Corp.	Republic Corp. of America	Beaconsfield Stud., also Hammer Prod.	None
Equity Brit. Films	Various	Various quota prods.	None
Butchers F. Serv.	Various	Various indep. prods. in ass. with Butchers	None
Ass. Produc. & Distrib. Co.	Various	Sound City Studios, UK Films & indep. prods.	None
Ace Films (shorts)	Educat. Film Corp. of America	Ace Films	None
Reunion Films	Mainly Continental films	Various indep. prods.	None

23 other renters distributed from one to six films (Brit. and/or foreign) in 1936. Total no. of Renters' Licences issued 1935/6: 65; total no. of producers of long films in 1935/6: 76.

*Note. Gaumont-British are the only English company having their own distribution organisation in the USA.

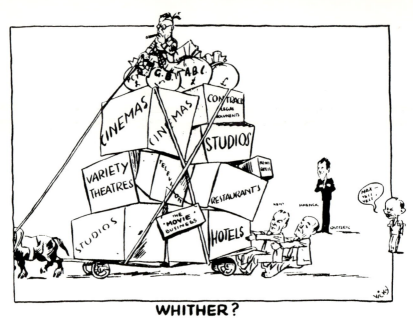

WHITHER?

Vicky cartoon in *World Film News*, November 1936. Maxwell made an unsuccessful bid for control of Gaumont-British. If Fox had agreed to surrender its holding, Maxwell would more or less have monopolised the industry.

The second recommendation made by the Moyne Committee concerned finance:

> The Government should, as soon as may be, take such steps as may be practicable to encourage financial interests to constitute one or more organizations to finance British film production, in approved cases, on reasonable terms.[19]

The evidence had showed that:

> The British film producing industry has an insufficient supply of capital for its needs and that the cost of the production of British films has been increased by the necessary money being obtainable only at a high rate of interest. . . . lack of finance is a powerful factor in enabling foreign interests to obtain control and is certainly an impediment to the industry's continued and satisfactory expansion.[20]

This recommendation again was largely influenced by Sir Cunnop Guthrie's evidence. He pointed out that the 'crisis' in the film industry was just beginning, and bankers would only support production with large collateral security and high rates of interest. He warned that

'Unless the financial hierarchy in the City of London obtain a lead from the Government they will not go much further in financing the film industry.'[21] Simon Rowson's evidence to the Committee showed that the industry was undercapitalised.[22] The trend was to use short-term money, and for film companies to obtain insurance policies at Lloyds on a bank overdraft. Rowson explained:

> An Underwriter at Lloyds undertakes to provide an insurance policy to guarantee an overdraft, and the bank provides that overdraft subject to that guarantee with a charge either by the bank or by the original guarantors on a specific asset, the picture in question, or on the companies which are responsible for making that picture.[23]

Often, if a producer wanted to make a film, the procedure would be for a loan to be arranged by an insurance broker. Once this was secure, a £100 company would be formed. According to Klingender and Legg, the total amount raised in the form of guarantees by production companies between January and October 1936 was over £4,050,000.[24] The main companies involved in these guaranteed advances were Aldgate Trustees, the Prudential Assurance Company, C. T. Bowring and Company, the Equity and Law Life Assurance Society, the Clydesdale Bank, Butchers Film Service and the Bankers Trust Company.[25] Klingender and Legg concluded:

> One of the most striking features of this expansion from a financial point of view, is the fact that on the production side it is based almost entirely on *expectation* without any concrete results to justify that optimism . . . the expansion has with few outstanding exceptions been financed not by increases in the companies' own working capital, but by a spectacular increase in *loans*.[26]

The Moyne Committee's recommendation was vague, and merely pointed to the formation of some kind of Film Bank. One member, J. Stanley Holmes, had been against a central organisation for film finance, preferring 'a number of organisations to provide the finance, in order to give rise to competition which would enable money to be obtained at a cheaper rate'.[27] Despite this, Arnold Wilson had informed the Committee, after a private consultation with the financial firm Helbert, Wagg and Company, that 'Steps towards the constitution of a Film Bank for financing film production were well on the way. . . . If the Committee recommend a long-term policy the bank would at once take shape.'[28] The possibility of a Film Bank was considered in 1937 by the Bank of England, when the financial crisis in the industry was at its height (see p. 82).

Most of the trade groups which gave evidence to the Committee were

TABLE XI
Number of films registered for renters' quota

Year ended 31 March	British	Foreign	Total
1929	128	550	678
1932	153	464	617
1934	190	484	674
1935	189	477	666
1936	212	506	718

unanimous in their view that the quota method of protectionism should be renewed. One of the main reasons for this was the increase in the number of long films registered for renters' quota (see Table XI).[29] The system had worked: it should be extended. The Report duly recommended that quotas should continue for another ten years, once the 1927 Act expired in 1938. As Simon Rowson commented:

> On educational, social and political grounds, the power of the film to serve important national interests has been fully established. An important industry has been built up at the cost of much capital, and gives considerable employment to a large body of labour. . . . There can be no doubt whatever that the withdrawal of protection from the industry which has been built up would lead to its rapid extinction.[30]

A protective tariff instead of a quota was rejected, as in 1927; and an *ad valorem* duty on imported films was impractical because it was difficult to assess the value of a film at the time of importation. Sir Cunnop Guthrie said that certain film magnates with exhibition interests would hardly accept radical measures to reduce the number of American films imported or shown.[31] A duty levied on film rentals of foreign product in Britain was not considered a solution either, because 'this would amount to discrimination between British and foreign producers by means of an internal duty'.[32] At the tenth meeting of the Moyne Committee, Sir Arnold Wilson mentioned his idea for a body like a Film Marketing Board, with producers handing over their films to the Board so that records could be kept about receipts for purposes of calculating a tariff.[33] However, this proposal was not included in the final report, although one other member of the Committee, J. S. Holmes, was sympathetic.

The quota percentages recommended in the Report were 20 per cent for renters of long films, and 15 per cent for exhibitors. Both were to rise to 50 per cent in ten years. The FBI wanted high quotas (as did Alexander Korda, who had proposed 50 per cent), whereas the exhibitors pressed for reductions. The main change recommended by the Committee was that there should be a quota for 'shorts', starting at 15 per cent for renters and at 10 per cent for exhibitors.[34]

Under the 1927 Films Act certain classes of film were excluded from quota protection. These were films depicting mainly news and current events; natural scenery; industrial or manufacturing processes; and scientific films. This effectively precluded most documentary films from qualifying for quota, and discouraged exhibitors from showing the films. The only way such films could qualify was if they could be shown to possess 'special entertainment value'. This, as Paul Rotha of the Association of Realist Film Producers explained, was no easy task. It was difficult to arrange the press show to establish whether a film had 'special exhibition value', since the films did not automatically qualify for quota and no renter would take an unregistered film. The Advisory Committee responsible for advising the Board of Trade on these matters had no documentary film-makers as members. Educational and cultural considerations were therefore seldom taken into account when 'special exhibition value' was assessed.[35] Consequently the footage of British short films registered with the Board of Trade fell from 170,000 feet to 68,000 feet between 1929 and 1935.

Since the passage of the Films Act the documentary film had become more significant, largely because of John Grierson's work for the Empire Marketing Board and, after 1933, for the General Post Office. Despite critical acclaim, few of the films were shown in commercial cinemas: exhibitors claimed they were unpopular. The proportion of short films shown in Britain during the year ending September 1935 was 4.21 per cent – a fall of 2 per cent from the previous year. The obstacles faced by documentary film-makers were exacerbated by the double-feature programme. This became standard in the 1930s, with exhibitors usually showing a newsreel rather than a short film between the two features. Grierson's memorandum to the Committee argued the case for a 'shorts' quota on commercial and national grounds:

> The short field is the logical training ground for directors and technicians . . . permits the exploitation of capital too small for large-scale production . . . provides for the trying out of new ideas. . . . I would urge that the leavening of the average programme with a single short item of more serious intention either socially or culturally would have the effect of improving the relationship between cinemas and the public. . . . The shorts field already in its documentary section demonstrated how different aspects of the national life can be described. . . . If the ordinary working and traditions of the national life are to be presented, one must look mainly to the shorts field for their presentation.[36]

Despite opposition from the exhibitors, the Committee proposed a 'shorts' quota. Even so, the attitude towards the films remained the same: by 1939 cinemas carrying double features devoted only 2¼ per cent of screen time to short films.[37] *Night Mail* and *North Sea* did better than most, but this was because they were less pedagogic than many documentaries. Attempts to portray industrial life – for example *Housing Problems*, *Coalface* and *Industrial Britain* – could seem patronising to the working class; and those who knew the realities of the Depression hardly wanted to see them in the cinema. But exhibitors opposed documentaries and shorts mainly because they did not possess the profit-making lure of commercial features. T. H. Fligelstone, giving evidence for the CEA to the Moyne Committee, defended his dislike of documentary films: 'The public come into our cinemas to be amused, not educated. If their amusement can be so guided that it is educational, that is all right, but they will not come in to be educated.'[38] This attitude illustrates the trade's definition of 'entertainment': closely related to commercial, rather than educational or cultural, values. This undermined the independence of the BFI; sealed the fate of the Moyne Commission's plan for an independent Films Commission; and strongly influenced the Board of Trade's films policy.

The report's main criticism was of 'quota quickies':

> It was admitted, however, even by the renters themselves, that in recent years the spirit of the Act has not, speaking generally, been given effect. In order to obtain the requisite length of British film to satisfy the renters' quota, the majority of foreign-controlled renters appear to have made arrangements for the production of British films at the minimum of expense, regardless of quality.[39]

The blame for 'quickies' was placed squarely on the American renters. R. D. Fennelly, of the Board of Trade's film section, produced a table showing that whereas British renters, especially those associated with the two major combines, acquired more than their statutory requirement of British films, the American renters only acquired the minimum.[40] The figures supplied by Simon Rowson for the previous year corroborated this argument (see Table XII). United Artists was considered an exception, as it handled the product of LFP and British and Dominion. It was felt that because UA was solely a distributing company, British producers trusted it to push their films in the USA since it did not also handle the product of a large American affiliate.

Not only did it appear that British films were being shown, but that they were becoming more popular, an argument supported by Tony Aldgate.[41] The Board of Trade's evidence showed that despite 'quickies' there was a demand for British films, as illustrated by Table XIII, which details the range of bookings of long films acquired by renters in 1932–3 and 1933–4.[42] Most exhibitors seemed to be exceeding their quota requirements. In 1932 their statutory quota was 10 per cent, but they managed to show 21.6 per cent British long films; and in 1934, when

TABLE XII
Comparison of British films registered by principal companies,
1933–4 and 1934–5, with their minimum quota requirement

	Quota liability ('000 ft)		Length Reg. ('000 ft.)	
British companies	1933–4	1934–5	1933–4	1934–5
Associated British Film Dists.	10	51	67	43
Assoc. Producing and Dist. Co.	3½	7	16	23
British Lion Film Corp.	11	12	39	42
Butchers Film Service	16	8	26	45
Gaumont-British Distributors	44	47	206	210
Pathe Pictures	32	38	33	39
Wardour Films	18	31	109	120
Foreign-controlled renters				
Columbia Pictures Corp.	37	68	37	68
First National Film Dists.	45	49	46	49
Fox Film Corp.	65	69	66	69
MGM Pictures Ltd.	98	89	98	89
Paramount Film Service	108	97	108	98
Radio Pictures	88	78	89	78
UA Corp.	59	27	90	52
Universal Pictures Ltd.		113		113
Warner Brothers Pictures	49	47	50	47

their quota was 15 per cent, they showed 28.4 per cent.[43] Yet exhibitors still claimed that their quota was too high, and that British product was not always easy to obtain. Why was this, and was there any truth in exhibitors' complaints about the popularity and availability of British films?

TABLE XIII
Range of bookings of long films by renters, 1932–4

Range in days	British films				Foreign films			
	1932–3		1933–4		1932–3		1933–4	
	No.	%	No.	%	No.	%	No.	%
1–2,000	50	31.6	60	32.1	104	21.8	101	20.8
3,000–5,000	75	47.4	82	43.8	340	71.4	341	70.3
+5,000	34	21.0	45	24.1	32	6.8	43	8.9
Total	159		187		476		485	

The exhibitors' argument was that not all British films were 'quickies', but that only the combines were certain of obtaining the better British product. They objected to 'quickies', not to British films as such. GBPC and ABPC were the major producers, and they naturally showed their films in their own circuits. This left independent exhibitors at the mercy of American renters who would, it was claimed, offer films in blocks which included good American films and bad British 'quickies'. The Americans used the same argument to defend themselves against the charge that they deliberately obtained 'quickies' to discredit British films. As Sam Eckman of MGM pointed out to the Moyne Committee:

> The best producers are Mr Maxwell's or Gaumont-British, or London Films, and they refuse to distribute through us. They feel the preponderance of our films is so extensive that we could not lend our best efforts to the distribution of their films. . . . Most good British films are controlled by companies that have their own West End cinemas, and that being the case, we have had no other alternative but to fall back to the less important films.[44]

Independent exhibitors accounted for well over half of the total number of 4,448 cinemas in Britain in 1935.

Exhibitors identified the 'KRS booking policy' as another factor in the combines' ability to obtain the best films. The KRS (Kinematograph Renters' Society) would only allow a film to be booked for more than one cinema if the exhibitor had financial control of the subsequent halls.[45] Similarly, the practice of 'barring' (under which no two cinemas in the same area could show the same film simultaneously) created problems for the independent exhibitors – a majority and an influential section of the CEA. When a circuit hired a film, the 'barring' process followed it all over the country, and independents often failed to obtain new films. Even Simon Rowson, a renter, acknowledged the difficulties that had arisen from the growth of the two combines:

> The exhibitor, unlike most other traders, is not free to provide his patrons with the programmes of his choice. Owing to the growth and power of the circuits, he can only choose a programme from a fraction, sometimes only a small fraction, of the films ready for showing. A one-theatre proprietor in a neighbourhood of theatres belonging to a group or circuit of theatres under the same ownership is often compelled to show only the least attractive films because the larger companies exert their greater booking power to reserve the better and best pictures for themselves. . . . There are certain cases up and down the country, principally at certain positions in a number of the large towns, where the supply of good British films has not sufficed to enable all the exhibitors in the locality to have a good alternative choice of high-grade product.[46]

In 1935 GBPC and ABPC between them owned 559 cinemas, or 13 per cent of the total number of cinemas, and 17 per cent of the seats. The nine circuits in Britain owned a quarter of all cinemas, a third of the total seating capacity, and half the first-run cinemas. The CEA informed the Moyne Committee that good British films were popular, and only two areas – London's East End and parts of Scotland – appeared to dislike British films, whatever the quality. Native audiences particularly appreciated British comedies (the Will Hay, Gracie Fields and George Formby films); the Conrad Veidt spy melodramas; and Jessie Matthews musicals. The films of Hitchcock, Korda, Asquith and Wilcox elevated the reputation of British product. The root of the CEA's opposition to the quota percentage was linked, therefore, with the growth of vertically integrated combines, and a genuine antipathy towards 'quickies'. When UA's chief executive, Joseph Schenck, visited England in 1934, he wrote to his home office of the success of Korda's films in Britain:

> Korda will produce at least six pictures a year. You cannot conceive what these pictures are doing for us here. Where other American producers are compelled to sell quota pictures . . . in the high class theatres they hiss these pictures off and in the rough theatres they throw bottles at the screen.[47]

Whatever the case, it was clear that the Act had been abused. And although there had been progress, British films still faced obstacles: America's domination of the market; the lack of stable financial support; disadvantageous booking terms; the stigma of 'quickies'; and the absence of an imaginative films policy.

The Moyne Committee heard evidence on two possible remedies for 'quickies' – a test based on cost, or one based on quality. In 1929 the FBI suggested a 'cost test', and in 1931, before the CEA opted for the 'quality test', the two organisations sent a deputation to the Board of Trade in favour of the 'cost test'. In its evidence the FBI wrote:

> Producers have given most careful study to the problem of the quota Act and have investigated many plans for elimination of the poor quality 'quota picture'. They do not suggest that high cost of production necessarily means good pictures or that a cheap picture cannot sometimes be a good one, but experience shows that films registered for renters' quota and costing less than the figure indicated are generally bad.[48]

The minimum 'cost test' suggested by the Association of Cine-Technicians (ACT) was that films over 6,000 feet long should have cost not less than £12,000 to qualify as quota pictures, and that films less than 6,000 feet should have cost a minimum of £2 per foot. The exhibitors, by that time, had decided that this might reduce the film supply, and favoured a test based on viewing films to ascertain a minimum standard of quality. The test was to be conducted by a Committee consisting mainly of exhibitors. Its main function would be:

> To establish as a standard a *bona fide* attempt to produce a film possessing entertainment and exhibition merit which would enable the renter to rent that film in a free market in competition with foreign films generally acceptable to the public.[49]

The Moyne Committee recommended a quality test because:

> A cost test such as that proposed to us of £2 per foot . . . might well prove ineffective in preventing evasion and the continuation of the evil. Further the imposition of a minimum cost test might be a serious hardship to smaller film producers. . . . The quality test we have in mind had nothing to do with censorship as now conducted. It would be concerned normally only with the entertainment value and general merits of a film.[50]

The exhibitors appeared to have got their way, but not over the administering authority. The Committee's most radical suggestion was that this should be independent of the trade and have considerable powers other than the viewing of films:

> The Commission should, in addition to exercising its normal administrative functions and acting as a tribunal to give impartial judgements on matters dividing the film industry, have powers of initiative and control. . . . Absolute independence from professional or any other pecuniary connection with any branch of the film industry is essential in all the members of the proposed Commission.[51]

The reason for strict independence – the Commission was to consist of a chairman and between two and four other members appointed by the government – was that many of the matters to be dealt with were internal trade ones, for example 'the redundancy of cinema houses, combinations in one section of the trade and counter-combinations in another, quicker turnover of capital and the furnishing of information required by the local licensing authorities in the exercise of their powers of control.' These were controversial questions, and impartiality was essential if decisions were to be made.

How did the Committee decide on this radical recommendation? When it considered 'the nature of the official, or body, who might have power to vary the quota in the future', Alan Cameron not surprisingly feared that 'If the Board of Trade had the deciding voice in the matter the question would be considered from the trade point of view rather than from the public and national standpoint.'[52] Dr Mallon suggested, at the same meeting, that a body of three independent persons was preferable to the Board of Trade in that the former would not be open to political influence'. A month later Sir Arnold Wilson produced a scheme for a British Cinematograph Industry Board, with three independent and seven trade members; but after opposition from Holmes, Wilson agreed to draft an alternative proposal for a body entirely independent of the trade.[53] Once this had been done it was decided that:

> Any proposal in the Report for the constitution of such a Commission should be separate from the rest of the Report so that if the Government did not see their way to accept a Commission on the lines proposed it would nevertheless still be open for them to adopt the other recommendations of the Committee.[54]

However, at the thirteenth meeting of the Moyne Committee it was finally decided that the Films Commission should administer the quality test, and it was agreed 'to make the proposal for the appointment of a Commission an integral part of the Report of the Committee, by which the whole Report would stand or fall.'[55] How this change came about is obscure, but at the previous meeting it was recorded that the views of the President of the Board of Trade would be sought. Nevertheless, it seemed that by October 1936 the Committee was convinced that an impartial body to regulate the affairs of the industry was its most important recommendation, and this became the central plank in the report. The industry's problems certainly needed to be examined: release-reform; overbuilding; standard contracts; distribution of box-office receipts; financial instability; high costs. John Grierson, in his preface to *Money Behind the Screen*, thought financial recovery depended on the Films Commission:

> If, through the Films Commission . . . order can be brought to the finances of our work, mismanagement eliminated and this rush of promoters abated, it is the creative worker who will most have reason to bless a measure of government co-ordination.

Other recommendations in the report concerned the definition of a British film, and booking practices. The 1927 Act provided that films made in the Empire counted as quota pictures, but this had not had the anticipated effect. As the FBI observed: 'There have been instances of films made in the Empire for purely local purposes being acquired by foreign renters here at negligible cost for the sole purpose of serving as quota to match foreign films.'[56] It was hoped that there would be an Imperial quota, but most Dominions had not passed legislation favouring British films, preferring in some cases to protect their own film industries:

Certain States of the Australian Commonwealth have introduced local quota regulations requiring that a proportion of home-produced films shall be exhibited, without extending the advantage of such quota legislation to films produced in the UK. This state of things is dangerous to UK films as they will be eligible for both Australian and British quota.[57]

To remedy this, the Moyne Committee recommended that films made in the Empire should pass the quality test, and suggested that:

The Government should approach those Dominion States in which film quota legislation is in operation to protect the local industry, with a view to urging that treatment given by them to films made in Great Britain should be as far as possible reciprocal in this country.[58]

The original Act stipulated that the author of a film's scenario should be British. However, conditions had clearly changed since 1927, when the provision was included in the Act to ensure that 'whatever the authorship of the work on which the scenario was based the actual treatment of the film should be British, so as to exclude a foreign atmosphere and prevent disfiguration of a story or event essentially British in a manner which would outrage British ideas'.[59] This had proved very difficult to enforce, since British scenario authors were in short supply, and it was not easy to ascertain who the author was when, especially since the coming of sound, more than one person usually worked on a scenario. The Committee therefore decided that the provision should be dropped. The anomaly prompted another cartoon from 'Vicky', for *World Film News* in November 1936. The irate figure on the right is Max Schach of the notorious Capitol Film group (see next chapter).

The labour provisions of the 1927 Act – that 75 per cent of the labour used in the production of quota films should be British – were reaffirmed by the Committee, and it was advised that a proportion of foreign films, up to 10 per cent of the total footage or up to 20 per cent of the studio scenes (whichever was the lesser), should be allowed in British films. This was because some films were refused quota registration if not all the studio scenes had been shot in the British Empire. The Committee thought it was unreasonable to expect producers not to use the services of foreign film companies or studios in their pictures, provided the film was produced by a British company.

The 1927 Act tried to eradicate certain booking practices – blind, block and advance booking – but the evidence showed that it had failed. Exhibitors and renters made verbal 'gentlemen's agreements' to book blocks of unseen films. In theory the law was not broken, but in practice contraventions were widespread. To encourage exhibitors not to make

'. . . And some have greatness thrust upon them.'

Cartoon by Vicky, *World Film News*, November 1936.

these agreements, the Moyne Committee recommended that booking penalties should fall only on renters, that the maximum fine should be increased to £250 per film, and that after a second conviction a renter could have his licence suspended or withdrawn. All films, the Report proposed, should be 'trade shown'; and, provided there was no advertisement, some films could be shown to members of the public before a 'trade show' for purposes of a 'try out'.

TRADE REACTIONS TO THE MOYNE REPORT

The report's main recommendations – the Films Commission and the quality test – were the subject of vigorous debate as soon as it was published. Writing in *Sight and Sound*, Ivor Montagu was pleased with the Committee's work:

> Their unanimous report is a shining witness to the fact that any reasonably impartial batch of citizens, guided by a conscientious civil servant secretary [Mr Patterson], can come to sensible conclusions about subjects that the expert representatives of mutually conflicting interests would quarrel over till all's blue without reaching any conclusion. . . . The Committee deserves congratulations on what is, frankly, an unexpectedly good report.[60]

73

The Board of Trade asked the CEA, the KRS and the FBI for their comments on the report in December 1936. All were against an independent Films Commission, and opinion was divided on the type of test required to eradicate 'quickies'. The FBI pointed out that a quality test based on viewing would make finance harder to obtain, since producers would not know whether their films would qualify for quota or obtain bookings. A test based on cost was thought to be a more reliable standard because:

> No independent Commission can possibly be as well qualified to judge what will please the public as the companies actually engaged in production, and if an unsuitable standard is insisted on not only may the British production companies be involved in heavy losses, but the number of British films produced will decline.[61]

The CEA was contemptuous of the Films Commission, calling it

> cumbrous, wasteful and expensive. We think that our proposal to constitute a small viewing panel of, say two exhibitors, a producer, renter and an independent chairman, to which a film could be referred within a short time of trade show is much more practical. . . . We dissent strongly from the idea that people knowing nothing of our business are, because of that independence of this trade, peculiarly qualified to view and to judge.[62]

The KRS was opposed to both the Commission and the quality test, and thought the former would 'bring grave risks to the millions of capital invested'. The Hays Office sent a memorandum from America which also attacked the Commission:

> The *sine qua non* of membership on the Commission is that the commissioners have 'absolute independence from professional or any other pecuniary connection with any branch of the film industry'. In other words, apparently, that they should know little or nothing of the vast and complicated mechanism whose destiny is to be placed in their hands.[63]

On the question of the 'shorts quota', the CEA and the KRS were opposed, whereas the FBI and the ACT were in favour. The FBI agreed with the recommended quota percentages, but the KRS thought they were far too high. The CEA did not object to the minimum figures of 20 per cent and 15 per cent, but strongly opposed the maximum of 50 per cent.

The report, with its recommendations for a Films Commission and a quality test, and the crucial references to 'foreign control' and the need for a Films Bank, set the stage for the debates on the renewal of the Films

Act in 1937–8. The story of the evolution of the 1938 Films Act was very much the story of how the trade and the Americans tried to make sure that the Moyne proposals did not become law, or provide the basis for a wider, more imaginative films policy.

4 Film Finance in the 1930s

> It was a classic example of money madness in the movies, or how to get something for nothing.
>
> Ernest Betts, 1960, commenting on the Capitol case, 1939

The financial instability of the film industry referred to in the Moyne Report was the subject of an inquiry by the Bank of England in 1937. There was a boom in British production from 1933 to 1936, but the costs of film-making increased. Between 1935 and 1937 new studios mushroomed. In 1928 there were nineteen stages in British studios with a total area of 105,650 square feet; by 1938 there were seventy with 777,650 square feet.[1] Between 1925 and 1936 640 new production companies were registered, eighty-eight of them in 1935 and ninety-four in 1936. By 1937, when the crash came, only twenty were still in operation.[2]

Alexander Korda's international success with *The Private Life of Henry VIII* (1933), a film that cost £93,710 to produce and earned over £500,000, inspired others to make films for the American market. This was a dangerous policy, because if a film failed to recoup its production costs losses could be catastrophic, especially if the picture was a lavish venture intended to appeal to British and American audiences. Despite the Americans' insistence that there was no discrimination against British films in the US, that they did not do well there simply because Hollywood's output was superior, British producers faced obstacles for economic reasons. In the 1920s and 1930s the situation was the same:

> British producers are denied access to the American market. . . . This market can now be profitably reached only through one or more of a group of not more than ten national American distributors . . . each of which is busily engaged in marketing its own brand of pictures through its own sales or rental organizations, and through the theatres owned, controlled or operated by one or more of this group.[3]

The mistake in the 1930s was that producers would not face up to these economic realities: America was more or less a closed market, and *Henry VIII* was an exception. As the critic Ernest Betts commented:

The success of Korda's *The Private Life of Henry VIII*, which took vast sums of money in New York, fostered the notion that with a proper show of stardom, spectacle and extravagance British films could lead the world. . . . Successive Governments supported this view with the same well-chosen words. By forcing exhibitors to show a high quota of British films on their screens, the Quota Act did everything to promote a boom and entice the City into disgorging its millions for scraps of celluloid.[4]

Korda was not the first producer in the early 1930s to put faith in 'international production', and he was not the last.[5] The costs of film-making had been rising since the coming of sound, and Korda did have a better chance of fair distribution in the United States because his films were handled by UA. Even so, the returns on Korda's films after *Henry VIII* were disappointing, and with the competition of American films 'UA found it difficult to market British pictures'.[6]

International productions characterised the boom, and Gaumont-British in particular tried to secure an American market. Michael Balcon wrote in June 1936: 'In order to progress further we must pursue a production policy ever less and less parochial and more and more international in appeal. "Internationalisation sums up Gaumont-British policy".'[7] *World Film News* anticipated problems a month later when it commented: 'It is generally admitted in the film trade that a collapse is imminent and that it may come any time within the next six months.' By January 1937 there were signs that the bubble would burst. When *Money Behind the Screen* was published and the basic instability behind the production boom was revealed, the crash was just beginning. Julius Hagen's Twickenham group of companies went bankrupt after an attempt to make pictures for world release. Hagen claimed that he had been promised £40,000 for the American sales of *Scrooge* (1935), but had received only £1,200.[8] In March 1937 Gainsborough published a loss of £98,000 for 1936, and it was announced that the Gaumont studios at Shepherd's Bush would close. In the summer of 1936 Gaumont-British had an overdraft with the National Provincial Bank of £1,149,785, of which £247,904 was in respect of film production. By May 1936 London Films showed a loss of over £330,000.

It was clear that in a space of months the industry had passed from boom to bust.[9] Isidore Ostrer complained that 'unless we can get a bigger return from the American market for British pictures Gaumont-British will be compelled to abandon production'.[10] Max Schach of the Capitol Film group moved out of Denham to work in a less modern but cheaper studio; Herbert Wilcox moved from Pinewood to Beaconsfield. By July 1937 the *Financial Times* could declare that production losses were likely to be over one million pounds, with financial support being withdrawn from film production.[11] The press constantly referred to the

"IS THIS THE BIG "HIT" WE'VE BEEN WAITING FOR?"

Cartoon by Vicky, *World Film News*, February 1937.

film industry's financial problems; and Klingender and Legg's revelations in *Money Behind the Screen* caused more 'thunder in the City', as illustrated by a *World Film News* cartoon in February 1937.

Since film production was a speculative venture, especially in Britain where the producer received by far the smallest share of box-office receipts, ordinary channels of finance were wary of investing money. Although costs had risen and producers had lost money when their films failed in America, the root of the problem in 1937 was the unstable method of film finance that had evolved in the boom period. In the first six months of 1937 over four million pounds was borrowed by production companies, mainly by short-term financing. A popular scheme was for a producer to use a type of credit insurance, based on receipts from a film. The producer would have to find a distributor to advance a percentage of the production cost, and an insurance company would then issue a policy guaranteeing against loss. The distributors' advance was often an inadequate return on the money, and the excess loss risk was therefore insured against. Banks would often only give overdrafts if they were guaranteed by insurance policies. In some cases the distributor contracted to pay a fixed percentage to a producer, but if the film's daily receipts fell below an amount stipulated in the contract the distributor could stop the film's exhibition, pay the producer the agreed percentage and then claim on his credit insurance policies. As the *Financial Times* put it: 'Very few British films turn out to be paying propositions such as to wipe out the losses of the many which never should have been made, and one can realise the anxiety felt in the insurance world and outside.'[12] The insurance companies were so concerned that a group of Lloyds underwriters appointed W. C. Crocker, an insurance solicitor, to investigate the situation in the summer of 1937. As *Money Behind the Screen* reported earlier, the boom was based on expectation rather than on results, and the expansion was financed not by increases in the film companies' working capital, but by increased loans:

> The fact of the ever increasing weight of loan money as distinct from shareholders' capital emerges incontestably, even for the large corporations, while in the case of the new production units, the superiority of the former is overwhelming.[13]

Klingender and Legg claimed that in the first ten months of 1936 loans of nearly thirteen million pounds were absorbed by the industry:

> Banks, insurance companies, legal investment trusts, even motor manufacturers are falling over each other in their eagerness to stake a claim. Men and women who have scarcely given a thought to films all their lives are clamouring for posts in the studios, attracted by the rumour of high salaries and speedy promotion.[14]

THE CAPITOL CASE, 1939

The Capitol case exploded the whole precarious system, 'shook the City and terrified Wardour Street. . . . It was a classic example of money madness in the movies, of how to get something for nothing'.[15] In May 1939, the Westminster Bank brought thirty-five court actions against fifteen insurance companies that had issued guarantee policies as security for bank loans to the Capitol group of production companies. The group had been founded in 1935 by Max Schach, who was, as Ernest Betts later described him, 'clever with money and clever with people, and he had the inexhaustible energy of the movie man'.[16] This reputation was illustrated, as usual with a touch of satire, by 'Vicky' in the July 1936 issue of *World Film News*.

The case lasted six days. It was revealed that the production companies had been able to get credit for £1,711,000, according to Sir Stafford Cripps K.C. who appeared for the Westminster Bank, 'with the express approval of the Board of Trade as being a good way of financing British film productions'.[17] The total losses amounted to one million

"ER . . . WHAT ARE YOUR PRODUCTION PLANS, MR. SCHACH?"

Cartoon by Vicky, *World Film News*, July 1936.

pounds, and some of the films had never been made. In this particular case the Capitol group went to a firm of brokers, Glanvill Enthoven and Company, to raise loans. Glanvill's used underwriters in the marine underwriting market to issue guarantee policies for a part of the required loan, and these guarantees provided security for cash advances from the Westminster Bank. However, out of the £1,711,000 advanced certain sums were subtracted – premiums paid to the underwriters, Glanvill's commission, and a sum set aside in a reserve account to guarantee the interest payments on the loans to the bank. Glanvill's had ingeniously established a firm called Aldgate Trustees Ltd, as Sir Stafford explained to the court, in order to

> take a charge from the producing company over all the receipts for the particular film in respect of which the loan was made. . . . That charge was made effective by giving instructions to the distributing company to pay direct to the bank money which it owed to the producing company in respect of a particular film. At a later date that charge, which was in the first case a specific one, was converted into an 'umbrella' charge which covered the receipts from all the films of a particular company. The bank had no part of any kind in those arrangements.[18]

This would appear to have been a safe method for the bank, since after a year, if the company had not paid off the loan, the underwriters were

80

technically liable to pay up. In practice, though, the policies were renewed, and 'most of the underwriters apparently reinsured the whole or part of their risk'.[19] There were two reasons why this system did not work: 'Incompetent and inefficient management of the producing companies, and secondly, the complete failure of Glanvill's to watch the interests of the underwriters.'

The case was eventually settled out of court, but confirmed the incredible confusion in the financing of British film production first revealed by Klingender and Legg. It was to this that the Bank of England turned its attention in 1937.[20]

THE BANK OF ENGLAND'S INQUIRY, 1937

Sir Horace Wilson, Chief Industrial Adviser to the government and a close associate of Neville Chamberlain, asked the Bank of England to conduct an inquiry into film industry financing because of the rumours of the impending crash, and because the Board of Trade had received information in December 1936 about the plight of London Film Productions. The Bank of England placed two of its officials at the head of the investigation, Messrs Bunbury and Skinner, who were assisted by Gordon Munro, a director of the City firm Helbert, Wagg and Company, which had given advice to the Moyne Committee. A report was submitted to the Governor of the Bank in April 1937.[21]

At this time, E. H. Lever, joint Secretary of the Prudential Assurance Company, was trying to enlist the support of Montagu Norman, Governor of the Bank, for a financial reorganisation of the film industry. This was unlikely because Norman had little sympathy for non-'basic' industries claiming assistance from the Securities Management Trust, a subsidiary of the Bank (which conducted the inquiry). He was particularly critical of the film industry, and expressed astonishment when his close associate Lord 'Wyndham' Portal of Laverstoke, whose firm supplied the paper for banknotes, told him that the company he had recently formed with Rank and others, the General Cinema Finance Corporation (GCFC), was considering a deal with Universal. Herbert Wilcox, also associated with GCFC, was present at Portal's meeting with Norman and recorded the Governor's response:

> Portal started to outline the Universal deal when Norman broke in with: 'Wyndham, you're surely not going to interest yourself with that awful film industry?'
>
> Portal caught my eye, and tried to make out a case, but Norman was adamant. 'It's no good, Wyndham! It's unsound. And those dreadful people are not your class. Keep out of it.'[22]

The deal with Universal did take place, despite Montagu Norman's

81

hostile attitude, and Portal later told Wilcox: 'Don't take the Governor too seriously. He has a bee in his bonnet about the British film industry.'

Lever wanted the Bank to prompt the City to pump more capital into film production. The Prudential was the largest shareholder in London Films, having purchased 25,000 deferred and 250,000 preferred ordinary shares in the company in 1934. Alexander Korda had created London Films (LFP) in 1932, and the company went public in 1934. Korda had been signed up by United Artists in May 1933; and *The Private Life of Henry VIII*, which they financed, was an astonishing success, scoring a world box-office record of £7,500 on its first day's showing at the Radio City Music Hall in New York. Montagu Marks, an Australian businessman who had joined LFP, together with Sir Cunnop Guthrie, persuaded Percy Crump of the Prudential to invest in Korda's company. The main reason for this, apart from Korda's successful reputation, was to enable LFP to develop the 'Hillman colour process' which had impressed Marks during a visit to England. Marks learnt that the company owning the process, Colourgravure Ltd, a subsidiary of Gerrard Industries, needed a successful film producer to buy and exploit it, and Korda seemed the obvious choice. However, LFP was less fortunate with subsequent films, losing £30,000 in the fiscal year 1934. And by May 1936 this figure had risen to £330,000.

Korda's base was Denham, a complex of large modern studios which cost almost a million pounds to establish and which were finally completed in May 1936, following delays caused by the exceptionally harsh winter of 1935–6 and a fire during construction. The Prudential had been concerned since October 1935 about Korda's overspending, but by January 1937 Lever was confident that a standard of economical production had been laid down and accepted by Korda. Lever told Gordon Munro in March 1937 that although the situation at Denham had improved, the 'crisis' made tenants difficult to find. He outlined the precarious method of short-term finance, arguing that, although it caused problems, 'This class of finance could, with proper supervision and adequate margins, be so organised that it is practically gilt-edged so far as the lender is concerned, but to achieve this it is essential . . . for the time being, it should be centralised in one institution.'[23] In other words, he was advocating a sort of Film Bank, with possible support from the Bank of England. His idea was that a syndicate of bankers should provide short-term finance, and that a permanent organisation should be established once the necessary experience had been gained. He also hinted that the government might involve itself more directly:

> Although ultimately such a bank should be a purely lending institution run on conservative and economical lines, it should in the early stages of the building up of the industry take some part of the real risk of film production and might in some form or other be the

channel through which the Government could give the industry direct financial support if it decided to do so.[24]

Lever also considered that the industry needed to be reorganised, and that steps should be taken 'to concentrate the production side of the business into two or three strong groups and to encourage much closer collaboration'. His ultimate dream was for British films to succeed in world markets.

The Bank of England based its initial investigations on this report, and also on a report submitted by Helbert, Wagg and Company in April. The latter report concentrated on the need to reform the whole industry, rather than just the production sector. It agreed with Lever that the best productions were those that aimed to penetrate overseas markets, and that short-term finance, properly directed, was a suitable financial method. Munro wanted a Film Finance Corporation, and an expert to be called in from abroad to reorganise the industry. This was part of a three-pronged strategy: an interim arrangement for the immediate crisis; reorganisation; and the eventual establishment of a Film Bank.

On 8 April 1937 a meeting took place at the Bank attended by representatives from Helbert, Wagg and Company, the Board of Trade and the Bank itself. The Board of Trade was concerned about the industry, but would not commit the government to direct financial involvement unless the Bank's inquiry showed this to be unavoidable. There was talk, though, of the government providing a guarantee for the interim period, when a syndicate would be established with control of about £2 million. Before interviews began with selected people in the industry, Munro submitted a memorandum outlining a possible scheme for the interim organisation.[25]

The information for the Bank's inquiry came from the minutes of evidence to the Moyne Committee, and from interviews with the following: E. H. Lever; R. D. Fennelly of the Board of Trade; Lord Portal of Laverstoke, chairman of the General Cinema Finance Corporation, the recently formed holding company for the growing Rank empire; R. P. Baker of Associated Film Distributors; F. W. Baker of Butcher's Film Service; C. M. Woolf, who had resigned from Gaumont-British in May 1935 and formed General Film Distributors; S. W. Smith, managing director of the British Lion Film Corporation; and Simon Rowson.

When Lever was interviewed, he said that at the end of 1936 the Prudential had about £2 million invested in LFP, and reiterated that Denham had difficulty finding tenants because the financial crisis discouraged production.[26] To remedy this, it had been decided that LFP should embark on a production programme of twenty films a year to keep the studios going, but finance for this was only available until mid-1937. Lever said the Prudential currently had £800,000 locked up in completed but undistributed films; and the total amount needed to keep LFP producing and Denham solvent was about £2 million. He was anxious that the Bank of England should support the formation of a Film Bank so that the Prudential could be persuaded to continue to back LFP. Bunbury commented on Lever's case:

> He may have lost more than he cares to say and wants to lessen his commitments on the production side, hoping eventually to float the studio as a Public Company. . . . He rather spoils his case for the independent producer in his anxiety for the Prudential and although the difficulties of Pinewood and Denham reflect the difficulties of the 'independent', a safe and satisfactory way of giving financial help to these people has not so far emerged.[27]

On 26 April, Bunbury and Skinner saw Fennelly and informed him about the interview with Lever. Fennelly doubted whether LFP would have to close, but he knew that the Schach group was in trouble and that Sound City studios could find few tenants. On the other hand, Maxwell's group was not about to collapse and other producers showed no symptoms of 'crisis'.

There was more news of LFP when Munro informed Skinner and Bunbury that Lever had failed to obtain money from Lloyds Bank. If no word came from the government about film finance, he said, LFP would have to close.[28]

The next interview was with Lord Portal. He placed the blame for the crisis on the independent producer who obtained money through the insurance brokers. He was opposed to Korda's expansionist policy, and thought it wiser to concentrate on economical productions budgeted at not more than £60,000. Portal said that C. M. Woolf was financially inept, so the General Cinema Finance Corporation had been formed and a £1½ million deal made with Universal to shore up GFD.

R. P. Baker agreed with Portal that Wilcox and Korda had overspent, and the lure of the American market spelt disaster. C. M. Woolf said that the small independents were the cause of all the trouble, but 'if the industry were to have another crash it would be the end. . . . He would like to see the worthwhile independents continue as such if we could feel the way'. Simon Rowson submitted memoranda on the need for reciprocity with America: 'It is probably impossible to contemplate the production of large scale pictures otherwise than under the protection of a reciprocal plan. Up to the present, however, no evidence exists that American interests are likely to agree any effective proposals for bringing it about.'[29]

The evidence so far showed that the 'crisis' affected LFP and many of the smaller companies, and was caused by three main factors:

extravagance and rising costs; unstable finance; and the onerous terms of the distribution contract. The Bank of England was in a difficult position, and was determined not to recommend intervention unless the case was 'exceptional'. Any remedy had to be permanent and self-sustaining, and the Bank thought some participation by the industry would be necessary. The inquiry was secret, which meant that only the opinions sought were considered. The investigation was originally intended to be more thorough: the list of people to be interviewed was much longer than those actually seen. For example, important representatives not examined were Messrs Crawley and Stevenson of C. T. Bowring Insurance, a major backer of film production in the 1930s; F. C. Ellis and L. H. Wilkins, who were directors of Glanvill Enthoven and Aldgate Trustees; representatives of the Westminster and National Provincial Banks and of the insurance companies. It seemed that the Bank of England wanted the inquiry to justify its instinctive stance of non-intervention, and was therefore selective when gathering evidence.

The LFP position deteriorated. It was disclosed that Lloyds Bank had been asked to advance money on the security of the film negative and insurance policies covering 70 per cent of the cost of production and the 30 per cent balance – or 'risk money' – put up by the Prudential. Lever said that not only had Lloyds refused to put up the money, but the National Provincial and Midland Banks had also refused. He needed £400,000 to complete films in production, and the City firm of Glyn Mills had been asked to supply £200,000. The total amount needed to pull LFP through the crisis was nearly £2 million. But Bunbury was more cautious: 'There is a degree of unanimity amongst those we have seen of extravagance, irresponsible management and lack of control in LFP and amazement that the Pru should have done what they have done.'[30] In February 1937 F. M. Guedalla, United Artists' legal counsel in Britain, reported on the increasingly precarious relationship between LFP and the Prudential:

> Reverting to the Balance Sheet I should think Korda and LFP must be in a terrible way, but inasmuch as the Prudential are owed mortgages for £1,100,000 and are stated to have another £900,000 invested in the business . . . I have thought and still think that the Prudential are bound to see Korda through his troubles. On the other hand, they are getting very sick of paying out month after month. . . . If they decide to stop financing LFP, then the whole show blows up immediately.[31]

In May, Lever sent Bunbury some figures relating to all LFP films produced since *The Private Life of Henry VIII* in 1933 (see Tables XIVa and XIVb).[32]

London Film Productions

Film	Cost of Production	(£) Receipts to 24/4/37
The Private Life of Henry VIII	£ 93,710	£210,000
Catherine the Great	127,868	127,000
Don Juan	114,239	53,700
Scarlet Pimpernel	143,521	204,300
Sanders of the River	149,789	143,200
The Ghost Goes West	156,062	158,039
TOTAL	£785,189	£896,239

The following figures were intended to show that LFP had reformed, and that some newer productions were less extravagant.

TABLE XIVb

Film	Cost of Production
Things to Come	£241,028
The Man who could Work Miracles	133,104
Moscow Nights	52,326
Rembrandt	138,945
Men are not Gods	93,362

Lever said that if no money was forthcoming the Prudential would be forced to wind up LFP, or sell out to the Americans. Later, Lloyds Bank agreed to advance against new films on the floor, but would go no further despite pressure from the brokers.

On 25 April, the Governor of the Bank was presented with an Interim Report.[33] It was agreed that the methods employed by the City over the last few years had been dangerous, and that a shakeout was needed. Any financial assistance, the report stated, should only be given to 'people of substance' and under 'stringent conditions'. The films produced with money from a new film finance organisation should be aimed at the British market, as costs over the past years had increased by as much as 60 per cent, LFP being one of the main companies responsible for the increase. The Interim Report recorded that the inquiry had suffered so far because an expert had not contributed, and the need for a permanent organisation had not yet been considered in the context of the wider debates on the Films Act. The inquiry had presupposed a crisis based on Lever's original memorandum, but many of the people interviewed had not backed up his argument of a general crisis.

Lever continued to press the government about LFP's plight. He wrote a letter to Dr Burgin, Parliamentary Secretary at the Board of Trade, which R. D. Fennelly of the Board described as being 'in the nature of an ultimatum' since it said that everything depended on the government's attitude:

> If that attitude is one of indifference my course is clear – if the contrary then I will willingly continue to help all I can and will do my best to persuade my directors not to take drastic action at this stage. . . . I can only do this however if I have a definite assurance that other finance will very shortly be forthcoming. London Films has to expend money and enter into commitments now for productions many months hence and I obviously cannot advise my Company to assist London Films to meet this expenditure unless I know that money will be available to see the programme through.[34]

On 1 June, Bunbury wrote a personal note to the Governor of the Bank, warning Norman about the dangers of extending the scope of the Bank's inquiry.[35] From then on the likelihood of the Bank becoming involved in a scheme to help production – or of a government subsidy – was more remote. Bunbury wrote:

> There is no evidence today of any breakdown in the fulfilment of quota. . . . A decision on the Film Bank is complicated by a hangover from the Aide-Memoire position in the form of LFP and I see great danger in our being put into a false position through the insistent applications from one quarter. . . . I think LFP must find their own solution. . . . For the Bank to take any further steps by way of enquiries would imply that something was likely to be done and I have no confidence that any further enquiries would disclose a practicable basis for any worthwhile Film Bank on commercial lines.[36]

One possibility was for the Bank to promise to induce commercial concerns to finance the more successful companies; and that the government should establish a Films Commission to regulate the industry.

In June, Norman wrote to Sir Horace Wilson, the government's chief industrial adviser, who had initiated the inquiry:

> It would appear that the recommendations of the Moyne Report in the matter of financial organisations were made without sufficient appreciation of the practical difficulties of proceeding on commercial lines at the present time. It may, however, be a matter for consideration by HMG whether in the absence for the present of any central Film Finance Organization a Films Commission, as suggested in the Moyne Report, might combine with such other functions as might be allotted to it, the functions of watching the financial develop-

ments within the industry. To this end a Films Commission might be empowered by law to call for appropriate and confidential returns by renters and exhibitors such as would enable the Commission to substantiate a case for a subsidy or for financial assistance in some form or another should such be necessary at a later date.[37]

LFP's immediate financial problems were relieved when Korda managed to raise £100,000 through the Chase National Bank of America, against the rentals to accrue from *Knight Without Armour*. Even so, LFP's problems continued, and Korda was forced to relinquish Denham in 1938. In June 1937 it was confirmed that the Bank of England's inquiry was concluded, leaving behind a vague promise for a Films Commission and some financial aid in the future. In the meantime, the quota remained the mainstay of the Board of Trade's films policy.

5 American Diplomacy and the Films Act

The film industry in this country is young and growing . . . it is essentially a type of industry with which the Government should interfere as little as possible.

R. D. Fennelly, of the Board of Trade's Film Department, in a minute to another official about the Films Commission.

The debate on the Moyne Report initiated serious discussion about the renewal of the Films Act. Films policy was due for reconsideration. And this time the issue of protection was less politically controversial, since Britain had abandoned free trade for a system of protection and Imperial Preference, based on the Ottawa Agreements of 1932. This was resented by the Americans, even though their own markets were protected by high tariffs.

From December 1936 to March 1937 the film trade submitted comments on Moyne to the Board of Trade. The general reaction was that protective quota legislation should continue, but that the Report's most radical recommendation, the independent Films Commission, should be rejected. The Board of Trade also opposed the idea because: 'It would place executive powers in the hands of a body over whom the President would have little control but for whose actions he would be answerable in Parliament.'[1] The Home Office thought a Commission would interfere with the position of the local authorities. The trade's main objection was that an independent body would meddle in strictly 'trade' affairs, such as overbuilding of cinemas ('redundancy'), film rentals and standard contracts. In other words, a body acting for the public interest was seen as a great threat to the trade's control over the industry. Such a body was not unprecedented. The sugar industry had a small body of commissioners, independent of the industry and appointed by the government, charged with 'the duty of considering not only the interest of the sugar industry, but the national interests generally, including the interests of the consumer'.[2] There was a similar body, with somewhat reduced powers, for the livestock industry. The Films

Commission had considerable support from the press – *The Times*, the *Daily Telegraph*, the *Manchester Guardian*, the *Financial News*, the *Daily Herald* and the *Observer*.

The CEA was the only trade group in favour of Moyne's quality viewing test, but it insisted that the viewing committee empowered to assess a film's 'entertainment value' should be dominated by the trade. The CEA feared that a 'cost test' might reduce the number of films available for hire.

In March 1937, at the CEA's Annual Dinner, Dr Leslie Burgin, Parliamentary Secretary of the Board of Trade, pleaded for the industry to confer and produce a scheme of reform: 'I make an earnest appeal to the trade to set up some body which can serve as a focusing point for matters affecting the trade as a whole and which can deal with some of the problems which arise between the various sections.'[3] In April, a Joint Trade Committee (CEA and KRS) met to discuss trade problems. The exhibitors were most concerned about 'redundancy', or the over-building of cinemas. Simon Rowson calculated that in the three years up to the end of 1934 302 new cinemas were built in Britain.[4] These added 351,500 seats, or 10 per cent of the total, and nearly half the new seating was for 'super cinemas' with over 1,500 seats. At the end of 1934 the total number of seats in the UK was 3,873,000. According to the CEA, 111 new houses opened in 1935, of which only 19 were replacements, making the net increase 92 cinemas, 27 of them being owned by the circuits.[5] Cinema-going was the mass entertainment of the working class – in 1935, 907 million admissions were recorded to the picture-houses of Britain.[6] Table xv illustrates the power of the combines, and how the trend was for smaller circuits to huddle together to compete with the booking strength of the larger groupings.[7]

The CEA Annual Report complained:

> Present day building tends to become more associated with the circuits. . . . Their purchasing power disturbs the equilibrium of the distribution of films which has hitherto prevailed amongst the existing kinemas. If this process continues at the present rapid rate, it will probably mark the last stage towards the goal of the super-saturation point.[8]

This was exacerbated by the 'KRS booking policy': renters refused to rent a film for a second or subsequent cinemas unless the exhibitor in question owned a 51 per cent interest in the cinemas. This increased competition between exhibitors, and encouraged circuit growth. It was claimed that the CEA and the KRS were near agreement over these contentious issues, but there was never any clear indication of a truce over the film hire question. The problem was exacerbated by internal rifts in both bodies between circuit representatives and 'independents'.

TABLE XV
Cinema circuits in Britain 1935–6

Size of circuit	No. of circuits		Total no. halls		Net increase of halls
	1935	1936	1935	1936	approx. 12 mths 1936
2–9 halls	128	138	615	824	209
10–19	22	27	288	333	45
20–49	4	5	130	151	21
50–99	1	2	53	106	53
100–199	2	2	242	320	78
+200	2	2	559	601	42
Total circuits	159	176	1,887	2,335	448

Walter Runciman, the President of the Board of Trade, announced in the Commons that the quota would continue for another ten years, but said that before the Bill was published there would be intensive discussions with the trade. In April the Lords debated the films question, and Lord Strabolgi proposed a motion, which was later passed by the government: 'That in the opinion of the House a flourishing British kinema industry is of increasing importance, and that all practicable steps be taken to assist its foundation on a firm basis.'[9]

In May, Neville Kearney of the Film Producers' Group of the FBI sent Fennelly at the Board of Trade details of the meetings between the CEA, the KRS and the FBI. They disagreed on certain fundamental points. The exhibitors still objected to a cost test, while the other groups recommended one of £15,000 as the statutory minimum cost for a renters' quota film. The CEA and the FBI worked out a scheme for statutory arbitration to resolve trade conflicts. The trade was to form a Joint Trade Committee. All questions except film· rentals could be discussed and the Board of Trade was to be asked to appoint an arbitrator, or arbitration board, with powers to decide any points of disagreement. Each decision was to be registered with the Board of Trade, and penalties could be imposed for breaches of the agreements. The producers stressed the advantages of flexibility in the Act's administration, as Kearney explained:

> We naturally do not want to antagonise the Americans. . . . Flexibility of powers in the Act . . . seems to me to be the key to the situation. If it is realised that tails can be twisted without the formality of new legislation . . . I feel pretty confident that the spirit of the law as well as its letter will be observed.[10]

In fact, the element of flexibility in the eventual Act did make it more acceptable to the Americans and the trade.

As for the quota percentages, the renters and exhibitors wanted the initial quotas to be 15 per cent for renters and 10 per cent for exhibitors, whereas the producers favoured 20 per cent and 15 per cent. The FBI and the ACT were the only major trade groups to advocate a 'shorts' quota; and in May, Kearney informed the Board of Trade of the FBI's latest scheme to reduce the number of American films:

> A further essential method of ensuring the protection and development of the industry would be the imposition of restrictions on imports of foreign films, coupled, if desired, with a considerable increase in the specific rate of import duty on such films.[11]

This was never enacted – it was too great a threat to American interests – but the FBI was keen on a scheme of reciprocity to promote the distribution of more British films in America, and this was included in the 1938 Act, although the eventual clause was more or less drafted by Fay Allport, the representative of the Hays Office in London.[12]

At that point an important disagreement occurred in the CEA over the quality test. The CEA's General Council was strongly in favour of the latter, even though its Committee recommended a cost test. The circuit representatives in the CEA, Major Gale and Mr Fligelstone, clashed with the 'independents' on the General Council, Messrs Nyman and Metcalfe. The trade met Dr Burgin on 26 May, and the Board of Trade was forced to conclude:

> In drafting legislation affecting a trade as intricate as this it is obvious that the Government would be in a happier position if they could rely upon a considerable volume of trade support. It is clear, however, that there is little hope of the divergent views being reconciled without a strong lead from outside and that the Government must proceed to formulate their own proposals. . . . The exhibitors seem to be on rather a bad wicket as it can be argued their agitation is one in support of foreign films against British films.[13]

In this instance the Board of Trade was not blind to the exhibitors' vested interest in keeping American films in plentiful supply.

In May 1937, Oliver Stanley became President of the Board of Trade. Stanley had come into contact with the film industry during his term of office as Under-Secretary to the Home Office (1931–3) and had piloted the Sunday Entertainments Bill through the Commons. Before taking over from Runciman at the Board of Trade, he had been at the Board of Education.

The Board of Trade released a set of proposals in June. These were that initial quotas for long films should be 20 per cent for renters and 15 per cent for exhibitors, rising by stages over ten years to 30 per cent and 25 per cent. A minimum cost test of £15,000 per film was proposed for renters' quota films, with films costing £45,000–60,000 obtaining double quota credit. A film failing the cost test could still qualify for renters' quota, provided it proved of 'special exhibition value'. A possible reciprocity option was mentioned, but no details were given. The Board of Trade was to have powers to vary quota levels and the amount of the cost test every three years. The proposals also stated that there should be a 'shorts' quota of 10 per cent for renters and 5 per cent for exhibitors, rising to 20 per cent and 15 per cent over ten years. There was to be no cost test initially for 'shorts', but the Board of Trade was to have the power to impose one subsequently. The only classes of film excluded from quota protection were newsreels and commercial advertisements. Finally, the Films Commission was rejected in favour of a body similar to the existing Advisory Committee.

On 8 July, Stanley wrote a memorandum for the Cabinet, outlining his proposals for a White Paper issued later in the month.[14] He explained his objection to the quality test: 'It would inevitably introduce a much greater element of uncertainty into film production; and one result of accepting this recommendation of the Moyne Committee would therefore be to add vastly to the difficulty of financing British film production.' The White Paper followed the same lines as the June proposals, except that the minimum cost test was to be calculated on a 'Form C' basis, i.e. £7,500 in salaries and wages as the minimum. The idea that expensive films should qualify for double quota credit was confirmed, but Stanley altered the minimum figure to £22,500 in labour costs. The possible reciprocity option mentioned in the June proposals was detailed in the White Paper. The producers, and individuals like Lord Strabolgi, Simon Rowson and later Maxwell and Ostrer, wanted more British films to be shown in America, although there were disagreements on the best method of achieving this. Stanley therefore recommended that if a renter acquired, for not less than £20,000, the rights for one foreign country of a British long film, he should be allowed to count the purchase as equivalent to the acquisition for renting in Britain of a British film of the same length. The quota figures were modest at the outset because of the time needed to allow the trade to adjust to the cost test. Other minor recommendations in the White Paper involved tightening up the existing restrictions on blind and advance booking; dropping the 'scenario author' provision of the 1927 Act; stipulating that films made in the Dominions could qualify for renters' quota provided they passed the 'cost test'; and allowing up to three unadvertised 'try outs' of films before a trade show.

TRADE REACTIONS TO THE WHITE PAPER

Soon after the publication of the White Paper the trade began to campaign in earnest for alterations. The American renters, represented in London by Fay Allport of the Hays Office, were quick to send a memorandum to the Board of Trade.[15] Their main desire was for an extension of the multiple quota credit principle. The White Paper provided that films costing three times the minimum should get double quota, but the renters wanted to go further and win triple quota for films costing four times the minimum. The other main provision demanded by the Americans was that more foreign labour should be allowed to work on British films. They also opposed a 'shorts' quota and the figure for the cost test, and asked for American representation on the Advisory Committee. The KRS was by this time dominated by American renters, and the British renters decided to be represented by the FBI during the quota debates.

In the 1930s the Americans had become more concerned about overseas markets. The Fascist regimes in Italy and Germany had effectively excluded American films. Nathan D. Golden, Chief of the Motion Picture Division of the US Bureau of Foreign and Domestic Commerce, complained in 1939:

> The intensification of difficulties abroad has resulted in a falling off, from 70 per cent to 65 per cent, in America's domination of the world's picture screens. . . . During the past year the ardent fanning of that spirit of nationalism has meant in numerous countries, an ever increasing fervour and energy in the attempt to build up the struggling local film industries – industries which, despite their obvious faults and feebleness are apt to be supported by governmental action.[16]

In 1938 about 35 per cent of the American industry's gross income came from abroad, mainly from the British Empire. In the late 1930s quotas, import restrictions and censorship regulations threatened to accelerate the protectionist trend and reduce the number of American films exhibited. The Hays Office was desperately anxious that the 1938 Films Act should not further shrink Hollywood's overseas markets.

The Americans were able to take advantage of the fact that at the same time as the debate on the renewal of the Films Act, Britain and America were contemplating an Anglo-American Trade Agreement. The crisis in Europe made such an agreement extremely significant for political reasons, since politicians on both sides thought it might reduce German expansionism. British statesmen, led by Anthony Eden, hoped for American support against the threat of Japan in the Far East and of Hitler in Europe. They were anxious not to anger Washington on the comparatively trivial film issue. On his side, Cordell Hull, the American Secretary of State, was anxious not to allow the film dispute to jeopardise the trade agreement negotiations, especially since Hays informed him that the film industry might unleash an anti-British press campaign

94

based on the injustices of the quota, using the issue as an example of the British attitude towards trade liberalisation. He was concerned that the criticisms of his trade agreements programme in Congress should not increase, and his hopes for an agreement with Britain rested on persuading his colleagues that it would reduce tension in Europe, promote multilateral trade and dismantle Imperial Preference. Several key areas in the US economy were anxious for freer access to British and Imperial markets to keep them out of the Depression. Both the Foreign Office and the US State Department had an interest, therefore, in not allowing quarrels over the film industry to endanger much larger issues.[17] In March 1937 Hull wrote to the US Embassy in London:

> At this time both Great Britain and the US are hopeful of world-wide trade liberalisation and are likewise hopeful that trade between the two countries themselves may be placed upon a more liberal foundation. I would view with considerable regret any move which would lay greater burdens on an American interest as important to us as the motion picture industry.[18]

The State Department supported the Hays Office in its attempts to influence the British legislation, and, as will be shown, was partially successful in securing, with Oliver Stanley's help, some of its demands in the eventual Act.

The CEA meanwhile persisted in its campaign for a trade-dominated Commission and a quality-viewing test. To reach some sort of compromise, the CEA and the FBI agreed on a trade committee to inform the President of the Board of Trade about 'trade' matters. The Board of Trade was doubtful, as Fennelly wrote to R. C. G. Somervell of the Industries and Manufactures department:

> Both the FBI and CEA are still hankering after some sort of a Films Commission, but I think I persuaded them that the utmost they could hope for was a clause to the effect that the President might, if he thought fit, refer to the Advisory Committee for investigation and report any question brought to his notice by a trade body recognised by him for that purpose. I pointed out, however, that such powers could rarely be exercised as I could not see the President permitting the Advisory Committee to consider redundancy or such questions as film rentals, which were necessarily commercial matters to be settled by the trade itself.[19]

The problem that the officials did not face up to was that, left to its own devices, the trade had never been able to sort out its problems. The CEA was worried about the renters' superior bargaining position, and its desire for an exhibitor-dominated Films Commission reflects this. The

95

KRS had recently introduced a 'grading policy' whereby films deemed by a KRS viewing committee as 'A', as opposed to less good 'B' films, were only offered for hire on percentage rather than flat-rate terms. However, since the Commission advocated by the CEA was to be trade-dominated, the chance of it producing agreement with the renters was remote. The obvious solution – the independent Films Commission advocated by the Moyne Committee – was rejected because of opposition from the trade and from the Board of Trade.

The Association of Cine-Technicians (ACT) wanted a fair wages clause in the new Act, and a restriction on the number of foreign technicians allowed to work on quota film productions. The union's membership of 98 in 1933 had risen to 1,122 by 1936.[20] Between October 1936 and August 1937 the number of unemployed technicians rose from 40 to over 200, or nearly one-sixth of the ACT's membership. Wages had also been cut in the slump, and the fear was that the White Paper's double quota credit provision would encourage more American companies to produce in Britain, using mainly foreign labour. Although there were provisions attached to the granting of work permits for foreigners by the Ministry of Labour, the ACT's spokesmen, Ralph Bond and George Elvin, argued that these were seldom observed. Permits stipulated that foreign workers had to train their British counterparts, but in practice the 'ace' technicians stayed on in Britain and were not gradually replaced by British labour. There was also a clause in the permit making the employment of a foreigner conditional on proof that there were no suitable British technicians and that native labour would not be displaced. The ACT claimed that Korda at Denham rarely employed British workers, and that unless something was done the British would never gain the experience needed to replace foreign technicians. The TUC supported the ACT in its cause, and the Norwich TUC passed a resolution:

That the contemplated legislation relating to British films shall provide for the maintenance and development of a British film industry free from foreign disparagement and influence and shall adequately safeguard the employment of those British workpeople now employed in the film industry.[21]

Already the American companies had started to increase production in Britain. MGM was making bold plans for its new unit headed by Michael Balcon, and Warners First-National continued to produce at Teddington. Paramount announced plans for a series of films for the world market. British technicians had every reason to fear the consequences, if the American tendency to use technicians from Hollywood continued, of the Board of Trade's policy of encouraging American finance to sponsor 'British' films.

The Bill's career through Committee, Report stage and final readings was eventful. The rhetoric was reminiscent of 1927. Oliver Stanley declared: 'I do not want our defences to be made in Hollywood. I want the world to be able to see British films true to British life, accepting British standards and spreading British ideas.'[22] The main changes were the adoption of a Cinematograph Films Council on the lines of the Advisory Committee of the 1927 Act; the rejection of the producers' separate quota scheme and Stanley's alternative; the institution of the triple quota credit provision to encourage American finance into British production; and the adoption of a fair wages clause.

Tom Williams, a Labour MP, reintroduced the Films Commission clause during the Report stage:

> My argument is based exclusively on the wisdom or otherwise of appointing a small commission to be permanently engaged watching every move, advising the Board of Trade, drafting regulations and orders where they are necessary, and generally keeping in far closer touch with the industry than has been the case during the past ten years.[23]

However, despite considerable support for the Commission at the Committee stage, Stanley made sure that the clause was not passed in the Report stage – it was rejected by 201 to 140 votes. In the end he succeeded in substituting a trade-oriented body consisting of eleven 'independents' and ten trade members (two producers, two renters, two employees and four exhibitors). With limited terms of reference, the body resembled the Advisory Committee of the 1927 Act. This disappointing result was predictable because of the hostility of both the industry and the Board of Trade to Moyne's Commission. John Grierson was particularly upset that the Board of Trade had rejected the proposal, and wrote in 1937:

> The long-term service of creative and national interests is being sacrificed to short-term financial ones. The Moyne proposals took a long view and aimed at a wise government of the film industry. The prospect has disappeared with the vital omission of the Moyne proposals for a commission which would stand above the conflict of commercial interests. It is natural enough for the Board of Trade to be jealous lest another body usurp its functions, but the loss of the Film Commission must disappoint all who wish to see the anarchies of the trade abated, the interests of minorities preserved, the quality and personnel factors encouraged, and the fierce commercial interests of the trade geared to national purposes.[24]

Towards the end of 1937 the trade unions and the FBI formulated a scheme known as the 'separate quota'.[25] The idea, advocated for example by Norman Loudon of Sound City Films, was that no film could qualify for both renters' and exhibitors' quota. The latter was to be reserved for films marketed by British companies, creating a small protected market for British films. Stanley did not agree; nor did the CEA and three influential figures – John Maxwell, C. M. Woolf and Maurice Ostrer. Stanley proposed an alternative along similar lines, stipulating that films qualifying for renters' quota could, if the renter wished, qualify instead for a special exhibitors' quota.[26] This was opposed by the trade, and the scheme was dropped.

The most controversial part of the new Films Act was the extension of the White Paper's 'double' quota provision, to include 'triple' quotas for expensive films. To register for renters' quota a film had to have cost a minimum of £1 per foot in labour costs, with a minimum total of £7,500 per film. If a film cost three times the minimum – at least £3 a foot with a total of not less than £22,500 in labour costs – it could count twice its length for renters' quota. A film of over £37,500 or £5 a foot in labour costs could count three times. This was what the Americans wanted, and the Board of Trade was keen to oblige since it accorded with the policy of inducing American companies to invest in British film production. In February 1938 the Foreign Office sent a telegram to the British Ambassador in Washington, Sir Ronald Lindsay, disclosing that 'certain amendments' (triple quotas and reciprocity) would be introduced when the Bill was in Parliament to meet some of the American demands. This was designed to appease the Americans, and the telegram stressed the importance of secrecy:

> It would be extremely embarrassing if news of these proposals reached either the industry here or the press before the President of the Board of Trade has had an opportunity to mention them. . . . Any suggestions here that HMG were in receipt of formal representations from the US Government on the subject of the Bill while it was still under consideration by Parliament might well destroy any sympathy in Parliament for the proposals.[27]

In March 1938, while the Films Bill was being debated in the Lords, Stanley had a meeting with the US Ambassador, Joseph P. Kennedy, and agreed to fight for triple quotas and reciprocity. These two proposals had been introduced in the Commons, but the government was forced to withdraw them because of two setbacks – Stanley was ill, and there was a Cabinet crisis when Anthony Eden, the Foreign Secretary, resigned on 20 February.

Kennedy, only recently appointed American Ambassador, doggedly pressed the government to make concessions on behalf of the American renters. He had personal experience of the movie world, having been involved in the foundation of RKO-Radio in the late 1920s, before concentrating on politics in the 1930s. Kennedy wrote to Cordell Hull after his meeting with Stanley:

> In my opinion the triple credit and reciprocity amendments should certainly be granted; if they are, my whole opinion of the Bill would be that we have a reasonable Bill from any American point of view but not so reasonable that we definitely should not consider that we have made substantial concessions to the British point of view.[28]

Both these amendments were passed by the Lords, and so the Americans had far less to fear from the legislation than they originally supposed.

Hull was especially keen that the British should include film in the forthcoming trade agreement, since it was a major item of American trade. The British, however, argued that it was outside the purview of international treaties because quotas were a matter of internal regulation, and film was primarily a cultural commodity. The Board of Trade argued that Britain did not intend to discriminate against American films, but wanted

> only to ensure a certain percentage of English films being shown for cultural reasons. The American film industry expects to have things too much its own way. Unfortunately . . . the US Government continues to look on films as a purely commercial item in the trade negotiations . . . while we regard them partly at least as a cultural responsibility.[29]

Using this argument the British succeeded in keeping film out of the discussions on trade, though the Americans tried to introduce it on several occasions. From the way the Board of Trade legislated for the film industry it is hard to imagine that it took cultural arguments seriously; but in the negotiations it was found expedient to present a cultural face. Hull saw the films dispute as a test case for better Anglo-American political and economic relations, and it was a disappointment to him when the British re-enacted quotas for the film industry and refused to allow them to be discussed in the trade negotiations. Even so, the 'triple' quota and reciprocity clauses favoured American interests, and confirmed the Board of Trade's policy of encouraging American investment as a tempting solution to the industry's chronic financial problems.

The new Films Act became law in March 1938. The quotas for long films were to be 15 per cent for renters and 12½ per cent for exhibitors. In the Lords they had been raised by Lord Moyne to 20 per cent and 15 per cent, but Stanley made sure, after considerable pressure from both the Americans and the exhibitors, that they were brought down again in the Commons. The quota for 'shorts' was 15 per cent for renters and 12½ per cent for exhibitors. Studio wages and labour conditions were safeguarded in the Act, and other provisions included the multiple quotas; the reciprocity clause; the inauguration of the Cinematograph Films Council to 'keep under review the progress of the British film industry and report to the Board of Trade'; and a stipulation that the Board could vary, within limits, the quota percentages and the cost test.

The Hays Office approved of the reciprocity clause, multiple quotas, the absence of a Films Commission, and a lower cost test than was originally proposed. However, it did not consider that the other clauses helped the American industry at all, even though the State Department saw the Act as a vast improvement on the White Paper of July 1937. In May 1938, once it was clear that quotas would not be included in the trade agreement talks, the Americans sent a list of unofficial 'suggestions' on the film issue to the Board of Trade. These included limits on quota percentages, and a request that the Board should give sympathetic consideration to American interests in any decisions concerning the availability of British production facilities and labour. These suggestions were rejected. The Hays Office had failed to thwart the legislation.[30]

The new Films Act followed the lines of the 1927 Act, but revealed the government's willingness to rely on American finance rather than try to reorganise the industry. The ACT's Annual Report commented that the new legislation was 'fundamentally unsound in that the basis of the Act is not primarily concerned with the development of a flourishing British film industry independent of foreign control'.[31]

THE ORIGINS OF MONOPOLY

The new quota legislation did not have time to take root before the outbreak of war in 1939. There was, however, a decline in production, from 228 films in the year ending 31 March 1938 to about 90 in the following year. The repercussions of the crisis of 1937 were still being felt, and as in the aftermath of the 1927 Act many small companies collapsed, leaving the field open for the growth of the two major combines.

In the late 1930s Rank's empire was evolving. After establishing GCFC in 1936, and securing the deal with Universal, Rank went on to acquire control of GBPC in 1941. GCFC bought a controlling interest in the Metropolis and Bradford Trust, the company controlling GBPC, and in 1942 Rank acquired control of GCFC through a company called Manorfield Investments. 1941 was significant for Rank also because in that year he acquired control of the Odeon circuit, through a company called Foy Investments which he had formed with Oscar Deutsch. When the latter died in 1942 Rank took over his shares, and thus controlled Odeon's cinemas and Odeon Cinema Holdings (OCH). OCH was linked with UA, and thus with Korda, who joined the OCH Board. In 1938 Denham was merged with Pinewood to form D. & P. Studios. Table XVI illustrates the origins of the Rank monopoly in 1939.[32]

TABLE XVI
The Rank monopoly

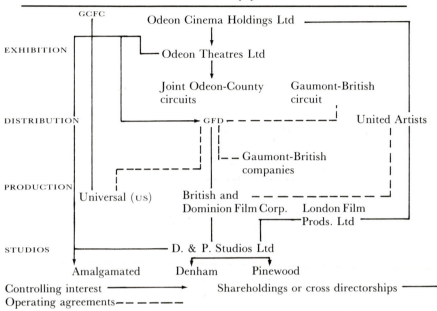

Controlling interest ——————→ Shareholdings or cross directorships ———
Operating agreements— — — — — —

The other major combine, ABPC, had failed to gain control of GBPC, but expanded in 1937 when the Union circuit was acquired, increasing the number of cinemas in the circuit to 450. When John Maxwell died in October 1940 his holding of 4,050,000 ordinary (voting) shares, out of a total of 8,000,000, passed to his widow. Mrs Maxwell needed large sums for estate duty and tax, and in December 1940 ABPC's lawyer, Robert Clarke, approached the Bank of England with a scheme whereby a Film Finance Corporation, being considered again at the time by the Bank, the Treasury and the Board of Trade, would acquire a 50 per cent interest in ABPC through the purchase of the Maxwell shares for £2 million. The Bank rejected this plan because it was not envisaged that a Films Bank would have fixed assets, and the deal might involve the government in the affairs of the industry far more than officials intended.

However, Warner Brothers were interested in purchasing, through their British subsidiary, a 25 per cent interest, or 2,007,000 ordinary shares. The Treasury was not anxious to prevent the deal because it provided an opportunity to bargain with Warners to pay for the shares with blocked sterling and dollars. As Rendell, a Treasury official, wrote to Somervell at the Board of Trade, in June 1941, the Treasury 'might indeed find it difficult in certain circumstances to justify a reluctance to jump at several million dollars in return for an interest in a number of buildings that are liable to be demolished at any moment'.[33] Max Milder of Warners convinced the Board of Trade that the company's interest in the purchase of the ABPC shares was to secure greater co-operation with the British film industry and the promotion of British production:

> It would have been quite possible for us to purchase the whole of Mrs Maxwell's interests, and in fact, her first thought was to secure an outright sale of her whole interests. It was partly because we understand and appreciate the national sensitiveness of these matters that we preferred to acquire only a 25 per cent interest and not a 50 per cent interest.[34]

By August 1941 the deal was completed. Warners purchased the shares for £903,150, and Max Milder was appointed Joint Managing Director of ABPC. Although control formally rested in British hands, it later became clear, when Milder took control of cinemas, that Warners had a more than effective voice in the company's management and booking policies. In 1945 Warners purchased more shares in ABPC, increasing its interest to 37½ per cent of the issued ordinary capital.[35]

By 1939 the post-war structure of the industry was already evolving. And the character, aims and limitations of state intervention were clear. Although ideas for a Films Commission and a Films Bank had been considered in the 1930s, neither had been implemented. The issues were, however, to be raised again during the war, and the Moyne Report remained as a reminder to the government that film 'is today one of the most widely used means for the amusement of the public at large. It is also undoubtedly a most important factor in the education of all classes of the community, in the spread of national culture and in presenting ideas and customs to the world.'[36]

6 Adaptation to War

> Except for a return to something like normal conditions
> almost anything is possible in the British Film World.
>
> *Kinematograph Weekly*, 26 October 1939

A QUESTION OF SURVIVAL

The film industry shared fully in the chaos and confusion of the first
weeks of war. The most immediate cause for alarm was that the Home
Office had sent instructions to all cinemas to close if war were declared.
It seemed at first that, just as the previous war had almost killed off film
production, the present one might put an end to the business altogether.
After 3 September screens were dark all over Britain for some days, and
the absence of the familiar queues made the blacked out streets appear
even more desolate. But the Home Office had been acting on the false
assumption that hostilities would begin with severe aerial attacks and
that in this event cinemas would become deathtraps. When no air raids
occurred, cinemas in some areas were allowed to reopen, and by the end
of the second week only those in Central London remained closed.

Although reprieved from instant extinction the trade still faced great
uncertainty. Exhibitors were worried about their supply of films;
producers wanted to know whether they would be allowed to continue
their work. The behaviour of the government just before the declaration
was rife with contradictions. Already some studios had been earmarked
as storage space by the Ministry of Food, and there was talk of
suspending the quota. Yet elaborate plans for a Ministry of Information
included provision for a sizeable department dealing with film; and the
Films Officer designate, Joseph Ball, invited representatives of the
industry to a lunch and asked them for their future co-operation in
the war effort.[1]

The film trade was prompt in putting its views before the government
and the public. Exhibitors appealed against the closure order; a group of
producers met within days of the declaration and on 9 September sent
representatives to the Board of Trade. The cause was taken up in
Parliament, but the President of the Board of Trade, Oliver Stanley,
avoided making any firm statements, simply repeating an assurance that
'any necessary changes in the present Acts will only be made after
further consultation with them and that there will be no unavoidable

delay in reaching a decision.'[2] In the Upper House, Lord Strabolgi defended the industry with his customary zeal:

> When the last Great War ended the British film producing industry had practically ceased and for seventeen years has had an uphill struggle to try to get back to the position held previously. The first reason that induced me to raise the matter is that we do not want that state of affairs to occur again. I believe that is also the Government view. The film producing industry, I am informed, still has labour and material and is carrying on on a reduced scale, but those concerned in it want to be assured as to the future. In the last Great War all the men were taken from the industry but the industry was not then so important, people had not recognised its importance for entertainment and in moulding the public opinion and, to speak bluntly, as a means of propaganda, disguised or open. There is now uncertainty and the people in the industry want to know in particular whether the Government have any intention of tampering with the Act of 1938 establishing a quota which the industry wish to have maintained.[3]

Oliver Stanley had alarmed the exhibitors by suggesting that he intended to cut the dollar cost of imported films by 75 per cent, an aim which might necessitate a drastic restriction on the number of American films imported; at the same time he had shaken the producers by threatening the complete suspension of the quota Act.[4] Throughout October the state of uncertainty continued. But as the government seemed committed to some method of saving film dollars, producers began to entertain the hope that instead of being put out of business they might be asked to push up their output to replace American films. An editorial in *Kine Weekly* captures the mood precisely: 'Except for a return to something like normal conditions almost anything is possible in the British Film World. Production may founder or it may skyrocket into a dimension hitherto undreamed of.'[5]

The long period of doubt and indecision was partly a product of the general lack of preparation and of poor intelligence which affected most aspects of life in the early stages of the war. But in this case the situation was aggravated by an extreme ambivalence which was only partly resolved as the war progressed. An obvious reason for promoting film production in wartime was that films might contribute to the propaganda effort. The Cinematograph Films Council remarked in their first wartime report: 'The only favourable factor contributed by the war was the enhanced value of the film as a medium for conveying information and for strengthening morale.'[6]

Questions relating to propaganda and morale were themselves the subject of considerable disagreement throughout the war, but controversy was focused on the use of radio and the press. Film, in comparison, received very little Ministerial attention. Duff Cooper has nothing to say about the Films Division in the account he gives of his work as Minister of Information in his autobiography;[7] neither of Brendan Bracken's biographers mention the Ministry's film work.[8] People in the industry occasionally pointed out that the enemy took a very different view of the importance of film,[9] and in a Parliamentary debate the government was reminded on one occasion that 'the Nazis consider film to be an important part of propaganda in total war.'[10] But such comments could backfire by seeming to suggest that Britain should adopt the propaganda methods of the notorious Goebbels. Quite apart from scruples about the morality of using the entire film industry for propaganda, many people doubted the efficacy of overtly propagandist films. Lord Strabolgi warned the head of the Films Division that

> If his department is going to make propaganda films he should be very careful. The obvious propaganda film never creates the effect intended. All films of course have some propaganda value. . . . Even the Hollywood rule that good shall always triumph over evil has a propaganda value.[11]

Doubts about the value of overtly propagandist films increased if anything as a result of work done to assess the effect of some of the MOI's productions for the home market (see page 115). And the more subtle kind of propaganda value which Strabolgi thought all films carried is, by its nature, hard to prove. As the war went on, therefore, the propaganda argument declined in importance. At the·same time the success abroad of a few patriotic films, notably *In Which We Serve*, encouraged the belief that films were an asset in terms of overseas public relations.

The argument which soon came to be taken more seriously as the experience of war was assimilated was that the cinema had a value as entertainment. For this adjustment in official attitudes the cinema could in part thank its audience, which came hurrying back as soon as the closure orders were lifted. Despite the black-out, continuing restrictions on opening hours and the lingering fear of air raids, takings, which had fallen by 30 per cent in September 1939, had returned to near normal by the end of October and were slightly higher than normal in November and December. When the air raids did begin seriously the following autumn, the government made no attempt to repeat the blanket ban of the year before. Cinemas not only stayed open but continued functioning right through raids, and indeed if the raid went on the audience often stayed all night.[12] While the public made their own demonstration of the importance they attached to cinema-going, the military authorities were discovering that entertainment had a considerable value in sustaining morale among the troops.

Official interest in the cinema, therefore, was related to a concern with the national image rather than with propaganda defined more narrowly. As Simon Rowson put it in an internal Board of Trade memorandum: 'The admitted reasons for maintaining such an industry are, first, that it might continue to contribute to the recreation of the people at home and throughout the Empire, and second, to "project Britain" all the time all over the world.'[13] In practice the first consideration rather than the second guided policy, and the exhibition side of the industry, essential as a provider of entertainment, was maintained at full strength throughout the war, whereas the production side, essential for 'projecting Britain' but not necessarily vital as a supplier of films, was run down to less than half its original capacity, with no firm commitment to keeping it going even on this reduced scale.

When conscription began, cinemas were from the first treated much more favourably than studios. In 1940 chief projectionists were 'reserved' (exempted from conscription) from the age of eighteen while senior production technicians were reserved from thirty; actors and some junior grades of technician were not reserved at all. The position for producers became at least less chaotic when, early in 1941, the system of reserving whole categories of jobs was effectively superseded by arrangements to defer the service of individuals, whether actors or technicians. All the same, producers continued to complain that films had to be postponed or abandoned because of manpower difficulties. Cinemas did not have to close for want of staff, although they did suffer shortages and, like many industries, came to rely more and more on newly trained women recruits. Special courses were organised to enable women to take up the work of assistant projectionists. It is of interest that far fewer opportunities opened for women in production, probably because, since most of the jobs involved were more prestigious, there was more resistance to allowing women to do them.[14]

In the summer of 1940 the Board of Trade took an active interest in plans being worked out by the CEA and the KRS to decentralise the method of distributing films so as to ensure that supplies could be maintained even if transport was severely disrupted. Yet, in the same period, the Board of Trade accepted arrangements which much reduced the producers' ability to make films. The most serious problem was space. By the spring of 1940 many studios had already been taken over for other uses: only six out of nineteen remained fully operative while a further four were only partially functioning. In the summer, the Ministry of Aircraft Production requisitioned another four studios and in the autumn threatened to take Denham, the largest and by far the best of the remaining studios. It was only this last claim, which would very nearly have put an end to feature production, that provoked some serious resistance. In the end Beaverbrook accepted other premises and Oliver Lyttleton, then President of the Board of Trade, made a clear commitment to preserve some production by putting in a claim to the Ministry of Works to earmark eight remaining studios for film-making.

Producers were also affected by material shortages since they used many controlled materials. In 1940 film production was classified as number eight on the list of priorities operated by local appropriation boards. Producers experienced some difficulties at this time, but it was not until the introduction of clothes rationing in 1941 that material shortages became a big issue. The government at first took the view that actors would have to use their personal coupons to obtain costumes. After some determined lobbying, the authorities relented to the extent of introducing a system enabling producers to make specific claims for additional coupons. The briefing given to the President of the Board of Trade in this context sums up the official attitude at the time:

> The president may wish to adopt the line that we should not wish to deny that films have a certain value for export purposes and morale. On the other hand if any cloth that is devoted to one object must be withheld from another purpose, films undoubtedly come pretty low on the scale of priorities.[15]

The discrepancy in the treatment of exhibitors and producers made sense only because a large proportion of films came from America. Such attention as producers did receive was partly due to doubts about the future of American imports. In the first two years of war there were fears that the supply might be affected by enemy action, or cut back by the Treasury, or cut off as a result of American retaliation against import restrictions. Even when the supply of American films seemed assured, the need to save dollars provided an argument for keeping some domestic production going in order to avoid complete dependence on imported films.

It was not surprising, therefore, that official attitudes to production fluctuated according to the state of the nation's finances and the behaviour of America.

THE FRAMEWORK OF GOVERNMENT

One factor which helps to account for the government's indecisive and often contradictory behaviour was that there was no body of the kind Moyne had proposed in 1936, a body responsible specifically for film matters. The relevant issues overlapped into the territory of a number of Ministries; and as the wartime administration took shape, the confusion grew as more bodies came to exercise powers in different limited spheres.[16]

The Board of Trade and the Home Office retained their former functions, and the Home Office acquired additional powers to regulate the opening hours of cinemas. The new Ministry of Information was made responsible for matters relating to censorship, propaganda and morale, but did not have a monopoly of power in these areas since the Board of Film Censors continued its normal work; the British Council promoted British film abroad; the armed services both produced and exhibited films. The Ministry of Labour decided which categories of workers or which individuals should be exempt from military service. The Ministry of Works dealt with competing demands for industrial or commercial premises. Several Ministries, in particular those of Food and Aircraft Production, were involved indirectly because they wanted to occupy studios. Local boards were involved in allocating goods. The Treasury already had an interest in Entertainments duty and the Bank of England had conducted the 1937 investigation, but one of the most significant developments associated with the war was that, as a result of the dollar problem, both these bodies became much more deeply involved in the industry.

As the disparate pressures increased, there was more than ever a need for a body to provide co-ordination and overall direction. The Ministry of Information was one obvious candidate for this role, and for a brief period there were expectations both within the Ministry and within the industry that the Films Officer would assume quite extensive powers. In the autumn of 1939 the Films Division was preparing documents about quota policy and negotiations with the American industry, matters traditionally dealt with by the Board of Trade.[17] The Division also received communications about general policy from organisations and individuals within the business. The initial performance of the Ministry, however, was so disappointing that it seemed more likely to lose powers already allocated to it than to extend its sphere of influence. The Board of Trade therefore remained the principal link between the industry and the government, and as such was called on to provide guidance on new problems and to liaise with other interested Ministries. Yet matters to do with the psychological effects of policy remained the province of Information, so that neither Ministry was in a position to make comprehensive proposals without consulting the other. Furthermore, proposals had little chance of becoming policy unless the Treasury also threw its weight behind them.

The effect of leaving the Board of Trade in charge of practical matters was to minimise the impact of the war on the industry. The Board of Trade's Film Department was set up to respond to the industry rather than to direct it, and its staff were inclined to resist equally suggestions for mobilising resources against their owners' will or attempts to shut down any part of the business. The Department had only one specialist adviser, Simon Rowson, and was therefore not equipped to engage in long-term planning on the industry's behalf. In theory, recommendations from the advisory body, the Cinematograph Films Council (CFC), could provide a basis for future policy, but in practice the Council did not have the kind of authority which would ensure that its advice was taken seriously. When war broke out the Council had little more than a year's experience, and in that time had not gained the confidence either of the trade or of the administration. Some of its own members had doubts about the Council's standing. Two independent members, Arnold Plant and Albert Palache, wrote a memorandum for their colleagues on the financial sub-committee in which they commented: 'Recent experience . . . suggests that the CFC itself cannot, under present circumstances, be certain that its meetings will be fully representative of the various sections and that a Report from its Committee will gain much in weight by the endorsement of the whole Council.'[18]

The Board of Trade therefore continued to maintain direct contacts both with individuals and with the trade associations. The exhibitors and distributors, represented respectively by the CEA and the KRS, each presented a united front. The CEA was a particularly effective lobby in that as a national organisation with a developed regional structure it could exert pressure at a local level as well as through its London office. The relative strength of these associations naturally tended to benefit American interests, since the KRS was by this time dominated by American distribution subsidiaries while the members of the CEA depended heavily for their profits on the supply of American films. Producers, on the other hand, lacked a strong organisation to represent their views. The film producers group of the Federation of British Industries was no longer functioning; the British Film Production Association, formed in 1940, collapsed almost at once as a result of internal disagreements. The British Film Producers' Association, set up in 1945, was to attract only the major producers. Even the short film producers were divided between two associations. The more influential, the Association of Short Film Producers, consisted mainly of the makers of sponsored films; the British Short Film Makers' Society represented makers of speculative entertainment shorts.

Despite their organisational weakness the producers became quite an active lobby. Personalities were important and many of the communications addressed to the Board of Trade came from individual producers. Among these Michael Balcon was, in the early part of the war, a major influence. He was President of the short-lived British Film Production Association, and he subsequently helped to organise a committee of feature producers which was able to liaise regularly with the Board of Trade. Balcon was highly respected as a working producer, but he was not as rich in his own right nor as well connected politically as some of his rivals. He was able to gain acceptance from the government as spokesman for production partly because, temporarily, competition for that role was limited. Alexander Korda, who had been more in the public eye and had the advantage of a personal friendship with

Churchill, was in America between 1940 and 1942, and his absence during this crucial phase of the war somewhat tarnished his reputation for a while.[19] J. Arthur Rank and John Maxwell were, without doubt, the most powerful men involved in production, but Maxwell did not personally command much respect within the Board of Trade. One of its officials commented in a note of 1940 that 'During most of the time that Mr Maxwell has been connected with the industry he has been notorious as pursuing a policy with which the rest of the industry is at variance.' The note added that his studio 'would have been enhanced if more money had been spent on a better grade of equipment. For many years this was notoriously inferior to that of any other studio in the country.'[20] Maxwell was in any case in poor health by this time and he died in October 1940. At the beginning of the war Rank was still a relative newcomer to the business and was not yet personally involved in trade politics, as he was to become in the next few years. His interests were still usually represented to the Board of Trade by Oscar Deutsch or Richard Norton.

In 1939, feature producers were particularly anxious to state their case directly because among their grievances was the question of their representation on the Films Council. Of the two places reserved for producers, one was occupied by a person representing the makers of shorts and documentaries (Grierson until November 1939 and subsequently F. A. Hoare, managing director of Merton Park studios and chairman of the Substandard Cinematograph Association); the other was filled by Captain Richard Norton, a business executive rather than a working producer, who, as head of Denham Studios and a close associate of Rank, was not considered to represent exclusively production interests. The Board of Trade apparently accepted the producers' case; and when Norton resigned in February 1940, Michael Balcon was appointed to the vacant place. Balcon worked hard on the Films Council and was able to exert considerable influence in the Council's recommendations. This, however, was to prove something of a Pyrrhic victory, since in cases where the views expressed by the Council conflicted with the advice of the major trade associations the Board of Trade proved more receptive to the latter.

Employees in production were also poorly represented on the Films Council. Although many different professions were involved and six unions organised the industry, only two places were allocated to employees. One of these was held by George Elvin, General Secretary of the ACT, and the other by Tom O'Brien, General Secretary of the National Association of Theatrical and Kinematographical Employees (NATKE), which had more members working in exhibition than in production. The trade unions, like the employers' associations, lobbied the government directly. Up to a point they were able to make a collective approach through the Film Industry Employees' Council

(FIEC), but on many issues they acted separately, sometimes putting forward conflicting proposals. The NATKE had particularly bad relations with the ACT and the electricians' union, the ETU, partly because it competed with both these unions for members, partly because, under Tom O'Brien's leadership, the NATKE was associated with the most conservative position within the Labour Party while the other two unions were strongly socialist. A pre-war demarcation dispute between the NATKE and the ETU left lingering tensions, and a similar battle was brewing between the NATKE and the ACT.

Political differences became very explicit after the ACT began campaigning for state ownership. In 1941 the union's annual general meeting adopted a document which recommended the nationalisation of part or all of the film industry as the most effective way to ensure continuous production of 'films springing from and expressing traditional and national ideas'. At this time the NATKE was highly critical of the ACT proposals and prevented the FIEC from adopting a similar policy. Tom O'Brien made a public attack on the ACT in 1944 at the NATKE annual general meeting, discrediting the demand for nationalisation with arguments about the threat of totalitarianism. The NATKE differed from all the other film unions on the slightly less controversial question of the need to alter the relations between exhibition and production. The ACT, the ETU and Actors' Equity all strongly advocated some form of intervention in favour of production, whereas the NATKE adopted a position closer to that of the exhibitors and backed the CEA in opposing any measures which might involve some loss of revenue, power or freedom for exhibitors.

The various film interests concentrated their attention on trying to influence the Board of Trade since, when other Departments were involved, the Board of Trade frequently mediated. There were, however, some problems which resulted in other links. From the autumn of 1940, for instance, a committee of trade representatives advised the Ministry of Labour directly on questions of deferment of military service.[21] Numerous contacts also came about through the use which the government and the Armed Services made of film themselves, and the task of mediating in this context was usually the responsibility of the Ministry of Information.

THE MINISTRY OF INFORMATION

While the Board of Trade was concerned with the economic health of the film industry, the Ministry of Information was responsible for involving it in the war effort. What this would mean in practice was far from clear since, although the Ministry had been elaborately organised, little thought had gone into the nature of its work. The first Minister, Lord Macmillan, told Parliament:

In the case of a new Ministry such as had been confided to me it is a little difficult, I think, for the public to appreciate precisely what are its functions. I may say that I have had considerable difficulty in ascertaining what are its functions myself.[22]

Lord Macmillan's problems were shared by most of his staff, with the result that within a few months the organisation as a whole had acquired an almost unrivalled reputation for incompetence.[23] The government's efforts to improve matters at first added to the confusion. Chamberlain briefly considered winding up the whole operation and did temporarily remove from it the sensitive work of censorship. In the first year, four internal reorganisations and three changes of Minister kept the Ministry in a fairly constant state of upheaval. The second Minister, John Reith, was not lacking in ideas but his ideas and his style were unpopular in many quarters, not least with Churchill. Under Reith's successor, Duff Cooper, some stability was reached; but it was only after the appointment of Brendan Bracken the following year that relations with the government and the public and the various media became satisfactory.

The work of the Films Division soon attracted scathing attacks from several quarters. The first Film Liaison Officer, Joseph Ball, was a tactless appointment from a political point of view. He was previously Director of Publicity for the Conservative Party and had been in charge of the party's 1935 election propaganda. From the point of view of Labour sympathisers he was suspect not only because of his record as a propagandist for the Conservatives, but because he had performed this role at a time when there was considerable concern about the extent to which the Conservatives reputedly manipulated and certainly censored the news in their own interests.[24]

The appointment was also calculated to displease those who thought an official Information Service should be educational or improving. Ball favoured the approach of the advertising agencies rather than that of the serious press. He was on friendly terms with many commercial film companies and shared their dislike of the 'uplift brigade'. Thus he ignored the companies and film-makers associated with the documentary movement and even passed over the GPO film unit, although it was a production facility already placed entirely at the service of the government.

The documentary movement retaliated with a barrage of criticism. Paul Rotha later characterised the time of Joseph Ball's office as 'a four-month period distinguished by inertia',[25] a view which is supported by other observers. Kenneth Clark, who replaced Ball, offers this scathing description of his predecessor: 'A small fat man sitting behind an empty desk with lines of cigarette ash stretched across the folds of his waistcoat. He could not have moved for a long time. . . . when asked about his staff

[he] said he had never met them.'[26] There was undoubtedly a political dimension to the allegations of incompetence. Joseph Ball was firmly identified with the entrepreneurs of the film business – producers, cinema owners, studio owners – who were worried by the prospect of possible competition from the state and hoped the Films Division would do very little except channel government work to private companies.

Many of the criticisms were made by film production employees, by documentary film-makers and others who hoped that the state film service would be developed and expanded. In their account of these events Frances Thorpe and Nicholas Pronay suggest that Ball's dismissal in December 1939 was brought about by the hostility of his political opponents and was a sign of the government's 'belated recognition of the importance of good relations with the literati'.[27] But while the literati were predisposed to object to Ball, they were by no means his only critics and it is as likely that the government was responding to the very trade interests that his appointment had intended to please. For the Films Officer upset his former friends quite as much as his traditional enemies. Although he spent much of his time pleading for favourable treatment for commercial interests, his efforts did nothing to resolve the crisis of uncertainty hanging over the industry. Then he provoked a sharp attack from the newsreel companies over the affair of the coverage of the Expeditionary Force. The newsreel crews were prevented by the Defence Notices and Control of Photography order from covering this important story, and the material shot by the army was, according to the newsreel companies, so amateurish as to be unusable. Furthermore, Ball not only failed to make use of the public sector but also generated very little work for private companies.[28] The first major propaganda film to be made, *The Lion Has Wings* (1940), was not commissioned by the state at all but was produced by Alexander Korda as a commercial venture and as his personal contribution to the war effort. Film companies were therefore unhappy about the lack of patronage; the press was able to fume about the lack of any results; and several government departments claimed that requests for films were being ignored.

The documentary movement did gain some advantage from the fiasco of the first months simply because the GPO unit was at least turning out a few films. It was not unreasonable to assume therefore that the documentary method rose in official estimation as much because it showed results as because it was championed by the quality press. In any case, after Joseph Ball's departure, the GPO unit was incorporated into the Films Division under its new name, the Crown Film Unit. Subsequently a considerable share of war work was contracted either to Crown or to private specialist documentary companies like Strand and Realist. Documentary film-makers became more influential than they were ever to be again. The magazine *Documentary News Letter* provided a platform for their views on information, propaganda and film policy. They took an increasing interest in the controversies surrounding government policy towards the entertainment industry, and were for many reasons practically less isolated from their colleagues in features than they were before or after the war. Because of the increased demand for documentary films and the shortage of facilities for making features, most of the feature companies turned partly to making factual shorts for the Ministry of Information. The shortage of technicians further encouraged an exchange of labour between the studios and documentary companies, and it was easier than before for a director, like Harry Watt, or a producer, like Sidney Box, to move from documentary to feature work. There was also a vogue for films which, stylistically, hovered between the two categories: dramatised reconstructions of real events and highly naturalistic portrayals of fictional events.

Within the Ministry of Information the documentary movement became an effective lobby but did not achieve a take-over. Kenneth Clark looked to the commercial industry as well as to the embryonic state sector, and according to his own account made a point of cultivating good relations with feature producers.[29] Three of the films put into production during his short period of office were commissioned from Michael Balcon. In April 1940, when Clark was promoted to the position of Controller of Home Propaganda, his place was taken by Jack Beddington, the former director of publicity of the Shell Group. Beddington agreed with many of the ideas associated with the documentary movement and had put them into practice by creating the Shell Film Unit; but, with his background in public relations and his experience in private industry, he stood a good chance of being accepted as well by the conservative elements in the entertainment business. Like his predecessor, he followed a policy of simultaneously developing the state film service and offering work to private enterprise, a course which he pursued so competently that, although he failed to silence critics, he retained his post to the end of the war, surviving the downfall of two Ministers and all the resulting changes in the Ministry.

During the spring and summer of 1940 the work of the Films Division developed rapidly. By June, twenty-eight documentaries had been completed and a further twenty-one were in production. Two different tactics were pursued to ensure that films reached an audience. On the one hand, a fleet of mobile cinema vans was acquired to provide non-theatrical film shows; on the other, a programme was launched for the production of five-minute films designed for free release in public cinemas, and arrangements were made with the CEA to ensure the widest possible distribution for them. Nevertheless, the Division was the subject of sweeping criticisms in a Report to the Select Committee on National Expenditure by the sub-committee on Home Defence Services. Work in the home field was found to be ineffective, the main reasons being that too much time was taken up with administration, too much reliance placed on long documentaries or features and, most harmful of all, that the aims were ill conceived:

> The third reason, and the one which perhaps most largely contributed to the lack of definite objectives, was the fact that British morale stands in so little need of artificial support. This consideration should have led to the conclusion that material for films was not to be found in interpretations of a vague theme of re-assurance but in messages to the people precisely related to particular needs. The aim should be not merely the enhancement of patriotic spirit but its direction into channels of activity.[30]

The sub-committee's remarks were directed partly at an approach to propaganda prevalent throughout the Ministry, but in so far as they were aimed more specifically at film work they can be seen both as a belated response to the initial phase of mismanagement and as an attack on the subsequent influence of the documentary lobby. The general intent of the recommendations was to restrict the role of the Division, to subordinate it more effectively to central government control and curtail its powers in relation to the commercial industry. More specifically, the committee wholeheartedly approved the programme of five-minute cinema films, but condemned the mobile cinema project as uneconomic and questioned the value of the GPO unit.

The sub-committee was also highly critical of one of the more controversial initiatives taken by Kenneth Clark: the provision of financial backing for feature projects thought to have good propaganda potential. This form of sponsorship was a new departure, since previously the production of propaganda or public relations films was associated with practices distinct from those involved in profit-making entertainment. In the case of the former, all the costs and a fee for the film company would usually be supplied by a sponsor, who would primarily be concerned about the effect, not the earnings, of his film; in the case of the latter, finance came in the form of investments, usually from several sources, and the investors were, theoretically, motivated by the hope of commercial gain. In practice the lines were not as clear cut as that since some sponsors expected returns from a cinema release and the motives of those who invested in entertainment film were often very mixed. The pragmatic question of cost, however, helped maintain the distinction, since full-scale features were too expensive for most sponsors and so belonged clearly to the category of commercial entertainment. The fact that manufacturers sometimes gave 'props' free or paid to have their brand name shown in a feature was hardly considered a source of ambiguity since their contributions were relatively small. The prospect of substantial government investment being channelled into features was seen as a very different matter, and was viewed with alarm from several quarters. The producers of commercial entertainment feared that the market would be distorted so that, if they were not themselves the recipients of such funds, they might find themselves at a competitive disadvantage. Outside the trade the scheme met with hostility from those who feared simply that it would waste public money; and from those who also saw sinister implications in it, because the two countries, Germany and the Soviet Union, where film production was known to receive state backing, were in the grip of totalitarian regimes.

The first project designated for state support proved abortive because the subject ceased to be of interest after the fall of France. The second was realised but not without a struggle. The film was *49th Parallel*. According to the director, Michael Powell, the idea was originated by Kenneth Clark and a friend of his, John Sutro, 'a rich young man who worked for Alexander Korda', whose father put up some of the production money. The Treasury's initial contribution was £25,000 out of a budget of £60,000, and was extracted against strong opposition. Michael Powell relates that he succeeded in convincing Duff Cooper, the Minister at the time, that the film should be made: 'In the end Duff Cooper stood up and said to the Treasury "finance must not stand in the way of this project" and walked out. So the Treasury very sourly folded up their briefcases and we were off in a week.'[31] Although the Ministry of Information won this particular round of the conflict, the Select Committee backed the Treasury and reported that its sub-committee 'consider that no more features should be undertaken even if the film now being made should be as successful as it is hoped it will be. A single success would not, they consider, justify the risks inherent in feature film production.'[32] Jack Beddington and his colleagues contested some of the sub-committee's conclusions, but eventually took action on most of the recommendations. Accordingly, plans for extending non-theatrical distribution were dropped although the existing service was maintained.

Even though *49th Parallel* did turn out to be a commercial success, the policy of investing in features was officially abandoned. Nevertheless, the Films Division did not adopt quite such a passive role in relation to feature production as the Select Committee had wished, but tried to exert influence through its responsibility for vetting scripts and its work of liaising between film companies and the government departments from which the companies needed facilities or information. An informal committee of screenwriters, film directors and Ministry officials was set up to facilitate an exchange of ideas with the industry. The Ministry's formal powers of censorship do not seem to have played much part in its relations with feature producers. In the case of features, the powers were in any case only exercised if the British Board of Film Censors judged that security considerations were involved. In practice it seemed that producers had less reason to worry about a Ministry veto than about complaints from more powerful departments. The most famous case of a finished film which risked being banned as a result of government disapproval was *The Life and Death of Colonel Blimp*, which was condemned not by the Ministry of Information but by Churchill personally.[33] Although no more projects like *49th Parallel* were launched, the state continued to provide some financial backing for films which, while not treated as features in production, obtained a commercial cinema release as either first or second features. Michael Balcon received £20,000 towards the cost of *Next of Kin*, made for the War Office; after 1941 both the Crown and the Army Film Unit themselves began to produce documentary features. The Crown unit made a number of dramatised documentaries like *Target for Tonight* and *Western Approaches*; while, with *Desert Victory*, the War Office launched a successful series of films based on actual combat footage.

Throughout the war the activities of the state film services remained a source of friction between industry and government. For producers the situation was complicated by the fact that the government was, in different contexts, both employer and competitor. Conflicts therefore occurred over a wide range of issues, from the handling of a particular contract to decisions about general policy. Michael Balcon acted as principal critic and watchdog. In June 1940 he wrote to the Board of Trade expressing a general sense of disappointment:

> Many of us have done our best to harness ourselves to the Films Division of the Ministry of Information with, alas, very little encouragement. We all hoped that the Ministry of Information would have codified its relations as between itself and the industry to guide it at least on policy, but this has not been done.[34]

A more specific cause for annoyance was the administrative methods employed by the Division. One of the strongest supporters in principle of a state film service, Paul Rotha, wrote after the war that:

> The Government's method of commissioning films during the war has been adequate but not so imaginative or effective as it might have been. The method has worked, but not without endless disputes and a loss of time and energy. A film tended too often to become a file and not a film.[35]

Many criticisms made of the Division were directed at bureaucratic defects of the kind Rotha refers to, but underlying the charges levelled by most commercial producers was an attitude of hostility to the expansion of state power. Certainly the substance of a series of further complaints made by Balcon or his company was that the state was offering unfair competition. In December 1940 Balcon accused the MOI of hampering the production sector's independent war effort by, among other things, the policy of offering short films free to the cinemas.[36] The following year, on the trade committee of the CFC, he argued that the government had launched its own film units without adequately considering the existing capacity of the industry and that those units were unfairly absorbing men and resources needed by companies like his own.[37]

Fear of state competition was also very evident as a source of conflict between the government and the exhibitors.[38] The CEA attacked plans for showing films outside cinemas, both the scheme involving mobile projection units and another one based on supplying projectors to public libraries.

There was also a clash with the Army over the question of free film shows for the troops. This row first blew up in October 1940 when the War Office announced its intention of making the Army Council responsible for organising film entertainment, a task previously performed ineffectively by the NAAFI. The CEA threatened all-out opposition to the plan on the grounds that the Army, instead of showing films, should provide transport to take the troops to public cinemas.

The behaviour of producers and exhibitors conveys a rather exaggerated impression of the extent of state competition. The MOI had no brief to effect fundamental changes in the ownership of the industry and did not set out to poach on the preserves of private enterprise. On the issue of exhibition, the Ministry quickly responded to the CEA criticisms, dropped the plan to include entertainment in the programmes to be distributed by mobile units, and assured the CEA that the projectors in libraries would not be used for showing entertainment films.[39] The military also took the path of conciliation, and by the end of 1940 relations were much improved and a trade committee had been appointed to work with the Army. In production, although the state's role as sponsor increased enormously at the expense of the industry in general, its role as producer did not increase proportionately. The volume and variety of films made for the state was unprecedented, but the Ministry did not expand its own facilities to cope with all this work, continuing to farm out most of it to private companies. In most years the Crown unit accounted for less than a third of total production expenditure. Between December 1942 and November 1943, for instance, Crown received £66,488 for its work while £296,935 was paid to private contractors. [40]

In one area of production of particular importance in relation to propaganda, that of the newsreel, the contribution of the state was minimal. After the initial debacle relating to the Expeditionary Force, the MOI concentrated on working with the five private newsreel companies. The Ministry persuaded them to operate a common pool of material in order to economise on resources; it arranged facilities for them with the military and vetted the finished films. Apart from this the state was involved in producing news for export. The British Council made a newsreel, *British News*, for foreign consumption and, for a while, the MOI produced an alternative programme. The Armed Services cameramen made a big contribution in documenting the war, but the cinema newsreels which provided the British public with regular reports of the fighting were the work of private companies.

The only plausible ground for claiming that the state film service was a threat to private interests was that it was growing very fast. The Crown unit, to begin with, had had rather a small share of prestigious contracts, obtaining, for instance, only one out of the first nine commissions for five-minute films for the cinema. But by 1943 it was allowed to concentrate on the productions of second features for the cinemas, the most prestigious of all kinds of films made by the MOI. Despite the curtailment of the original plans for non-theatrical distribution, the scope of the mobile cinema service increased quite significantly. While in 1942 there were 94 vans, the number reached 141 in 1943.[41] Realistically, cinema owners had little reason to feel threatened. This was a time at which their own audience was growing fast and the audience reached by the mobile cinema, 10 million in 1943, was less than 1 per cent of that reached by the cinemas. The position was different for producers because their business had been precarious before the war, and during the war their activities were cut back severely. The Crown unit was using resources they might otherwise have used and was therefore a direct competitor; and, although from the scale of its work it was hardly a formidable one, the connection with the government was considered an unfair advantage.

The danger which the state units represented was, however, trivial compared to the danger from American competition. As far as the future health of British films was concerned, the arguments about the Ministry of Information and its activities were a sideshow. The important struggle was around the policy to be adopted towards America.

7 A Wartime Policy for British Films?

A purely British industry – always a doubtful starter – will now never run.

Internal memorandum to the Governor of the Bank of England, 10 October 1941.

RELATIONS WITH AMERICA

The burden which the war would put on foreign exchange, particularly dollar reserves, at once placed in a new perspective the old problem of American domination of the film trade. The cost of film imports became the focus of government concern; the need to reduce the cost was the main determinant of policy. From the government point of view the value of British film production was closely related to the contribution which it might make to the drive for dollar savings. Decisions, therefore, on questions like the future of quota and the allocation of resources to film production depended on the strategy adopted in relation to American imports.

Discussions between the Treasury and the Board of Trade about film imports had begun by the second week of the war but were slow to reach any conclusions. Film interests were inclined to consider the President of the Board of Trade, Oliver Stanley, personally responsible for the delays, but they seem to have been due more to a past history of administrative torpor for which he can take only a limited share of the blame. The crisis revealed that officials did not know what the value of film imports were, and had only a hazy conception of the way the American film industry functioned.

There were no statistics on the rentals earned by American films, nor on the payments made by American distribution subsidiaries in London to their parent companies in America. The Board of Trade was therefore unable to provide the Treasury with anything better than a number of guesses as to the size of the sum at issue. The extent of official ignorance is best illustrated by a letter from Somervell of the Board of Trade to the Treasury in which he reminds his colleague that 'as you know we have always taken it to be £5 or £6 million', and then tells him that a new informant claims that the figure is nearer £10 million, a possible reason for the discrepancy being that 'the American companies are very unwilling to disclose the true figures because there is something very shady attaching to the balance of £4 million.'[1] Subsequent enquiries from the CEA produced nothing more definite than the opinion that the figure was nearer £10 million than £5 million.

Although Board of Trade officials were well aware that the American film companies relied heavily on their earnings from the British market, they seem to have underestimated the extent of opposition which the American film lobby would organise against any measures to reduce these earnings. For during the initial discussions which took place without consultation with American interests, ideas involving direct restrictions on imports and cuts in earnings of at least 75 per cent were put forward as if relatively unproblematic.

The Americans reacted quickly to the first rumours of these plans. On 22 September 1939, Joseph Kennedy, the American Ambassador, called on Stanley to ask for details and was shocked to hear that the British intended to restrict American remittances to 50 per cent for films already in the country and to $5 million per year on new films. In a telegram to the State Department he commented: 'As I see it this is very close to destruction for the American film industry and I should think a catastrophe for the theatres in England.'[2] A State Department circular was put out with the information that in normal years revenue from the British market was $40 million a year and that the British proposal, if carried out, would cut this by $35 million. The Hays Office immediately began to formulate counter-proposals, and Stanley was persuaded to postpone discussions until these were ready.

The details of the agreement were thrashed out during October, the principal points at issue being first, the exact sum to be blocked and, secondly, the possible suspension or relaxation of the quota. While the Treasury insisted that no more than $14 million should leave the country, the Americans dug their heels in for $17 million. The Americans also hoped to use the opportunity to strike a blow at the quota regulations, while the Treasury was anxious to avoid making quota concessions at this stage, because the renters' quota was seen as one means of encouraging the Americans to channel some of their blocked earnings into British production, so reducing the accumulation of funds which at some time would have to be released.

In the course of the discussions the American Ambassador explicitly drew attention to possible repercussions for Anglo-American relations in general. It was reported, for instance, that at a meeting between the Ambassador, the President of the Board of Trade and the Chancellor of the Exchequer the Ambassador had pointed out that

any substantial diminution in the revenue from the UK would constitute a crushing blow to the American industry and would have

121

disastrous results not only upon the actual producing companies but upon real estate investment represented by cinemas throughout the US. In fact, there would be created in those circumstances in every small town throughout the length and breadth of the States a focus of ill will towards Great Britain whose action had caused this widespread dislocation and hardship.[3]

The British finally gave way on the question of the sum to be released but forced a stalemate over the quota. The Americans accepted that the Act would remain in force until March 1940, to allow time for further discussions. The agreement on remittances, signed in November 1939, was to last for a year. The American companies accepted that their remittable income would be limited to $17.5 million and undertook to supply as many films, in relation to American output, as they had in previous years. The uses to which blocked funds might be put were specified, the most significant being the acquisition of rights to British films, investment in British production and the purchase of lease or real estate. The agreement also included provision that consideration would be given to replacing quota by arrangements under which American companies would agree to make a sum of money, equivalent to obligations under quota, available for film production in Britain. The immediate beneficiaries, however, were the British exhibitors, who were assured of a year's supply of films; and the American producers, who would maintain their share of the market, even though temporarily they could withdraw only half their earnings from it. British producers could no longer hope for a reduction in American competition and they still had to contend with uncertainty about the future of the quota. The Treasury had obtained a small dollar saving, but very much less than had originally been intended.

The British also reaped a less tangible benefit by avoiding a showdown with American film interests. The points which the Ambassador had made about public opinion could not be ignored. Until America's entry into the war, public opinion in America was a sensitive issue. This was a reason for the British to seek good relations with Hollywood for its own sake, not only because the film lobby had influence in Washington. Hollywood was inclined to be anti-Nazi and so pro-British, a tendency accentuated by the sizeable British community there. Several films made before America's entry into the war were overt propaganda for the British cause. British films were themselves given a more favourable reception than usual. The bias was so apparent that isolationists accused Hollywood of war-mongering, and in the autumn of 1941 a Senate sub-committee began to investigate charges.[4] All this would not necessarily have been changed by more effective methods to cut down profits from the British market, since there was more at issue than the short-term proceeds from Britain. But it was to be assumed that a head-on collision would have some unfortunate effects on the British propaganda campaign. And the fact that, during these first years of war, Hollywood was producing so much pro-British material took some of the force out of the argument that the British film industry had to be promoted for the sake of projecting the British case. Such considerations complicated the political dimensions of the problem and contributed to discouraging the British government from taking a tough line with the American producers.

When discussions about the Quota Act were resumed in the New Year, the trade had some grounds for optimism in that Oliver Stanley had been replaced as President of the Board of Trade by Andrew Duncan, a businessman who was thought to have a far better grasp of industry affairs. These hopes were justified to the extent that negotiations were conducted on the basis that quota requirements, in some form, would be retained. The details of the scheme finally adopted, which became known as the monetary quota, were, however, dictated primarily by the interests of the Treasury on the one hand and the American companies on the other. The Treasury requirement was that any new regulations would oblige the Americans to spend the same amount as they would have done under the existing regulations. The Americans were ostensibly looking for a formula which would go further than the existing double and triple quota provisions in enabling them to concentrate investment in a very few expensive productions. This would have the advantages for them that, making fewer films, they would be less involved in the problems of wartime production, and that they would probably be able to release the films they did make in the United States, in which case the investment would serve as an indirect means of getting their blocked sums out of Britain. One of the main stumbling blocks to arriving at a formula was that the quota requirements had been expressed in terms of footage and labour costs rather than investment; and the Americans also hoped to manipulate the adjustment of the regulations so that they would end up in practice free to spend less than before.

The first proposals devised by Fay Allport, acting on behalf of the Motion Picture Association of America (MPAA), were for this reason unacceptable, and the Board of Trade negotiated a further period for deliberation, extending the Quota Act as it was until June. The arrangement then decided on was that renters were to acquire films with an aggregate British labour cost of not less than £1 per foot of the length of British films which they would have had to register under the Act as it was. In addition, it was stipulated that there should be one film made for every 100,000 feet of imported film and that for each film labour costs were to be at least £3 per foot. This was to prevent any of the money being spent on 'quota quickies' and to place some limit on the sums that could be concentrated into one production. In each quota period renters could choose to operate under the old regulations or under the new system, the monetary quota.

The change, introduced by an Order in Council in July, was unpopular with British trade interests. Exhibitors feared that, with renters offering fewer British films, they would have difficulty fulfilling their quotas; producers feared that the high-cost American-financed films would displace their own products both in the British market and abroad. *Documentary News Letter* complained:

> There is little doubt that this legislation, in a very few months, will have produced a situation comparable to 1918–1927, when the British film industry was completely dominated in every department by American interests. No doubt this action of the Board of Trade is part of a much wider system of financial adjustments between this country and the USA. In fact the film, and all the world good will that that word suggests, is as usual being treated as of secondary importance.[5]

The scheme did represent, as this statement suggests, a compromise between American wishes and Treasury requirements on which British film interests had had little influence. As such it was a symptom of a general approach which opened the door to American domination, but it is doubtful whether, in itself, it did more than confirm a trend. The Americans had already been taking extensive advantage of the double and triple quota provisions and had been spending considerably more than the minimum required of them under the Act. During the period before the changes were introduced the six principal renters between them had a liability in single quota pictures for 47 films at a total labour cost of £357,000; they actually made only 27 films, and yet spent in 'Form C' (British labour) costs as much as £962,000. Besides, even under the monetary quota the companies claimed that they had had great difficulty meeting their obligations, owing to a shortage of space and personnel, so it seems improbable that the old footage quota could have been enforced.

The sharp increase in exhibitors' quota defaults which occurred in 1941 cannot be blamed only on the monetary quota. A number of other decisions had been taken which excluded the possibility of increasing or even maintaining the pre-war output of films. In recognition of this, the Board of Trade, after consultation with the CFC, made an order under section 15 of the Cinematograph Act to prevent the quota percentages rising as originally allowed for. For the next three years renters' quota was held to a proportion of 20 per cent for long films and 15 per cent for short films; exhibitors' quota to 15 per cent for long films and 12½ per cent for short films.

In 1942 the obligations placed on the renter were further eased by a relaxation in the requirements of the monetary quota. According to the amended regulations, the renter had to produce one film of at least 7,000 feet in length with labour costs of not less than £3 per foot, and to produce a film or films the British labour costs of which would equal £1 per foot of the number of feet of film which the renter would have to make according to the footage quota. Following the progressive weakening of quota arrangements there was a slight reduction in defaults both by renters and by exhibitors in the first year, but by the end of the war defaults had increased again (see Table XVII).

TABLE XVII
Quota defaults and prosecutions 1938–45

Year	Renters		Exhibitors	
	Defaults	*Prosecutions*	*Defaults*	*Prosecutions*
1938–39	12	nil	437	3
39–40	?	nil	316	3
40–41	10	nil	1,402	4
41–42	12	nil	1,721	4
42–43	8	nil	846	2
43–44	11	nil	977	6
44–45	13	nil	1,014	6

The first Anglo-American film agreement and the subsequent introduction of the monetary quota took the urgency out of plans to achieve dollar savings through increased production of British films, but did not immediately make such plans redundant. In this respect the autumn of 1940 was the turning point for British producers when the decision was finally taken that film production would contract, not expand. Although the pressure on resources was an important influence on government thinking, the determining factor was the outcome of negotiations with the Americans about the arrangements which would follow the expiry of the 1939 agreement.

The Treasury had been highly dissatisfied with the 1939 agreement, and subsequent changes in the exchange rate had aggravated the position in that the sterling equivalent of $17.5 million increased from £3½ million to £4½ million. That summer, while the outcome of the Battle of Britain still hung in the balance, the Treasury and the Board of Trade began discussing plans for a far more restrictive agreement. The Treasury proposed in August that the aim should be to cut remittances down to as little as $5 million. Of remaining earnings it was estimated that about $10 million might be spent on production and on buying rights to British films to satisfy the requirements of the Quota Act. All other funds would be blocked.

The Board of Trade was well aware that the American companies would vigorously resist such a proposal, but was unsure how much political support they would be given or how far they would eventually refuse to co-operate if the Treasury proved intransigent. In an exploratory conversation at the Treasury, the American Ambassador adopted an uncompromising position, arguing that any further restrictions on their remittances would put the companies out of business. Shortly afterwards the American Consul stated that the British proposal would be rejected out of hand by the companies and that they would have the active support of Mr Kennedy (the Ambassador). The Board of Trade started considering very seriously the prospect of an American boycott.

During September the film section was working on the assumption that the Treasury would not back down. Simon Rowson wrote a memorandum on the likely effects of a boycott. Some groundwork for this had been done the previous June, when Rowson had discussed with the chemical industry the possibility of increasing production of film stock to replace American imports. He found that only one-sixth of the stock required was made in Britain, but the manufacturers had assured him that they could expand if the companies making their machines could supply new plant.

The problem to which Rowson turned his attention in September, the supply of films to cinemas, was less amenable to precise quantification since the quality of the films was obviously a relevant factor. Addressing himself only to the question of numbers, Rowson reported that cinemas were consuming between ten and twelve new films a week and that the maximum output which the British industry could achieve would be from four to five films. In order to achieve this it would be necessary to derequisition studios and provide a revolving fund of £3 million. In the year ending March 1940, only 108 long films had been completed. Rowson suggested that, in order to cope with the inevitable shortfall, cinemas might close one week in two. Less drastic solutions put forward were enforcement of single-feature programmes or limitations on the frequency with which cinemas could change their programmes. Measures of this kind were also thought of, then and during the post-war crisis, as a means of saving dollars which could serve instead of, or as well as, blocking funds.

It seems surprising that relatively little effort was put into developing some scheme for cutting down the number of films shown. The demand for up to twelve films a week was the result of three circuits showing two programmes a week, each consisting of a double feature – a pattern which, although it might maximise profits in a boom period, was not dictated by commercial necessity. In France a single-feature programme was imposed during the Occupation and did not result in a mass defection of the audience. A few years after the end of the war the trade in Britain was voluntarily changing its practices: long runs became more and more common, and eventually the three circuits were reduced to two. The least damaging idea for the trade was probably the abolition of the double feature, but this was of limited interest to the government because it would not, in the short term, do much either to save dollars or to solve the film supply problem, since programmes were not made up of two equal films but of a first and second feature. Only a small proportion of rentals would be saved by cutting second features, while few second features were of a high enough quality to run on their own as the main attraction. Nevertheless, there would have been some long-term advantage in that the British industry could have switched all its resources to first feature production, and by making fewer but better films would have been able to supply a larger proportion of programmes. As we noted earlier, however, it was precisely a mechanism for long-term planning that the Board of Trade lacked.

While looking into ways of coping with a possible boycott, the Board of Trade sought the views of people in the trade on whether it was likely that the Americans would go so far. The conclusions drawn from the various lines of enquiry were that the Americans would probably not impose a boycott but that plans should be prepared in any case. The Board of Trade's ideas were summarised in a report at the end of September:

> I think (and Simon Rowson agrees with me) that it is most unlikely that the American companies would in practice boycott this market. This, however, will not necessarily prevent the bluff from being made and if we are to be in a position to call it, we must have ministerial authority, including the Foreign Office and Treasury, and also plans to meet the situation if unexpectedly the boycott were brought into force. I have discussed the position with Mr Rowson and he considers that short of a complete break with the American companies in which they repudiated their outstanding contracts (which are fixed for six months ahead) we could make such regulations (e.g. compulsory single feature programmes, limitation to one picture a fortnight etc.) as would make it possible to keep the cinemas adequately supplied, though naturally at the cost of some deterioration in the kind and amount of entertainment, for at least a year.[6]

The Treasury was informed and granted official approval to the scheme. The American Consul was told the Treasury's terms for a new agreement, and reported that the Ambassador regarded them as 'unfair, unreasonable and unrealistic' and would advise the companies not to accept the paragraph which committed them to continuing to supply the market.

Everything seemed set for a collision which would have offered British producers an unprecedented opportunity and challenge, when outside events intervened. Plans were interrupted because of a change of President of the Board of Trade: Andrew Duncan was succeeded by

Oliver Lyttleton. A further delay was caused because it was just at that time that Lord Beaverbrook in the Ministry of Aircraft Production was making his bid for Denham Studios and, reasonably, the Board of Trade officials wanted this matter settled before irrevocable decisions were taken which might commit them to a programme of expansion. When negotiations resumed in late October 1940, the Treasury suddenly backed down and offered to release $12 million. This decision seems to have been taken by the Chancellor alone, during a meeting with the American Ambassador which had been called at the Ambassador's request. The explanation offered to Somervell at the Board of Trade by the Treasury official handling the matter was that it was 'as a result of Mr Kennedy's insistence upon the importance of the political aspects of the case'. Presumably Kennedy had indicated that an unfavourable settlement would damage Anglo-American relations in other spheres, a serious threat at that juncture, when America was not even committed to Lend Lease, let alone to entering the war herself. Nevertheless, the Treasury official was sufficiently taken aback by the turnaround to express himself in unusually emotive language: 'I need hardly say that I left the room in a rather shocked condition,' he wrote. 'I can only apologise for putting you up to do our dirty work and then selling out over your heads.'[7]

From that time the idea of expanding, or even maintaining, the level of production was abandoned. The pressure on studio space and manpower was increasing to an extent that, even given higher priority, the industry probably could not have pushed up its output to the extent Rowson had suggested. After the agreement, with the prospect that American imports would continue at their customary level, the main grounds for giving it high priority were removed. As for the case based on the propaganda value of film, one full year of war had engendered a degree of scepticism, reflected in the comments of the Home Policy Committee Policy Report about the susceptibility of the masses to propaganda. The policy gradually adopted for the remainder of the war was based on the aim of preserving a 'healthy nucleus', which was interpreted to mean the production of about fifty films a year.

The arrangement of blocking funds had its own disadvantage, which would in fact have been greater if the proposal had been forced through without a boycott. The difficulties were firstly that it was only a temporary expedient, and secondly that large reserves of blocked funds were an embarrassment in that they encouraged the owners to seek irregular means of remitting the earnings. In January 1941, the Treasury estimated that by September the American companies' blocked funds would amount to £8 million. In July, the exchange control conference recommended that measures should be taken to check the rate of accumulation. The idea of restricting imports and boosting the British industry was briefly revived but not given such serious consideration as before. The recognition that the problem was a long-term one, however, did increase interest in maintaining a 'healthy nucleus' with a view to returning to some such plan after the war. But the Treasury also hoped to interest the Americans in long-term investment in British films, an aim which seemed to preclude too tough an approach to imports.

In the event, when negotiations began on the 1941–2 agreement, political pressures were again brought to bear. The Permanent Secretary at the Board of Trade, Sir Arnold Overton, wrote afterwards to the Bank of England that the attempts to drive a hard bargain were doomed to failure because the American film companies would get representation from the State Department so that 'considerations of higher political importance would force us to give way to them'.[8] The Americans insisted that the discussions were conducted between the Ambassador and the Chancellor, in itself an indication of the importance they attached to the question. The outcome was an arrangement similar to the previous ones except that it was less restrictive. The companies were allowed to complete transfers of funds due under the earlier agreements, and to transfer up to $20 million in the year of the new agreement.

By the time the agreement was due to expire the position had been greatly changed by America's entry into the war. In the autumn of 1942 the companies pressed for the complete release of funds. The Board of Trade warned that such a step might damage the British film industry since the blocked sterling had, they considered, been an inducement to the Americans· to exploit a number of British films in the American market. Nevertheless, in October all existing blocked funds were released, although negotiations continued about future earnings. The American attitude during Lend Lease negotiations convinced the Treasury early in 1943 to drop the attempt to maintain restrictions. Leisching, a Second Secretary at the Board of Trade, commented that 'the Treasury are evidently shaken and feel that they must not expose themselves to criticism by imposing restrictions on these film remittances in the future'.[9]

THE FILMS BANK AND THE COMMISSION

One side effect of the dollar problem was to put back on the agenda the question of how to improve the financing of British films. It was anticipated that the chronic shortage of finance would be aggravated by uncertainty about the future and by the additional risks associated with the war. Producers were naturally worried, but exhibitors were also concerned since they could no longer count on receiving an adequate supply of American product. In the autumn of 1939, therefore, the government was under pressure from both sides of the trade to take some action. Sidney Bernstein of the Granada chain proposed a plan for the co-operative financing of films by exhibitors,[10] while ideas floated by producers included the suggestion from Associated Talking Pictures, the company in which Balcon was then involved, that loans should be made from the Entertainments tax.[11]

More significant than the exhibitors' sudden regard for the welfare of production was that the government was itself becoming receptive to the notion of helping producers, and it was the Treasury, that most cautious of Departments, which was largely responsible for this. In November 1939, a Treasury official, writing to the Bank of England in connection with the American agreement, ventured the opinion that: 'In the long run, from the exchange point of view it seems to be very desirable to do something to foster British film production in order that British films may replace American ones.'[12] The Cinematograph Films Council was asked to advise, and a confidential report was prepared by a sub-committee, formed to study problems arising out of war.[13] This document, submitted to the full CFC in January 1940, recommended that the government should immediately establish a Film Finance Corporation with a minimum capital of £1,800,000 furnished entirely by the government. There followed lengthy consultations between the Treasury and the Board of Trade, the Bank of England, the CFC and the trade. But conditions changed, and the basis for agreement between the industry and the government evaporated. By the autumn of 1940, in the light of the worsening wartime shortages and the new Anglo-American agreement, plans for expanding the industry were abandoned as impracticable. Consultations continued, however, since it was recognised by then that the dollar shortage would be a long-term problem. Although in the end nothing came out of that round of discussions, the arguments used and the positions adopted are interesting to the extent that they set the scene for the post-war debate.

The case for the Film Finance Corporation made by the CFC sub-committee was based on arguments about potential export earnings as well as about the needs of the home market. As far as home market needs were concerned, the committee calculated that out of a requirement of 600 films per year 450 would continue to be supplied from America, leaving 150 to be met by British production. Of these, 35 would be financed by American companies to meet the quota requirements, and existing British sources of finance would take care of only a third of the remaining 115 films. The committee suggested that in existing circumstances the target for wholly British production should be dropped to 90 films and that the Film Finance Corporation should undertake to finance two-thirds of these, 60 films in all. The difficulties of attracting private capital were highlighted by an analysis the committee undertook of the costs and earnings of a sample of 61 films (see Table XVIII). This suggested that, while the more expensive films were less likely to go into profit than the cheaper ones, they were far more likely to earn some

TABLE XVIII

Costs and receipts in respect of 61 British feature films produced in the period 1 January 1937 to 30 June 1938

Films costing	No.	Cost	Gross UK rentals	Receipts Estimated net UK	Net from overseas	Estimated total net	% overseas of total net receipts	Cost × 100 total net receipts
Under £15,000	13	£119,677	£174,301	£122,011	£2,998	£125,009	2.4	95½
£15,000 – 36,000	15	314,001	345,186	241,630	10,004	251,634	4.	125
£36,000 and over	33	2,674,757	2,277,899	1,594,529	691,114	2,285,643	30.	117
TOTAL.	61	£3,108,435	£2,797,386	£1,958,170	£704,116	£2,662,286	26½	117
£36,000 and over further analysed								
(a) £36,000 – 75,000	20	£1,033,760	£1,270,157	£889,110	£205,730	£1,094,840	19	94½
(b) £75,000 and over	13	£1,640,997	£1,007,742	£705,419	£485,384	£1,190,803	41	138
TOTAL.	33	£2,674,757	£2,277,899	£1,594,529	£691,114	£2,285,643	30	117

131

foreign currency. The lesson the committee wished the government to draw from these figures was plainly stated:

> The sub-committee emphasise the fact that films costing over £75,000 each, derive 41 per cent of their net receipts from overseas. It is obvious that the manufacture of products which are capable of furnishing foreign exchange upon this scale should be fostered. [. . .]
> The figures set out in the table speak for themselves and provide ample evidence to explain the difficulties which have been encountered so far, and which continue to be encountered, in inducing private capital to enter this field of activity.
> In the light of the foregoing there remains no doubt that a Film Finance Corporation must be formed and that this can only be undertaken by the Government, which will have to furnish the necessary permanent capital.[14]

The sub-committee was apparently asking the government to subsidise the production of high-cost pictures for export, but it was aware that the industry's reputation for extravagance and poor judgment would be used as an argument against any element of public subsidy:

> There is good ground for the expectation that a system of finance providing expert scrutiny and control of production costs, from the first inception of a project till it reaches the screen, would succeed in large measure in placing the production of the more expensive type of film on a profitable basis.[15]

The sub-committee envisaged that the corporation might exercise some control over the exploitation of the films financed by it, 'including setting up a separate department for the sale or renting of foreign rights and for the study of overseas markets.'[16] The President of the Board of Trade, Andrew Duncan, rejected the possibility of funding such a corporation entirely from government sources and asked the Bank of England to consider some alternative arrangement. The Treasury and Sir Frederick Whyte, Chairman of the cfc, had already asked the Bank of England for advice about the possibility of setting up a bank based on private capital and the Governor's answer in December 1939 had been negative: he would not be able to find private money and would not be willing to sponsor such a body.[17] The present suggestion, however, was for some form of partnership between government and private capital. At the Bank of England the cfc document was examined together with the Bank's own reports of 1937, and the outcome was that Montagu Norman agreed to do a new report on condition that the matter was kept secret from the cfc and the trade.

132

It is worth noting that one of the people asked by the Bank to work on the report was Albert Palache who, three years later, was to chair the CFC committee which produced the controversial report on monopoly. Palache was a partner in a City firm of financiers, A. R. Wagg, and had been nominated by the Bank of England at the end of 1939 to fill a vacancy on the CFC as an independent member with financial expertise.[18] Someone else who was brought in to work on the report and who, for a short time, had an important influence on events was a financier called de Stein, described in the relevant notes as 'bad in meetings and as a thinker but whose influence might be helpful if we wanted industrial money'.[19] Among those consulted Ernest H. Lever of Prudential Assurance figures prominently, and the report mentions that the industry people approached all 'belong to what one would call the established British element'.[20]

The view taken by the Bank of England was that the industry needed reform more than money, one of the main problems being the 'indifference of the British renter to the fate of his colleagues'.[21] The purpose of a film bank should therefore be to improve co-operation and organisation and this was to be done by influencing private enterprise rather than by setting up in competition by acting, for instance, as a renter or producer. The long-term aim, as the Bank of England saw it, was to make the industry self-supporting. For the present, the Bank reintroduced the idea of a Films Commission 'to effect co-ordination and direct the future development of the industry – in other words to govern it',[22] and made the provision of finance conditional on the creation of such a body. Other conditions were that screen protection should be maintained, that the government should put up some of the money and provide a guarantee fund, and that the industry should also contribute some capital and should participate in risks. Finance should be channelled through renters, and renters wishing to use the bank would be obliged to spread loans over their entire programme of production, an arrangement which would guard against the danger that the bank would be asked to back only the riskiest projects which other financiers did not want.

Some further recommendations concerned relations with America. There was, it was found, no need for additional finance simply to ensure the existing level of British production. It would be needed in so far as the government wished to replace some American pictures with British and to produce films which it might insist the American companies purchased. These aims, however, could not be achieved by finance alone. Legislation would be needed to exclude a proportion of American pictures by means of a tax, and to ensure reciprocal treatment for British films in America.

While the Bank of England was working on its report, officials of the Board of Trade made a survey of existing structures of legislation which they regarded as being potentially relevant.[23] They looked at the Bankers' Industrial Development Company, founded in 1930 to help with the rationalisation of industry; the Agricultural Marketing Act of 1931, which set up Boards of Producers; the Lancashire Cotton Corporation, formed in 1929 for amalgamating mills and eliminating surplus capacity; and the Special Areas Reconstruction Association, established by Act in 1936. The list is indicative of the extent to which film policy was conceived of within the context of a general industrial policy for tackling problems of inefficiency, obsolescence and low profitability. The funding mechanisms for libraries, museums and even the BBC were not seen as offering any lessons.

By April 1940 the Bank of England and the Board of Trade were discussing the specific share structure of the proposed bank. In May, Andrew Duncan reported that the Chancellor agreed that they could proceed on the basis of setting up a statutory Films Commission and the film bank. The plans were interrupted, however, by the fall of the Chamberlain government.

There were no further developments until August, when the government's proposal was put to the CFC and the financial sub-committee began to consider a response to it.[24] The first reaction indicated that the broadly based trade support for a bank along the lines suggested by the CFC would not be extended to the scheme under review. The principal stumbling block was the Commission, the fact that it would be a body of independent persons which would have some powers over the trade. The Americans at once expressed unambiguous opposition, while within the British industry the prevailing view was hostile. On the CFC sub-committee, Arthur Jarratt was of the opinion that the trade might prefer to do without money if the Commission were to be the price; D. E. Griffiths, speaking for the American renters, said that they were a hundred per cent opposed; even F. A. Hoare, representing short film makers, did not favour the idea of an independent body; while Professor Plant, one of the independent members, queried the need to link the bank with the Commission.

The deliberations of the CFC sub-committee lasted until October and were so inconclusive that its recommendation amounted to little more than that the Board of Trade should consult the industry. At that time, however, the advice of the relevant Board of Trade official was that the industry would never accept the Commission, and that if the government wanted it established it would have to impose it.

The government's views about the merits of the bank and the Commission had been changing. In August 1940 the bank was still regarded as a priority: the Treasury was asking for further drastic cuts in dollar remittances; the introduction of monetary quota the previous month was likely to reduce the number of British films made with American finance; at least one major British production was threatened by lack of completion money.[25] In the autumn circumstances were changed by the terms accepted in the second Anglo-American agreement and by further reductions in the capacity of the British industry. The Board of Trade no longer considered that finance was urgently needed, but had been convinced by the arguments of the Bank of England that the industry needed regulating. The priorities were therefore reversed in that the Commission came to be regarded as a primary objective and the bank as a means for achieving it. In December, Oliver Lyttleton, as President of the Board of Trade, wrote to the Governor of the Bank of England: 'I do not think it would be possible to get the industry to accept a bill containing proposals for a Films Commission unless it also contained powers to set up a film credit organisation.'[26] The Treasury, however, continued to advance arguments in favour of the bank in its own right: it would serve as a bargaining counter when they entered the next round of negotiations with the Americans; the Americans might be induced to invest some of their blocked dollars through the bank; it would be valuable after the war to help the industry expand.

Consultations with the industry, which began in February 1941, were supposed to be confidential. But following a 'leak' to the press, the plans became the subject of a very public and quite angry debate. The CEA, which had supported plans for a film bank the year before, was totally opposed to the Commission,[27] and Jarratt was right in predicting that even many producers would think the Commission too high a price for the bank. Maurice Ostrer of Gainsborough and G. W. Parish of British National registered their opposition to the whole scheme.[28] The only real support in the trade came from some of the independent producers, among whom Michael Balcon argued in the press in favour of the government proposal.

The government did not seem to be deterred by the trade's response, but began to lose confidence in the scheme three months later as a result of advice emanating ostensibly from the City, but more precisely from sources connected with the trade. It was at this point that de Stein's role became crucial. The Bank of England had, throughout the negotiations, expressed concern about whether suitable people could be found in wartime to staff the bank and the Commission. When the government determined to go ahead with the creation of the bank in the spring of 1941, they recommended that de Stein should be asked to head the bank. De Stein, however, proved unwilling to take on the job, partly because he considered the work he was already engaged in more important, but also because he considered that the industry was no longer in need of finance, an opinion he had formed largely as a result of discussions with Mr Farrow, a financial expert who was also a director of General Film Distributors, the distribution arm of the Rank organisation. De Stein's refusal called the whole project into question and plans were brought to a standstill. It was also instrumental in bringing into the story Nigel Campbell, another partner in the same City firm as Palache and Munro. Campbell had been at the meeting at which de Stein had spoken of Farrow's views, and he sent a note to the Board of Trade stressing Farrow's connections with distribution and expressing doubts about de Stein's views. Following this, he was asked to make a further study of the finance question for the Board of Trade.

The Campbell report, delivered in September 1941, was highly critical of the industry and identified the cause of its problems as being low standards, inefficiency, mismanagement and high costs of distribution and studio facilities. It recommended that the Commission should be established but that, for the time being, no finance should be offered:

> We are strongly of the opinion that in the present state of affairs – the standard of commercial morality prevalent throughout the industry, the absence of any corporate objective or co-operative spirit, the inability to produce a reasonably continuous supply of box-office worthy films – any attempt to put the industry on its feet by placing at its disposal increased financial facilities is doomed to failure.

The Commission was necessary because:

> We are satisfied that in the present stage of development of the industry it is hopeless to look to it for any voluntary co-operative effort aimed at the good of the industry as a whole.[29]

As another way of improving the quality of British films, Campbell favoured the plan, also at various times mentioned by the Treasury, of encouraging American production in Britain. He subscribed to two already familiar arguments: that British producers would be able to learn from the Americans; and that American-produced 'British' films would be released in the United States and would therefore establish British stars with the American public and make British films acceptable to American audiences. Campbell thought it would be desirable to induce the Americans to make not less than forty-eight films in Britain for the next seven years. The government should at the same time pursue other ways of obtaining better treatment for British films in America. The particular strategy he proposed was to stop the double feature on the grounds of making wartime savings; then, after the war, the possible need for continuing this restriction could be used as a bargaining counter.

Opinion in the Bank of England on the Campbell report was that it was effectively a death sentence for the British, as distinct from an Anglo-American, industry. This was an opinion in no way linked with strong views about the cultural value of a British industry. Indeed, from previous discussions, it was clear that the Bank officials thought American-financed films were 'largely British in their characteristics' and could therefore promote British culture. If there was an argument for a British film industry, it was based on the need to free the market from complete dependence on American suppliers. The Bank official commenting to the Governor on the Campbell report suggested that the omission of the film bank ruled out any independent growth of the British industry, while political factors would affect the feasibility of bringing in American finance on the scale suggested.

> Duncan will know whether the virtual handing over of the British industry to the Americans (albeit a Hobson's choice) is politically possible. A purely British industry – always a doubtful starter – will now never run.[30]

The Campbell report was better received at the Board of Trade, where Somervell commented that he agreed with most of the suggestions. Nevertheless, none were acted on at the time. The Anglo-American agreement, signed only a month after the report was delivered, resulted in less rather than more American participation. With the release of some of their blocked earnings, American companies which had been planning to produce British films changed their minds. The single-feature programme was considered on several occasions subsequently but no detailed plans were prepared. A good deal of progress was, however, made with the Commission, which at one point seemed certain to become a reality. When Hugh Dalton became President of the Board of Trade, he initially pushed the scheme on the grounds that even though the Commission might be of limited value in wartime, it would be needed afterwards and should be set up without delay to be ready to tackle the post-war situation. The case was put to the Lord President's committee in the summer of 1942 in a joint proposal from the Board of Trade and the Treasury which acknowledged the difficulties but recommended that the government should proceed:

> The objections to establishing such a Commission are the lengthy and controversial legislation required, for which it will not be easy to set aside time, the difficulty of finding three men of the right type to be Commissioners, and the fact that the project will at first probably meet with little support from the industry and even with opposition from some sections.
> On the other hand, if the Commission is to succeed it must become firmly established and secure the confidence of the industry before having to deal with post-war issues. Nor is there reason to suppose that as time goes on, the industry will become better disposed to these

proposals, or the men for the job any easier to find. The fact that legislation takes time is an argument for starting at once.[31]

The Lord President's committee were favourable but asked for a more detailed scheme to be submitted.[32]

Work on a more detailed scheme, however, was never finished because towards the end of 1942 there was a complete change of heart within the Board of Trade. The paper submitted to the Lord President's committee early in 1943 explained that the departments concerned had lost confidence in the project:

> We have become increasingly doubtful as to the wisdom and necessity of our original proposal. Some of the strongest arguments for setting up a Films Commission have lost much of their significance, while the difficulties in the way are greater than we had at first supposed.[33]

The decision seems to have been influenced by pressures both inside and outside the Board of Trade. There were disagreements within the department. The official working directly under Somervell thought that the Commission was neither necessary nor desirable and engaged in a battle of minutes with Rowson. The balance of opinion shifted against Rowson when Hugh Gaitskell became involved. Gaitskell was then a temporary civil servant at the Board of Trade acting as Dalton's personal assistant and he disagreed strongly with the line which the department had been taking on the film industry. From the first he was critical of the attention which had been paid to films and in his first memorandum on the subject he wrote: 'There is no reason why films should be singled out for special treatment rather than, say, motor cars.'[34] The main factor, however, appears to have been a very effective public relations campaign mounted by Rank, which succeeded in convincing both Gaitskell and his colleagues that many of the arguments for a Commission were out of date. One of the main reasons advanced for reconsidering the proposal was that:

> There have been developments within the industry which point to the emergence of strong groups under the control of business interests which seem likely to operate according to the normal standards of commercial efficiency and honesty, which have not so far been conspicuous within the film industry. Furthermore, we understand that these interests are already negotiating with the American industry for a fairer share of the American market. The argument in favour of allowing the industry, if it can, to work out its own salvation without Governmental intervention is very strong when it comes to bargaining with the American film industry since a Films Commission appointed by the British Government would find itself in a most

difficult position in view of the talks on post-war commercial policy in which the two Governments will be engaged before long.[35]

The other arguments were those which had previously been considered but rejected: that there would be strong opposition to the Commission, and that it would be hard to find suitable Commissioners.

The Lord President's committee accepted the advice that plans for a Films Commission should be abandoned. So the outcome of two years of lengthy discussions and consultations was that no steps were taken to set up either a bank or an independent authority.

MONOPOLY AND ITS CRITICS

The emergence of the Rank organisation as a major power in the industry was clearly one of the factors which influenced the debate on the film bank and the Films Commission, and this development was to have far-reaching effects on industry politics. From about 1943 controversy began to centre as much around the role of big British companies and competition within the British industry as around the question of competition from America. The new debate also began to alter the terms of the older one since a key issue was whether British monopoly helped or hindered the activities of the American companies.

The story of Rank's entry into the industry has been told many times.[36] As one of the myths of the film business it has a distinctly prosaic, British quality: the devout Methodist flour miller sets out to co-opt the big screen into the service of God and, finding his goal frustrated by a conspiracy of renters and cinema owners, resolves the difficulty by buying out half the conspiracy. Reference has already been made to Rank's rise to power, but it may be as well to summarise the main events. From a commercial point of view the story began in 1935 when Rank acquired an interest in a film distributor, C. M. Woolf's General Film Distributors (GFD), and in Pinewood studios; the following year he formed the General Cinema Finance Corporation which took over both GFD and Pinewood; in 1938 GCFC bought an interest in the Odeon circuit and Rank appointed John Davis to reorganise the business. The same year the Denham studios were acquired from Prudential; in 1939 Rank and his associate, Farrow, joined the Odeon board; in 1941 Rank put in a successful bid for a controlling interest in the Metropolis and Bradford Trust which controlled Gaumont-British; Oscar Deutsch died, leaving Rank in complete control of the Odeons; in 1943 C. M. Woolf died, leaving Rank in control of GFD. As a result of these acquisitions Rank, in 1943, owned two of the big three cinema circuits, the most important British distributor, GFD, two big modern studios and four smaller ones; he controlled the production companies Gaumont-British and Gainsborough, was chairman of a group of small production

139

units, Independent Producers Ltd, and financed Del Guidice's Two Cities production company.

The Associated-British Picture Corporation (ABPC) had not grown so recently or so rapidly as the Rank group but it comprised a comparable empire, consisting of the ABC cinema circuit, production and distribution interests and two studios. In relation to ABPC, public concern was focused less on the prospects of further expansion than on the possibility of an American takeover. This seemed likely after the death of the company's founder, John Maxwell, in 1941, when Warners bought 49 per cent of the Maxwell shares, acquiring a 25 per cent interest in the ordinary capital.

Rank also had ties with American companies. GFD had bought an interest in Universal in 1936; Universal itself had an interest in United Artists, and there was another connection with this company through British and Dominion. When Rank bought his holding in Gaumont British, he inherited an association with 20th Century-Fox, the other major shareholder.

In the debate about monopoly the Rank Organisation, whether cast as hero or villain, figured much more prominently than did ABPC. This was partly because, during the war, competition between producers was focused on studio space and resources as much as on screen time. In this respect Rank seemed the major threat because he controlled more than half the available studio space and was actively in production, whereas ABPC had less studio space, had lost more as a result of requisitioning, and had temporarily withdrawn from production. The character of the Rank production programme was itself controversial because of the extent to which resources were invested in high-cost films for export. There were, at that time, two schools of thought about production policy. One, represented by Michael Balcon,[37] considered that the future lay in the production of modestly priced pictures of a distinctly British character primarily for the domestic market; the other, of which Rank was a leading exponent, recommended the strategy of trying to break into the American market by emulating the production and marketing methods of Hollywood. This question tended to merge with the monopoly debate even though Korda, for instance, who was not linked with a combine, as well as Rank, was associated with the export policy.

Another reason for the emphasis on Rank was that he was a much more formidable politician than the leaders of ABPC. He was associated with powerful City interests and had on the boards of his companies men with 'solid' backgrounds in banking and insurance, men like Philip Hill of Philip Hill and Partners, Lord Luke, Chairman of Lloyd's Bank, and E. H. Lever, joint secretary of the Prudential. He was also a prominent Methodist. As a 'man of substance' and a man of God he had certain advantages in dealing with officials who tended to regard the film industry as a sump of both financial and moral corruption. He also earned political credit as a patriot by pouring money into films during the war. ABPC, on the other hand, was not well regarded. John Maxwell himself, as we have seen, was not on good terms with the civil service, and after his death some ugly conflicts on the board jeopardised the reputation of the new management.

In the early 1940s monopoly was a topical issue. During the spring of 1942 a series of articles appeared in *The Times*, the *Economic Journal* and the *Economist* commenting on a general tendency to concentration in industry, encouraged, it was thought, by wartime regulations. Fears were expressed about the possible effects on individual freedom; arguments were put forward for some kind of state intervention. There was, therefore, a body of opinion outside the film industry ready to respond to accusations of monopoly.

Accusations from within the industry came at first mainly from production interests. The trade union, the ACT, had led the way with a pamphlet published in 1939, *Film Business is Big Business*,[38] which analysed the ownership of the industry and showed how there had already been a process of mergers. This was followed in 1941 by *A State Film Industry*,[39] a report advocating the nationalisation of part of the industry, which included criticisms of the combines. A number of independent producers joined the attack on monopoly. In this context they stressed their 'independence' as a virtue, and the term came to be used extensively and rather misleadingly in the ensuing debate. Independent producers were simply those who did not have permanent close ties with either circuit. This did not mean, as was sometimes implied, that they were free to choose the films they made, for they could only proceed with projects which were acceptable to a financier and which were likely to obtain a circuit release. At this time Michael Balcon was the leading activist among the independents. In his memoirs he describes how, with his associate, Major Baker, he took up the question of monopoly on the Films Council:

> Baker and I were both pretty vocal on the tendencies towards monopoly, which became increasingly apparent. Although Associated British were also concerned, it must be admitted that our fire was mainly concentrated on Rank . . .
>
> At the Films Council, aided and abetted by Miss Thelma Cazalet, MP (Mrs David Cazalet-Kier), and Sam Eckman Jr, we conducted a campaign against Rank's activities which resulted in a committee being set up, presided over by Mr Albert Palache, a City financier, to report on 'tendencies to monopoly in the film industry'.[40]

The first step towards setting up this committee was a statement added in a postscript to the fifth report of the Films Council warning that:

'During the year under review a marked trend towards monopoly control of the film industry became evident and it was clear that changes in the control of certain large companies would involve important issues of public policy.'[41]

At the Board of Trade, Hugh Dalton's first response to the Films Council report was to write in June 1943 to Rank and to Sir Philip Warter, acting for ABPC shareholders, asking for a personal undertaking from them that they would not 'take any steps to secure control, directly or indirectly, of additional cinemas or their booking arrangements, or of production studios, without the prior consent of the Board of Trade'. Rank gave such an undertaking in July; ABPC gave a similar one in February 1944. The Films Council considered this arrangement inadequate, and in December 1943 Dalton asked them to offer 'their advice on what further practical measures, if any, are necessary to check the development of monopoly in the film industry'.[42] It was as a response to this request that the committee referred to by Balcon was appointed, consisting of four independent members of the Council: Albert Palache as Chairman, Sir Walter Citrine, Professor Arnold Plant and Mr Philip Guedalla (although illness soon forced Guedalla to resign).

The committee held nineteen meetings for the purpose of taking evidence and heard about forty people from the trade and ten from relevant government service. Their report, entitled *Tendencies to Monopoly in the Cinematograph Industry*, was submitted to the full Films Council and to the President of the Board of Trade in July 1944. In approaching its task the committee had put an open-ended interpretation on the Board of Trade's request. They wrote:

> We understand the phrase 'development of monopoly' in the President's letter to the Films Council to refer to tendencies which appear to threaten the future prospects of an independent and unfettered British film industry. By independent we have in mind both freedom from foreign domination and freedom from dominating British control. By unfettered we mean enjoying reasonable access both to means of production of films and to screen time, and freedom from restrictive practices in the field of film distribution.[43]

Having defined their brief in this way the committee made a broad survey of the industry and offered proposals about the general objectives and character of future film policy rather than outlining specific measures. Their report, the first public report of its kind since Moyne, unambiguously supported the case for state intervention.

The report stated coherently the reasons for concern:

> It has been made clear to us that, save in quite exceptional cases, a booking by one of the three major circuits, Gaumont-British, Odeon

and Associated British Picture Corporation, is indispensable for successful exploitation of a British feature film in the United Kingdom. . . . The survival of independent British production is therefore dependent on the Gaumont-British and Odeon circuits, ultimately controlled by a single person, and on the controller of the ABC circuit. If these two persons should both decide not to book a film, or if on booking it they choose to allot to it the least remunerative playing dates and locations in their circuit, the picture is almost certain to be a failure and the producer may in consequence be ruined.[44]

The authors showed how this situation was linked to the question of American competition. Drawing attention to the Warner holding in ABPC and to a recent agreement between Rank and 20th Century-Fox whereby 'two directors of the latter Corporation have joined the Board of Gaumont-British', they outlined what they considered to be the implications:

It appears therefore that the statement that ultimate control over the three major exhibition circuits reposes in as few as two hands may not adequately convey the gravity of the situation in which independent British producers have suddenly been placed. For it may further be the case that these two hands are or may ultimately be guided by American interests. If this were true, the future of independent production might indeed be precarious. Whatever other action may be necessary in relation to these circuits, it is abundantly clear to us that great vigilance should be exercised and all necessary steps promptly taken to prevent the effective control over the circuits, no matter where the control *nominally* resides, from passing into foreign hands.[45]

In order to achieve this end, they recommended the introduction of a trustee arrangement comparable to that of *The Times* or the *Economist*.

As an investigation of monopoly the report had the merit that it examined the relationship between the structure of the British industry and the all-important question of American interests; but it suffered from a lack of precise statistical evidence for many of its observations. In the event this was probably unavoidable because few statistics were published, the committee had no power to require witnesses to disclose information, and, as they had to treat all information as confidential, they were unable to publish some of the facts they did obtain.

The extent of 'dominating British control' could be most clearly demonstrated where visible assets were involved – studios and cinemas. The report showed that of available studio space Rank alone owned 56 per cent and the two combines between them owned 70 per cent, but it could only record opinions about the effects of this. It established that the combines between them owned a quarter of all cinemas and a third of cinema seats, but had to rely on estimates for other important factors determining their control, such as the proportion of box office receipts taken by them and the proportion of 'first run' houses controlled by them. In relation to the very significant question of the London release, the authors remarked: 'As soon as we attempted to pursue our investigations any distance into the realm of detail we found ourselves groping in a statistical twilight.' Yet, as they observed: 'The main reason . . . for the dominating position which the circuits enjoy is the hold they have in the London region.'[46]

The sections of the report dealing with distribution suffer especially from the absence of precise information. Although figures were given for the proportion of screen time occupied by American films, the report had little to say about American distributors except that no evidence was offered that they engaged in 'collusive action' or formed a 'conspiracy to frustrate competition', or that the KRS was 'guided in its policy more by American than by British influence'. On the relationship between distributor and producer the report commented that distribution charges seemed high, and advanced reasons for assuming that independent producers suffered discriminatory treatment and that the integration of the circuits with vertical combines could be expected to aggravate this:

> When the exhibition circuits themselves are so controlled by an interest which controls competing production, and which has long-term arrangements in addition to distribute American feature films, the independent producer must assume that the best dates and locations will be reserved by the circuit for the associated producers and the American companies.[47]

The report also drew attention to complaints made mainly by independent exhibitors about particular restrictive practices: excessive time and distance bars; conditional booking, whereby a distributor gave the exhibitor the right to show a film only on condition that he booked also the supporting programme or other main films for other dates; the ban operated by members of the KRS which prevented independents booking as co-operatives.

The committee made a number of recommendations for measures to safeguard the position of the independents in relation to the combines. They suggested that legislation should be introduced to prevent further growth of the existing circuits or the creation of new circuits, to separate booking in the London area from booking for a national release, to make conditional booking illegal, and to compel distributors to treat co-operative booking by independents on the same terms as they treated

144

circuit bookings; that the Board of Trade should try to obtain agreements with the combines which would secure adequate screen time for independent productions and a reasonable share of new films for independent exhibitors; that an independent tribunal should be set up to arbitrate in the case of disputes about the allocation of studio space and, if the above mentioned agreements failed, to handle disputes about screen time and the allocation of product.

Following the brief they had set themselves, the committee also considered factors inhibiting the development of independent production which were not directly attributable to monopoly. They singled out the lack of permanent production finance and recommended the solution suggested by the Films Council in 1940, the establishment of a films bank. They also repeated the suggestion made then that the bank should have its own renting organisation.

The main strength of the report, for its supporters – and the main weakness, according to its detractors – was that the authors' case rested ultimately on cultural arguments. The authors recalled the attention paid to the cultural importance of film in the Moyne report in 1936 and at the 1926 Imperial Conference, and then expressed their own position in a passage which, through frequent quotation, was soon to become quite famous:

> The view is held in some quarters that the British Cinematograph business is to be regarded merely as one business among others, which may claim no special consideration and that it is out of place for Parliament to show special concern for its conduct and future development. We do not share that view, and we are confident that Parliament will continue in its endeavour to safeguard its future by means of special legislation not applicable to industry in general. A cinematograph film represents something more than a mere commodity to be bartered against others. Already the screen has great influence both politically and culturally over the minds of the people. Its potentialities are vast, as a vehicle for the expression of national life, ideals and tradition, as a dramatic and artistic medium, and as an instrument for propaganda.[48]

The extent to which the committee's advice was influenced by critical and cultural judgments was particularly apparent in the last section of the report, which discussed the relative merits of producing primarily for export or primarily for the home market. The committee decided unreservedly in favour of production for the home market on the grounds that:

> It would indeed be an unsatisfactory outcome of years of special encouragement for British film production if while this country

continued to be served mainly with foreign product, British production in its turn should become more and more dominated by the desire to appeal first to the foreign market.[49]

In their view the 'desire to appeal first to the foreign market' was not even the best approach to exports because: 'This country has its own contribution to make and does not need slavishly to imitate the idiom of other producing centres of the world.' [50] The main reason, then, why the committee championed the cause of independent production was that they thought independent producers were committed to working within a specifically British cultural context, while the combines looked first to the American market.

The Palache report was to remain an important point of reference in the post-war film debate because it neatly set out most of the ideas associated with the case for intervention: the stress laid on cultural considerations, the importance attached to national culture, the value of the independent producer, the twin dangers of American and British monopoly. It was also for this reason a highly controversial document.

On publication, the report received considerable press coverage which reflected the broad political division of opinion about its contents. Support was associated with a Liberal or Labour perspective. An editorial in the *Manchester Guardian* commented: 'The Board of Trade, already convicted of complacency, will not escape a graver charge if it fails to act promptly on these recommendations.'[51] The *Daily Telegraph*, on the other hand, quoted some highly critical trade comments, including the remark from E. T. Carr, the managing director of Eagle Lion, that 'while there are 3,800 independent cinemas in Britain any talk of monopoly is absurd', and Korda's assertion that 'the Films Council Committee wants a large number of mediocre films and Hollywood will make bigger and bigger films and if we do not then it will be the end of the British industry.'[52]

Although it was evident that some trade interests would be highly critical, the Films Council passed unanimously a motion giving the report qualified approval.[53] Soon after this, however, in September 1944, the tenure of office of that Council expired and neither Balcon, the leading critic of monopoly, nor the other producer member were reappointed. In their place the Board of Trade appointed Rank and Korda, a move which attracted a good deal of adverse comment. J. B. Priestley, for instance, wrote in the *News Chronicle*: 'It is unfortunate that the man who has now been dropped from the Films Council, Mr Michael Balcon, should be the one producer who . . . has been consistently working on the right lines, turning out sensible medium cost pictures and building up a team of enthusiastic young producers and directors.'[54]

146

The new appointments reflect the fact that opinion in the Board of Trade was against the Palache report. Hugh Gaitskell, who by this time had made a considerable impact on the film department, turned his initial assessment of the report into a scathing attack. This was hardly surprising, as he had himself been advocating the reverse policy of encouraging the kind of structure exemplified by Rank. His first major intervention had, after all, been to oppose the Commission on the grounds that the growth of the Rank Organisation had made state intervention unnecessary. In his comments on the report he wrote:

> The real difficulty is the approach of the Report to the whole question of monopoly, though if by monopoly one means large-scale production, then we must accept the fact that we have got to have it. The industry can never be run by a large number of small independent producers. What one can have, however, is a small number of large-scale producers, and in my opinion this is what we should work for since it gives us the prospects of making first class films, of acquiring an export market, and at the same time avoids what most people mean by monopoly.[55]

Although his critique of the report derived from a basic disagreement with its premises, he was able to discredit some sections by pointing to imprecisions and inaccuracies. In particular, he drew attention to the fact that the authors had not specified what they meant either by 'medium cost' or by 'independent'. Gaitskell objected, with justification, that if an independent producer was taken to mean one unconnected either with an American interest or with a British circuit, hardly any would qualify. The observation pinpointed one of the weaknesses of the report, which was that it failed to make a distinction between the entrepreneurial and the creative function of the producer. What the authors presumably had in mind was that, while there were virtually no producers independent in Gaitskell's sense, there was a body of creative producers who, it could be argued, would be able to work independently if the proposed state structures were set up.

The report could not be expected to receive much support from the industry which it had so severely criticised. Since its recommendations were primarily intended to help a group, the independent producers, who as yet hardly existed, there was no major interest group among the employers ready to speak for it. All that was needed, therefore, to ensure that the report could not be implemented was for the Board of Trade to base its decisions on the balance of advice offered by trade organisations. This was the procedure adopted.

Consultation began in August 1944, when the report was sent to all the recognised trade organisations with a request for comment. Neither the employers' associations nor the Board of Trade showed any desire to reach an early conclusion, and it was not until the following spring that most of the answers were received.

The one organisation which wrote back promptly and expressed 'unqualified support' was the ACT. Later, the screenwriters' society also indicated unqualified support and Equity gave its general approval. NATKE was somewhat critical, particularly about the emphasis on medium budget production, and neither accepted nor rejected the report. The replies received from the employers, although all more or less critical, displayed a characteristic degree of disunity. The only matter about which there was unanimity was the tribunal, which they all opposed; although the recommendation that the Board of Trade should allocate studio space was opposed only by the BFPA, and the proposal for a film bank was opposed only by the circuits. The circuits were consulted separately from the CEA and it is clear that, although a major influence in the Association, they were not able to dictate policy. The CEA agreed with the recommendations about conditional booking, co-operative booking and the need to allocate films to independent exhibitors, while the circuits, the KRS and the BFPA opposed them. The voice of the combines was far more apparent within the BFPA than in the CEA. The only measure designed to help independents which was supported by the BFPA was the allocation of screen time. The BFPA was vehemently opposed to measures designed to encourage medium-cost production and, concerning the circuits, disagreed that restrictions should be imposed on their further expansion. The KRS displayed its distaste for government intervention of any form by opposing all the recommendations which would interfere with the pattern of distribution and exhibition except, oddly enough, for the recommendation that the film bank should set up a renting organisation.

The Board of Trade officials were able to draw wholly negative conclusions from the results of consultation because they very largely discounted the views of labour. Their remarks reveal that they thought trade unions should confine their views to matters in which labour questions were directly involved. Thus in relation to the tribunal, official advice was:

> The President may well form the opinion that there is, in fact, no sufficient reason for setting up a tribunal for which no desire exists among the directly interested sections of the industry (i.e. producers, renters, circuits and independent exhibitors). This is not the view of the Association of Cine-Technicians (George Elvin's union) but labour questions would not fall within the tribunal's purview and Mr O'Brien's union . . . has made no presentment either for or against the tribunal.[56]

If the union view was disregarded, then trade opinion seemed to be completely at variance with independent opinion. Before Palache, the Moyne committee, the Bank of England and the author of the Campbell report had all concluded that the industry required external supervision. The Board of Trade officials, however, remained unimpressed and, as they had before, supported the trade position. Just as Gaitskell had dealt with the Campbell report by arguing that conditions had changed since it was written, so the departmental memorandum on Palache maintained that some of the problems highlighted in this report had been partially solved. This had happened, supposedly, as a result of a meeting between the President of the Board of Trade and industry representatives at which all sections of the industry had agreed on a procedure for internal arbitration on the lines of the Joint Conciliation Committee, a trade body which had already been set up in response to the complaints which led to the inquiry.

On the rest of the report the officials offered advice which, in its discouraging approach to intervention of any kind, was entirely consistent with their rejection of the tribunal.[57] They advised against making special provision for the production of medium-cost pictures 'because the industry is the best judge of what type of film is now likely to be profitable'. They advised against the film bank because 'in principle it is undesirable to multiply specialised corporations each dealing with a particular industry', and because there would be a danger that competent producers would prefer to use private finance and the bank would 'find itself left with the thankless task of looking after the sharks and the duds'. Although they conceded that it would be desirable to prevent further expansion of the circuits and to introduce a trusteeship arrangement, they recommended that because such measures would be difficult to implement no action should be taken until further consideration and consultation had taken place.

The character of this briefing underlines the extent to which the views of the civil servants concerned coincided with the wishes of the major trade interests. In these circumstances it was not surprising that the campaign against monopoly made little headway. In the two years since the Films Council had raised the issue, the only steps taken to counteract tendencies to monopoly were entirely dependent on the voluntary co-operation of the industry. The combines had given an undertaking not to increase the strength of their circuits; the relevant trade interests had agreed to establish a system of internal arbitration to settle trade disputes. The civil service, however, did not complete its briefing until just after the general election of 1945, so that the final decision was left to a new President of the Board of Trade, who was a member of a Labour government.

8   A New Scenario?

> The war has not produced films (with one exception) of the
> first magnitude. . . . But it has set the English film on the
> path in which masterpieces may be created; it has
> established precisely what was lacking in the English cinema
> before 1940, a traditional English style.
>
> Dilys Powell, *Films since 1939*

THE POLITICAL CONTEXT

At the end of the war the condition of the film industry appeared
superficially healthy. Cinemagoing had reached a peak of popularity,
with weekly attendances rising from 19 million in 1939 to 30 million in
1945. British films were proving more attractive than ever before, and
were earning unusually good reviews not only in Britain but in America.
But the present was not uniformly bright and the future was very
unsettled. The production sector, in accordance with the government
decision to maintain only a 'healthy nucleus', was operating on a
drastically reduced scale. The early release of studios and manpower
from war service was not all that was required to assure a rapid recovery.
New capital would also be needed and, although British films were
reaching bigger audiences than before, investment in production
remained highly speculative. Costs had risen so steeply that even
successful British films were not necessarily profitable. Even for the
prosperous exhibition side of the business the future did not look entirely
secure. The recent boom was widely attributed to wartime conditions,
and the trade expected some decline in attendances over the next few
years, a trend which, it was feared, might be aggravated by the
reintroduction of television broadcasting. The increased takings had,
moreover, been partly offset by a sharp rise in Entertainments duty
which, by the end of the war, accounted for 36 per cent of gross box office
receipts. For the industry as a whole, however, the biggest element of
uncertainty was that the two major problems – American competition
and domestic monopoly – remained unresolved.

The Labour victory in itself did not have clear implications for the film
industry. There was no policy for films as such. The election manifesto
had had very little to say about leisure and the arts in general, and one

150

passage which did indicate a commitment to state investment in such areas made no mention of the cinema:

> National and local authorities should co-operate to enable people to enjoy their leisure to the full, to have opportunities for healthy recreation. By the provision of concert halls, modern libraries, theatres and suitable civic centres, we desire to assure to our people full access to the great heritage of culture of this nation.[1]

There was in the manifesto, however, a critique of monopolistic big business which corresponded with the kind of allegations which had recently been made more specifically against the film industry combines:

> The 'hard faced men' and their political friends kept control of the Government. They controlled the banks, the mines, the big industries, largely the press and the cinema. They controlled the means whereby people got their living. They controlled the ways by which most of the people learned about the world outside. . . . These men had only learned how to act in the interests of their own bureaucratically-run private monopolies which may be likened to totalitarian oligarchies within our democratic State. They had and felt no responsibility for the Nation.[2]

In the economic sphere promised remedies included public supervision of monopolies and state control over essential industries and services. Since there was strong evidence to show that the film industry was a monopoly and, in the war, entertainment had been treated almost as a necessity, it was easy to assume that the Labour government would wish to adopt the Palache recommendations. The opposite conclusion, however, was suggested by Dalton's management of the industry, as President of the Board of Trade during the last three years.

Dalton had had the opportunity of bringing the film industry under some form of public control, but had not taken it. He had rejected existing proposals for an independent commission; then, when presented with the Palache report, he had simply avoided taking any decision by allowing consultations to drag on until the election. Neither the constraints of the coalition nor the influence of a Conservative administration account for his failure to act. State intervention in the film industry was not then an issue of party conflict, and Dalton's Conservative predecessors had considered setting up a films bank or a commission or both. As for his advice, it came primarily not from the regular civil service but from his personal assistant, Hugh Gaitskell, himself a Labour man.

Gaitskell made his sympathies quite public after he left the civil service and was elected MP for South Leeds. For he accepted an invitation to become Vice-President and Economic Adviser to the BFPA. Gaitskell was not then in a position to influence government film policy officially. Dalton, however, who had apparently accepted Gaitskell's general analysis, was now Chancellor of the Exchequer, and the Chancellor's opinions were likely to have at least as much impact on policy as those of the new President of the Board of Trade, Sir Stafford Cripps, who as a radical and a puritan might be expected to sympathise with some of the arguments in the Palache Report.

In Parliament there was no unified Labour position on the film industry. Left-wing MPs such as Michael Foot, Ben Levy and Woodrow Wyatt frequently alluded to the twin dangers of monopoly and American domination, and criticised their own front bench for failing to intervene. The Conservatives were also not of one mind. Some regarded all controls as anathema, while others outdid their Labour colleagues in demanding restrictions on American film imports. The content of the film debates in both Houses therefore tended to reflect constituency pressures and personal interests rather than party allegiances. The exhibitors, who were well represented in all constituencies and organised through the CEA, formed a vociferous lobby, particularly in Scotland where the leading exhibitor, Alexander King, was a well-known figure in local affairs. By contrast, production work was confined to a few areas of London and the Home Counties with a particular concentration in Eton and Slough, Ben Levy's constituency. Ben Levy also had a personal interest in entertainment since he was himself a playwright and was married to the actress Constance Cummings. Many of the other MPs who regularly spoke on film issues were connected with the industry. On the Labour benches Glenvil Hall, the Financial Secretary to the Treasury, was a former Vice-President of the BFPA; Tom O'Brien was General Secretary of NATKE; Eric Fletcher was Chairman of the ABC; J. Reeves was Secretary Manager of the Workers' Film Association; Michael Foot had worked on the script of *Yellow Caesar* during the war and in 1948 married a militant film producer, Jill Craigie. From the Conservative benches the views of the combines were often voiced by Earl Winterton, a close business associate of Rank and director of three Odeon companies, while other frequent contributors were E. P. Smith, a member of the Screenwriters' Association; Walter Fletcher, a former independent exhibitor; and Beverley Baxter who, apart from being a prominent journalist, had worked for the Gaumont-British Picture Corporation before the war.

Even though a third of the population went to the cinema at least once a week, film issues were treated in the House as a specialist concern. *Kine Weekly* complained in 1948 that the film debates were poorly attended: 'Entertainment is not a subject that MPs take seriously. It is regarded as a sign of grace in a Member when he boasts that he seldom visits the cinema.'[3] Looking back in 1950, Michael Foot painted an unflattering picture of the standard procedure:

> First of all we usually have a speech from my Right Hon. Friend the President of the Board of Trade in which he shows his good intentions about the industry. . . . Then we have the Right Hon. Gentleman, the Member for Aldershot (Mr Lyttelton), who shows how gracefully and wittily he can comment on a subject which he approaches with such a fresh and open mind. Then we have my Hon. Friend the Member for Nottingham North-West (Mr O'Brien), who tries to berate the Government very often for not adopting his advice, although often he does not remember what that advice was.
>
> We also have the Noble Lord, the Member for Horsham (Earl Winterton) . . . who tells us how brilliantly successful the Rank Organisation has been and how, if the Government will let them get on with their work, they will make a worse mess of it than they have done already.[4]

Whether the discussions were fruitful or not, they were frequent. Even in 1946, when no relevant bills were presented, film issues were raised several times in the Commons and the debates were well covered in the press. The industry and its problems were extensively reported and lengthy battles of ideas were fought out in the correspondence columns. Among the various contributors, the distinction between industry spokesmen and informed outsiders was often unclear. Just as many MPs were directly or indirectly involved in films, there was a considerable overlap between film and journalism. The critic Ernest Betts worked at one time as a scenario writer, was linked briefly with Del Guidice's Pilgrim Pictures, and subsequently became Public Relations Officer first for 20th Century-Fox and then for MGM; Nicholas Davenport was a financial journalist but was also involved in Gabriel Pascal's company during the war and subsequently worked for Korda; Paul Rotha was a writer as well as a film-maker; and very many people involved in film production wrote occasional articles. It was the nature of the film business that it courted and thrived on publicity, and the many links between the world of film and the press helped to keep it in the public eye. But the subject attracted attention for other reasons also, because it was connected with a number of more general issues which were at the time a focus of interest and controversy.

The very question of whether the fate of the film industry should concern the government at all was one which touched on class and class conflict. Films were popular; and although they drew their audiences from all classes, the working class accounted for a major proportion of admissions, a slightly larger proportion than could be accounted for simply by their preponderance within the population.[5] Thus an association was made between a serious interest in the cinema and a respect for, or a concern with, the tastes of the working class. Ideas about culture and democracy had been evolving rapidly during the war around the work of CEMA (the Council for the Encouragement of Music and the Arts), and there was a relationship between the aim of popularising the culture of the elite and recognising value or potential value in a cultural form which was already popular. A wartime editorial in *Documentary News Letter* drew attention to the role of class assumptions, making this invidious comparison between America and Britain:

> In America the cinema is a part of everybody's life from the Executive downwards. . . . Whereas here, certainly the governing classes (and this includes Labour, Liberal and Conservative politicians and civil servants) regard the films as something vaguely not quite nice – the 'flicks'.[6]

Although, as these remarks suggest, there were politicians from all parties who treated the cinema with some contempt, in the post-war debates it is notable that those who seemed most anxious to disparage popular taste were also the most ardent advocates of *laissez-faire*. Earl Winterton, for instance, asserted in a debate on the Film Institute in 1949: 'Again and again when a certain film has been produced, which is supposed to be of great aesthetic or artistic value, and some cinemas have shown it, it has proved to be a complete and absolute failure.'[7]

The idea that popular taste must be 'bad' taste, or at least quite different from that of the elite, often went hand in hand with the theory that the mass audience used the cinema only as a form of escape. One producer, writing a eulogy in 1946 on the influence of Rank in the industry, described the cinema as 'a kind of proletarian dope tantamount to alcohol but, as it were, an alternative to it'.[8] Beverley Baxter gave a more lyrical rendering of the idea in a House of Commons debate in 1947:

> In parts of Lancashire where life is very grim and one sees the local cinema palace and its perhaps slight vulgarity, but there it is, a magic door at which people can leave the hardships of reality and, for two or three hours, be carried away on wings of song or phantasy.[9]

A similar patronising attitude can be detected in some of the interventionist arguments, although in that context the 'drug' theory is advanced from the standpoint of a temperance campaigner. Thus Ellis Smith, Labour member for Stoke-on-Trent, told the House in 1944:

> I am concerned with the effect upon the lives of our young people of too many films coming from Hollywood especially on Saturday afternoons when you can see thousands of young children, from

154

working-class areas in particular, going to matinees and seeing films which they ought not to see. They ought to be seeing films of an educational character, or films bringing the best out of life rather than films which cater for the emotions.[10]

The schoolmasterly approach which characterised some of the work of the documentary movement between the wars lingered on in the rhetoric of the movement's post-war campaign for public instruction, a rhetoric full of terms like 'leadership' and 'enlightenment'.[11] Within film education itself, a condescending manner was apparently so prevalent that the authors of a report from the Youth Advisory Council found it necessary to urge that discussions about films should be 'neither solemn, priggish or superior'.[12]

Most would-be improvers of public taste were Labour supporters, but a left-of-centre political perspective was also associated with a tendency to defend popular taste. Stafford Cripps, for instance, suggested in a speech to the Association of Specialised Film Producers that both the trade and some educationalists made the mistake of underestimating their audience:

> It is a curious fact that whether you are dealing with film exhibitors or buyers of consumer goods they all tend to place the taste of the public much lower than it really is and they are often surprised and slightly resentful when they discover that they are wrong. . . . I myself believe that the best will always justify itself in the public estimation provided it is not used to deceive the public – as for instance by pretending you are out to entertain them when really your design is to educate them.[13]

Another film problem which was intimately related to a national problem was, of course, that of American dominance, and it is clear that the demand to reduce American influence on the screen was in part sustained by general anti-American attitudes. On the far left there were those who objected to America as the champion of *laissez-faire* capitalism and who therefore tended to consider American films as agents of capitalist ideology. Their complaints became more pertinent with the development of the Cold War and of overt anti-communist activity in the United States. Ivor Montagu drew attention to the relevance to Britain of these developments in an article in *Documentary News Letter* in 1947. He quoted Eric Johnston's statement to the House Committee on Un-American Activities that 'films are serving capitalism effectively as a propaganda medium' and pointed to 'an ugly scuffle among the major companies to be first with the titles *Soviet Spies* and *Iron Curtain* etc.'. He then listed some of the films which were to be investigated by the Un-American Activities Committee, including *Hitler's Children* ('so anti-Nazi that it must have been inspired by Communists') and *Strange Incident* ('an anti-lynching film') and concluded: 'I do not think it can be a matter of indifference to us if a large part of Britain's American diet comes to us following this sort of "screening".'[14] Moral and religious criticisms of America were common and sometimes overlapped with the political objections, as in this statement from the Electrical Trades Union:

> We hold the view that for private enterprise to control this medium of mass communication, exercising as it does such a potent influence on the adolescent minds of this country, is to abandon the youth of this country to an ever-increasing diet of American films obsessed with crimes of brutality and an unhealthy preoccupation with sex, to such an extent as to make the Committee's defence of private enterprise utterly unrealistic.[15]

A further source of anti-American feeling was a distaste for American culture, or for a certain image of American culture. America was often portrayed as the home of vulgarity, of values debased by mass production, as in this characteristic explanation of Hollywood's success in the magazine *American Outlook*:

> One reason Hollywood has 'gone over big' is that it tailors its films to fit millions of people. Some that seem shapeless are pinned together with a bit of everything that is 'box office' – i.e. that will attract crowds. Others, unadorned with substance, have been stripped of all that could offend. In short they are like American cheese: good enough to lure lovers of cheese when they can't get the best, but not rank enough to affront potential eaters.[16]

Anti-American feeling was partly a response to Britain's material and military dependence on America, but this itself was only one aspect of the very emotive question of Britain's changing place in the world. The outcome of the war was confusing. Britain was nominally victor but faced many of the material problems and political humiliations of a defeated power; her influence on world affairs was waning; her Empire was shrinking. This situation coloured the film debate, and many of the contributions to the debate concerned ways in which films could enhance British prestige and influence abroad. There were many whose imaginations were fired by the idea of using films as agents of cultural colonialism. The following remarks in a 1944 Commons debate are typical:

> It is essential, now that our Colonial Empire is to have the benefits of the Colonial Development Act and will be progressing slowly along the paths of constitutional government, for us to show the greatness of

our country and the great elements which make up the British character and the advantage and generosity of our own rule. Suitable films could be shown in the backward colonies in order to teach them that at least our code of life is highly desirable and should be emulated.[17]

The theme of projecting Britain could be martialled in support of Rank's export-oriented policy but was not necessarily used this way. Those who wanted the home market given priority could argue that pictures made for a British audience would be more truly British than those made for export, and would therefore better serve the purpose of projecting the national character.

The wide-ranging considerations drawn into the film debate testify to the extent to which films were seen to have ideological significance. This was as true of Conservative politicians as of those of the Left. Indeed, one of the arguments they frequently advanced against state involvement was that the party in power might use films to promote its own aims. In one of the debates about the National Film Finance Corporation, in 1948, Churchill asked whether Harold Wilson, as President of the Board of Trade, could guarantee that 'now that the Government are definitely entering the film business with the taxpayers' money there will be no attempt at exercising political control as, of course, is done in Soviet Russia, over the character of the films produced in the interests of one particular party or point of view.'[18] The spectre of a Labour government using the film industry to preach socialism was the counterpart of Montagu's comment about the American industry serving capitalism, or of the warning in the Palache report about the danger of a private monopoly representing only the ideas of its owner.

The terms of reference of this public debate were scarcely reflected, however, in the process of decision-making. The traditions of the Board of Trade and the character of the administrative structure made for a much narrower view of the possible aims of government. Film questions were handled by the Films Branch, a small sub-department of the Board of Trade which was responsible both for administering the existing Films Acts and advising on new legislation. It was headed by an Under-Secretary who was also responsible for another area of work but who nevertheless himself conducted the more important negotiations with the trade and to a large extent decided on the content of reports to the politicians. R. C. G. Somervell, who figured during the wartime discussions, held this office from 1938 to 1952. Under him was an Assistant Secretary, aided by two principals, one dealing with production and one with the administration of the Acts. The total staff in 1950 numbered only twenty-two, of which ten were occupied with the quota and four with registration. The Films Branch was not, therefore, equipped to do its own research and analysis. There was not even any provision for collecting statistics, except for information about admissions and box office takings of the kind required for tax purposes and to administer the quota. The civil servants were expected to work closely with the trade, to liaise between the trade and the government, rather than to contribute original ideas. The standard procedure for preparing a brief consisted in contacting the organisations considered representative of major sections of the trade and some companies or individuals singled out either because they were especially powerful or because they were thought to be particularly well informed. The method of work provided little scope for considering the interests of the cinema audience. But in practice it was even more limiting because, although the trade unions were included among the organisations consulted, the civil servants attached very little importance to information or ideas supplied by them.

We saw earlier how the ACT's view about the proposed tribunal to adjudicate on the allocation of studio space was dismissed because the tribunal would not handle labour disputes. As the incident suggests, the civil servants tended to disregard union evidence unless it had a direct bearing on the working conditions of the union's members. Another illustration of this is to be found in the comments made by the Assistant Secretary on the various documents submitted in 1944 in response to a request for information about the post-war requirements of the industry. The ACT sent in a document (*Industrial Post-War Reconstruction*[19]) which summarised the case for anti-monopoly measures, the establishment of a films bank and the partial nationalisation or municipalisation of exhibition, but which also discussed likely technological developments and the need for an organised industry training scheme. The list of expected technological developments seems, with hindsight, fairly sensible: process photography; increased uses of colour; growth of film libraries; expansion of 16mm; high-speed processing; television; stereoscopy. Yet, in a memorandum addressed to Gaitskell, the Assistant Secretary wrote:

> It is not by any means an impressive or statesmanlike document. It contains in embryonic form one or two sensible suggestions . . . but there are no really constructive proposals on matters directly concerning us. . . .
> A good deal of the report is clearly addressed to the gallery – i.e. the rank and file of the ACT members.[20]

The last remark reveals a fairly fundamental distaste for trade unions in general and the notions of democracy which, in theory at least, are mirrored in their structure. The memorandum's conclusion left little doubt about the chances the ACT might have of influencing this civil servant: 'I suppose we shall have to see the authors of this report and give them a chance to let off steam; but I think this can stand over until we have received the expected report from the BFPA.'[21] The BFPA report, when it eventually arrived, consisted mainly of a shopping list of short-term requirements: the release of studios and manpower, the continuation of the quota. It contained little analysis and gave less information about new technology than the ACT document, but it was apparently the kind of response which the civil servants were looking for.

It is difficult to tell quite how much influence the administration had on policy during the Labour government's term of office. In the first years, officials were certainly involved as much in the formulation of aims as in the execution of political directives. Because the film industry was considered hard to understand and its affairs treated primarily as a technical matter, the politicians relied very much on their officials' analysis of the kind of measures required to improve the industry's performance. But in the last years – when, with Stafford Cripps as Chancellor and Harold Wilson as President of the Board of Trade, it seems that the politicians were moving towards a more determined policy of intervention – there is evidence that their intentions were undermined by the civil servants.

The influence of the Board of Trade would, of course, have been very much reduced if the government had taken the decision to treat the cinema more as an aspect of culture and less as a branch of commerce. There was sufficient support for such a decision outside the trade for it to be a realistic option.

AN EDUCATIONAL AND CULTURAL MEDIUM

The debate about cultural policy and the debate about commercial and economic policy might have reflected the same conflicts underneath, but they involved two quite distinct forms of argument: different principles and different precedents were invoked. Whereas wartime economic controls were presented as temporary expedients, measures extending state power in social and cultural matters were accepted by some members of all parties as a step towards necessary reform. Before the Labour Party came to power there had been a considerable move towards greater state involvement in education and the arts. The Education Act of 1944 in theory extended the opportunity of a good secondary education to everyone. Through CEMA, public funds had been used to promote and popularise art forms previously enjoyed mainly by a very small elite. In the hope that the trend towards greater state support for the arts would continue in peacetime, the Dartington Hall Trust in co-operation with PEP had initiated the 'Arts Enquiry', a detailed survey of the state of various arts which was intended to serve as a basis for future policy-making. Under the Labour government the creation of the Arts Council took the principle of a public policy for the arts a step further.

But there had been no absolute break with the past. The changes were recent and were contested. Within a section of the literary elite they provoked a conservative backlash, signalled during the late 1940s by a spate of obituaries for culture, art and learning.[22]

The suggestion that the cinema might be included among the arts, and so become eligible in this capacity for state direction and support, met with considerable resistance. This was partly because financial interests were involved on a much bigger scale than in the case of the live theatre or music, but it was also because the suggestion threatened a number of ideas in which the intelligentsia had a vested interest. The subsidising of the art forms most valued by the intellectual elite might render that elite rather less exclusive, but seemed unlikely to undermine the traditions and assumptions which confirmed its superiority and enabled it to set the standards of 'quality' and 'taste' which would guide policy. To treat the cinema as an art was to disrupt the notion that only the discerning few could recognise or appreciate art. For not only were films made for a large audience, but most of the films which the critics endorsed were apparently appreciated, at least in their country of origin, by the general public. Except for those professionally involved in the film industry very few intellectuals were much better informed about the cinema, its techniques or its history, than were some relatively uneducated film enthusiasts.

In this last respect the position was beginning to change. The view that film might be a legitimate subject for serious study had been gaining ground. It is significant that film was not at first included in the work of the Arts Enquiry; but a working party was later to study the factual film, and some years after this the PEP brought out a very comprehensive study of the feature industry. The nature of the change, however, was ambiguous. During the war the increased interest in film was partly related to propaganda work. A number of sociological studies were undertaken to provide information about the composition and reactions of the cinema audience, and even works of critical appreciation such as Roger Manvell's *Film* placed considerable emphasis on the influence of films. In this respect the authors of these studies betray a preoccupation with managing the population coupled with an implicit assumption that they, as part of an elite, have the right to manage.

Indeed, the most influential academics of the 40s who, whether as critics or sociologists, wrote seriously on the cinema were deeply influenced by the very culture which their choice of subject appeared to challenge. The two writers who set the direction that film criticism was to follow until well into the 1960s, Ernest Lindgren (*The Art of the Film*[23]) and Roger Manvell (*Film*[24]), both accepted the prevailing theory of art promoted by, among others, R. G. Collingwood: a theory of art as an individual expression of emotion produced by specially endowed individuals and appreciated by a discerning few. Rather than examining these ideas, they argued that film could be assimilated to them: 'The film is a co-operative art,' wrote Manvell, 'but, as in all creative work, a single mind with a single purpose must dominate the whole.'[25] Similarly, when justifying his concern with a popular medium, Manvell offers a quite orthodox account of cultural hierarchy:

> The standards of our civilisation are the mixed standards of the privileged who are able to acquire culture, and the recognition of values which culture implies, and the standards of the culturally under-privileged, who, after a brief acquaintance with the tools of thought – namely reading, writing and arithmetic – apply them to reading the cheaper Sunday press and the enjoyment of the cheaper thrills of the cinema. The proper study of mankind must, however, include the assessment of these debased standards as well as those more finely acquired.[26]

The sociologist J. P. Mayer criticises Collingwood for his dismissal of film as 'amusement art' and Leavis for his 'contempt for the masses', but his own perspective is that of a member of the same cultured elite who shares similar values drawn from a liberal classical tradition. In the introduction to *British Cinemas and Their Audiences* Mayer offers fifth-century Athens as a model of a healthy society and the Roman Empire as a warning of what modern society might become. He does not question the position of the elite but rather what he sees as an abdication of responsibility: 'Neither escapism nor traditionalism can be accepted as solutions to make the film medium into a responsible instrument of contemporary culture. We cannot isolate ourselves from the masses. We cannot all go into monasteries.'[27] Instead the elite should be actively involved in providing cultural leadership. 'A democratic State, fully aware of its task, requires a leading and responsible elite not only in the sphere of politics but also in the realms of culture.'[28] Within the intelligentsia, therefore, the major division of opinion was between those who wanted to exclude the 'masses' and those who wanted to lead them. The former tended to have no interest in the cinema, and the latter tended to approach it in the spirit of a missionary.

A concern with morals was far more widespread than the desire to raise aesthetic standards, and this concern was focused particularly on the possible influence of the cinema on children. The government responded with the appointment in 1948 of the Wheare Committee on Children and the Cinema. The Committee took evidence from a wide range of organisations and individuals in the field of education, youth work, welfare and juvenile crime, as well as from the trade. Their report testifies to the prevalence of a vague anxiety about the amount of sex, crime and escapist fantasy in films, and of fears that children were 'exposed to harmful influences' which might undermine 'the child's social sense and may from its beginning vitiate his training for citizenship'.[29] But the authors found little evidence to link cinemagoing with behaviour regarded as anti-social or immoral. Accordingly they declined to draw any sweeping conclusions about the nature of the cinema's influence or the need to restrict young people's viewing, and their recommendations dealt mainly with the regulations governing safety and hygiene at children's shows, the quality of presentation, and suggestions for minor changes in the method of classifying films, including the introduction of the 'X' certificate, one of the few recommendations which was eventually adopted.

The Wheare report reflects some of the tensions between those who saw the cinema as a wholly pernicious force and those who adopted an attitude of guarded optimism coloured by a strong belief in the power of education. These differences emerge more explicitly in the educational context, where a generalised hostility to the cinema proved a formidable barrier to the development of film education. The British Film Institute had been established partly to promote a more enlightened approach to film by the teaching profession, but after fifteen years very little headway had been made in this area.

There was widespread dissatisfaction with the Institute and its work. Criticisms of the kind originally made in Walter Ashley's book *The Cinema and the Public* were still being levelled against it. And by the end of the war it was apparent that the Institute's activities in the field of educational film, as opposed to film education, were duplicating the work of other bodies. The Films Division of the MOI was producing films which were intended to be educational in a broad sense, while the National Committee for Visual Aids in Education was concerned with film as a teaching aid. The need to take some decisions about the BFI was the more pressing because in 1945 the government had to make plans for the kind of information service which would succeed the wartime Ministry of Information. At the end of the year, therefore, a series of meetings was held to consider the Institute's future. Representatives were present from the Privy Council Office, the Board of Trade, the Ministry of Education, the Office of the Lord President of the Council, the Home Office, the Scottish Office and the Scottish Education Department.

One of the documents considered at these meetings was the draft report of the Arts Enquiry, which contained a section on the work of the BFI. The account was highly critical:

> The Institute has tended to spread its services too wide for its resources, and has accomplished little. Much of its work has been superficial and half-hearted. Its activities have been constantly frustrated by the nature of its constitution and governing body, members of which sit as representatives of political organisations. It

has failed to serve the needs of education or the film industry, or to promote co-operation between the two. . . . Inability to fulfil its functions adequately and the general trend of its policy have now created among those who should be its warmest supporters disillusion and even mistrust.[30]

The evidence provided by the Education Ministry agreed that the work had been ineffective, although the blame was not attributed entirely to the Institute:

The Film Institute has never attracted the support of more than a small minority of Local Education Authorities and teachers; this is not necessarily a criticism of the Institute but reflects a certain lack of interest or belief in the educational value of the film.[31]

The document also explained one of the factors behind the animosity directed towards the Institute:

The Institute is much criticised for its relations with the trade. The substance of this criticism is that it is much too closely associated with Mr Rank's organisation and it is, therefore, cordially disliked by those who dislike and fear the tendency to monopoly in the film industry.[32]

More precisely the complaint was that the trade had used its influence to divert the Institute's activities away from the field of entertainment films and into a narrow concern with 'classroom films'. The problem was seen to stem largely from the Institute's constitution and the representative character of the governing body. In this respect the presence of government representatives as well as trade ones was seen as a danger. The Arts Enquiry had stated:

It is important that with the tendency towards monopoly in the industry and with the development of Government sponsored production and distribution the Institute should be able to safeguard the public interest. It must be able to criticise, where necessary, all films and film activities, including those of the feature industry and the Government. For this purpose it must have adequate status and finance and be independent of any Government department sponsoring or distributing films.[33]

Another reason the Institute was regarded in some quarters as hopelessly compromised was that its director, Oliver Bell, was a former member of the Conservative Party Central Office and thoroughly unsympathetic to the documentary movement and to the wider aims of 'uplift'. He could be expected to accept the trade view on most questions of policy.

The conclusion reached by the Arts Enquiry was that the Institute should be replaced by a new body which they called the British Film Academy. Its purpose would be

> the reconstitution of the British Film Institute whose main function should be to encourage the use of the film for educational, cultural, scientific and recreative purposes and to protect the public interest and assist the British Film Industry.[34]

Its governing body was to be a board composed of persons with authority to speak for education, the arts and learned and scientific associations. It should be better funded than the BFI and have better premises, including its own three-hundred seat cinema. It was conceived of more as a service to the industry, and its functions were to include research into cinematic technique, a statistical service, and the critical appraisal of films, as well as the provision of an educational advisory service. It was to organise the making of experimental films, to exhibit films itself, and to encourage the exhibition of films of cultural and sociological interest.

The Enquiry's report was eventually published in 1947 under the title *The Factual Film in Great Britain*, and provided the basis of a more public campaign for the reform or transformation of the BFI. In the same year the British Film Academy was founded 'by many leading British film makers, to advance film art by discussion and research and to encourage creative film-making everywhere'.[35] This was not the Academy the Arts Enquiry had called for, since the Council of Management was composed entirely of people working in the film industry, most of them feature film directors; it had no official status and no state grant. Nevertheless, the personnel involved included several opponents of existing BFI policy: the director was Roger Manvell; the staff included John Gillett and Karel Reisz; Paul Rotha was on the Council of Management. The founding of the Academy called attention to the failings of the BFI, and in particular to its impotence to make any cultural intervention relevant to the feature film industry.

The interdepartmental meetings of 1946 had established that there was a need to do something about the BFI, but left open the question of what should be done. The outcome was that the Lord President of the Council appointed a committee at the end of 1947

> to consider and report on any changes which may be desirable in the constitution and scope of the BFI and the relationship which should exist between the Institute and other bodies concerned with the film as a cultural and educational medium.[36]

The committee's chairman, Sir Cyril Radcliffe, had acquired a reputation for committee work and had recently returned from the

164

sensitive and arduous task of chairing the Punjab and Bengali Boundary Commission. The other members represented the arts and the field of public relations: Sir Ernest Pooley, chairman of the Arts Council; the film critic Dilys Powell; the art critic Charles Robertson; Sir Stephen Tallents; and the director of the Institute of Public Relations, Norman Wilson.

The Radcliffe proposals, which were nearly all adopted, went some way to satisfying the criticisms of the Institute but provided neither for the degree of independence nor the extension of powers and facilities which many people considered desirable. The Committee opted for adapting the BFI rather than replacing it with a new body. The governors should in future be appointed directly by the government; the Institute should receive a grant from the Exchequer; and its aims should be redefined to enable it to concentrate on encouraging the use and appreciation of film as an art, leaving to other appropriate bodies the responsibility for promoting film as a teaching aid. Its new objectives would be:

a) To encourage the development of the art of the film, to promote its use as a record of contemporary life and manners and to foster public appreciation and study of it from these points of view.
b) To explore and promote new or extended uses for the film.
c) To encourage, support and serve other bodies working in the same field.[37]

Its three main tasks were defined as:

a) The administration of the National Film Library.
b) The conduct of a first-class information service.
c) The development of a central and regional organisation to promote appreciation of the film art and new or extended uses of the cinema.[38]

The Radcliffe report laid the foundations for subsequent development, but in the short run did little to make the Institute more influential within the feature industry. The report gave little guidance about the level of funding required; the description of the work to be undertaken was left vague, whereas the kinds of work the Institute should not undertake were specified. One particularly significant negative recommendation was that the Institute should not collect statistics, although it was supposed to provide 'a first-class information service'. Apparently the service was not intended to include information about how the commercial cinema functioned. Restrictions of this kind naturally tended to perpetuate the Institute's isolation from the industry, reducing the possibility either for co-operation or conflict between the two.

A severe practical limitation on the scope of BFI activities was that the Exchequer grant (£68,000 in 1950) did not allow for a rapid incursion into new areas of activity such as exhibition or experimental production. The new method of appointing governors did not eliminate pressures from the trade against any developments which seemed to conflict with commercial interests. Although governors were officially appointed as independent persons, nominations were solicited from the same bodies and interest groups which had previously been represented, with the result that the Board continued to include members who, to all intents and purposes, spoke for the major trade associations. During the next two decades the Institute did slowly begin to assume new functions on the lines suggested by the Arts Enquiry. It took over the Telekinema, inherited from the 1951 Festival of Britain, as a venue for public exhibition in 1952 and in the same year helped to establish an experimental film fund; in the 1960s it expanded its activities outside London with the opening of a number of regional film theatres; its work in information and education gradually came to have more bearing on the conduct of the cinema and television industries in Britain. But it was only in the 1970s that the Institute came to play the kind of role envisaged for it by the Arts Enquiry, and by then the British cinema had itself become a marginal concern within the entertainment business.

The post-war reorganisation of the Government Information Services, which had added some urgency to the debate about the BFI, raised directly the question of how the Films Division and the Crown film unit would function in peacetime. It had always been assumed that the Ministry of Information would be disbanded at the end of the war. During its short life it had received more publicity for its shortcomings and blunders than for its achievements, and the Labour government was anxious to dispose of this potential source of embarrassment as quickly as possible. Plans were hastily drawn up to establish a different kind of body to handle government public relations. This was the Central Office of Information, a non-ministerial common services department which, unlike the Ministry, had no brief to formulate policy and was expected only to respond to requests from other departments.

The documentary movement foresaw that there would be less scope for the development of its work within that framework and made a case for the creation of a separate and differently constituted body for film. Various suggestions were put forward but all were influenced by two existing bodies, the BBC and the National Film Board of Canada. The Arts Enquiry suggested there should be a National Films Office which would function both as a government film service, advising the government and liaising with producers, and as a relatively autonomous producer and distributor of factual films. An MOI committee took much the same line, suggesting that the government should establish a body modelled on the National Film Board of Canada.[39] To make their voice

166

better heard, the documentary makers joined together in 1945 to form the Federation of Documentary Film Units. The aims were similar to those of the Association of Realist Film Producers, which had been dissolved during the war. Despite the movement's public and private campaigning, the government rejected their ideas. According to Basil Wright, the Treasury was strongly opposed to the establishment of the kind of public production organisation envisaged. Doubts were also expressed as to whether, if the government were to be the main customer, it was appropriate to create an independent body. The Films Division and the Crown unit therefore became part of the COI. The fears about the COI soon proved justified, and from 1946 the documentary film-makers found themselves dissipating their energies in a long wrangle both about the terms of contracts and the nature of policy.

In November 1946 the Federation of Documentary Film Units passed a resolution complaining that:

> The record of Government film production since April 1st . . . does not measure up to the past achievements nor to the demands of the moment. No major film comparable with those produced during the war, has been completed. Delays and obstructions have been increasingly characteristic of the commissions which the documentary units have received.[40]

Most of the film-makers personally affected thought the decline of documentary was brought about mainly by the COI and the government. Paul Rotha, for instance, claimed that 'the COI must be held responsible for the lack of drama and vitality that regrettably characterises its current product'.[41] Basil Wright perceived the problem in terms of 'having to work with a socialist Government who hadn't the faintest idea what education or propaganda or art films were about'.[42] This view has been challenged by younger critics and film-makers, who place the blame rather on the documentary movement itself. Both interpretations, however, underplay the complexity of the relationship between government institutions and the film-makers concerned.

During the war the development of government-sponsored film took place under special circumstances. This was recognised up to a point by the documentary movement. Rotha noted that the popular success of the MOI documentary features had been made possible firstly because the trade had been compelled to accept that it was 'in the national interest' to give them a release, and secondly because the subject matter was exceptional: 'They were dramatised actuality, with all the physical excitement and dramatic action of raid and battle and shipwreck.'[43] But another factor, which was not publicly discussed to the same extent, was that the film-makers had been able to present an interpretation of events, a 'line', which corresponded with government aims, was acceptable to the trade and produced an audience response, at worst of good-humoured ridicule and at best of intense identification. This was because there was a consensus about the need to win the war. War films, both commercial and government-sponsored, projected the idea of consensus by showing people of very different social backgrounds fighting or working side by side for victory. Such films dramatised an experience that the audience could recognise, although it was only a part of their experience. For the war also drew attention to the deep divisions in society; and at least one film, the popular commercial feature *Millions Like Us*, tried to articulate the tensions as well as the unity, and included dialogue which commented on the recent and tenuous nature of class harmony and questioned whether the apparent progress towards social equality would be sustained when the fighting was over.

At the end of the war, by electing a Labour government, the public showed that for the majority the underlying conflict was more 'real' than the harmony. But the election was only one move in a complex struggle. Every aspect of post-war reconstruction was controversial. For documentary to retain credibility with cinema audiences it needed to develop ways of expressing controversy. This was where the documentary movement had failed badly in the past, despite its avowed commitment to dramatising real social issues. The requirements of the sponsors and the reformist political theory of the film-makers had resulted in films which might depict industrial labour or conditions of working-class life but were not informed by working-class struggle. But by the end of the war some of the film-makers were beginning to question the record, to express dissatisfaction even with the publicly praised war work. An article published in *Documentary News Letter* in 1945 criticised the Films Division of the MOI for 'lack of contact with the public it serves, timidity, parochialism', noted that it had never made films about trade unions or co-operatives, and made the interesting suggestion that all films officers should spend at least a quarter of their time working in the regions.[44] The weakness of this kind of criticism was that it implied that the necessary changes could be brought about within the context of a government film service without examining the fundamental constraints associated with official sponsorship. For the government could hardly be expected to finance and encourage film which criticised it or exposed incompetence, while if a film defended too vigorously a controversial measure the government would be accused of using public money for party political purposes. The film-makers seemed to assume that such problems could be overcome if the film service was a policy-making body which could generate work as well as accepting commissions. But it is doubtful whether this would have created the conditions necessary for handling politically sensitive issues, for it would be extremely difficult for an organisation responsible for government information to establish itself also as a source of independent information.

168

Subsequent experience with the BBC and the IBA has shown how relative any definition of autonomy or objectivity must be in a divided society. Nevertheless, the straitjacket of 'balance' as interpreted by the television authorities has provided a little more space for the development of documentary than would have been the case with direct government control. The public service principle adopted for broadcasting, however, would have been difficult to apply to documentary production alone because of the problems of exhibition and distribution. The wartime compromise with the CEA had enabled government films to receive cinema release, but in return the MOI had agreed to limit the development of alternative methods of exhibition. Thus at the end of the war the government was still dependent on the good will of the CEA to reach a mass audience.

The COI managed to negotiate an agreement with the CEA for 1946 allowing for the exhibition of one ten-minute film a month and trailers tacked on to newsreels. But there was resistance to this within the CEA, and the executive was subsequently put under pressure to terminate the agreement. The CEA General Secretary, F. R. Fuller, admitted that the pressure was 'party political' in origin. This served as an additional constraint on the COI's production policy and, when the agreement came up for renewal, the COI explicitly promised that the films would be 'entirely free of controversial opinion'.[45] The agreement was renewed mainly, according to *Today's Cinema*, because the CEA hoped it would provide leverage in their campaign for a reduction in Entertainments Tax. Complaints about 'propaganda' continued, however, and Fuller admitted that some exhibitors 'object to anything good being said about anything with which the present government is connected'.[46]

The power and the nature of the political sympathies of exhibitors were particularly evident in relation to the COI films – sponsored, as they were, by a Labour government – but the problem was not specific to the COI or to documentary, since all films had to be 'sold' to the exhibitors before they could be 'sold' to the public. If documentary was to develop outside the context of public relations, its future needed to be considered in relation to the future of the film industry as a whole. In this respect the politics of the documentary movement were ambivalent. Many of the leading exponents of documentary, in particular Grierson, Rotha and Edgar Anstey, continued to argue that the system of sponsorship could provide satisfactory opportunities for development. At the same time the Federation of Documentary Film Units and many individuals were actively involved in the anti-monopoly campaign, and Rotha himself proposed a reorganisation of the industry along lines similar to those advocated by the ACT.[47]

9 Conflicts and Crises 1945–1949

Is it conceivable that if cinema had been invented even as late as broadcasting – cinema with its infinite possibilities for national education, national expression, international get-together and get-to-know-each-other – it would ever have been allowed to get into the largely foreign and exclusively profit-interested stranglehold that grips it now?

Ivor Montagu, 'Improving Britain's film business', *Documentary News Letter*, August–September 1947.

STAFFORD CRIPPS AND MONOPOLY

Since the lengthy consultations over the Palache report on monopoly were concluded just about at the time of the General Election of 1945, the new President of the Board of Trade, Stafford Cripps, was immediately confronted with the question of what action to take on the report. There was considerable pressure on him to reach an early decision. The ACT had already complained several times about the delay in implementing the recommendations. Early in November a question was asked in Parliament about the government's intentions, and later that month there was a debate on the industry in the course of which Michael Foot spoke at some length on the dangers of monopoly.

The advice of the civil service almost wholly contradicted the advice offered by the Palache report, and a heavy burden of decision fell on Cripps himself. Initially he seems to have been swayed by some of the arguments in favour of Rank, but at the same time he considered that it would be necessary to intervene in favour of independents. In November he wrote a note for the department:

I am anxious to leave the strong Rank combine effective for meeting and possibly dealing with American competition but at the same time I want ample opportunity for independent producers to make reasonably priced films to be shown primarily in this country.[1]

He suggested that a film corporation should be set up to help the independents by providing finance, securing studio space and allotting

170

screen time and, in addition to this, to supervise and encourage education and documentary production. In the autumn of 1945 Cripps also asked the documentary producer and director, Paul Rotha, to prepare a memorandum on how such a corporation might function. The resulting study, presented in December, stressed that the corporation should be of a permanent nature with a long-term perspective involving responsibility for script development, training and the production of short films. One of the most important proposed additions to the plan sketched by Cripps was that the corporation should be involved in exhibition, that it should both develop non-theatrical outlets for all films and also acquire a nationwide network of cinemas, firstly to provide an outlet for its own films but secondly to show European and occasionally American films 'not considered by the trade to be of wide appeal'.[2] Cripps' initial idea about securing screen time was that an additional quota should be established for corporation films. It was on this basis that a study group was set up at the end of 1945, involving Board of Trade officials, to work out the details of how the corporation would function.

Early in 1946 the plan began to run into difficulties. A major problem was lack of parliamentary time. Labour had an immense urgent programme of legislation to put through Parliament and it was decided that additional films legislation should be combined with the new Quota Act, which would not have to be passed before the existing one expired in 1948. Somervell therefore urged Cripps to accept a voluntary agreement with the circuits in place of the additional quota. The second problem was that the Treasury officials refused to recommend that the Treasury should guarantee a loan for production finance. Somervell then advised that in the circumstances all that could be done was to obtain an agreement from the circuits to show independent films and establish a committee of the Board of Trade to choose which films should occupy it. The producers would have to find their own finance.

Cripps considered taking steps against the circuits. He discussed the possibility of breaking up the monopoly in the London area by forcing the combines to dispose of some of their London cinemas; he also considered setting up a tribunal on the lines proposed by Palache. He was persuaded to reject both measures, the first on the grounds that the recent boom had inflated the value of cinemas and 'it would be difficult to secure the transfer of cinemas to other owners at the top of the market with every prospect of a falling off in attendance as other outlets for expenditure increase';[3] the second on the grounds that the voluntary Joint Consultative Committee of renters and exhibitors was effectively tackling trade disputes. Cripps therefore did nothing for the time being except implement the plan outlined by Somervell for securing screen time for independents. Nevertheless, in his policy paper prepared for the Lord President's Committee, he referred to this as an interim measure and described his aim of establishing a finance corporation. In his statement to the Commons in March 1946, he also mentioned that other measures would be considered in relation to the forthcoming discussions on quota legislation. When the time came, however, his proposals for the quota legislation did not include any effective measures to help independents or to check the power of the combines.[4]

The abandonment of Cripps' earlier intentions did not reflect any slackening in the public campaign for intervention. On the contrary, pressure was stepped up by a stream of letters, articles, and interventions in the House. During the year two pamphlets were published: *Films, An Alternative to Rank*, by Frederick Mullally, an assistant editor of *Tribune*; and *Monopoly, the Future of British Films*, by Ralph Bond, a documentary director who was an active member of the ACT and a member of the Communist Party. Both authors concentrated their criticisms of the existing industry against the Rank Organisation and its export drive, arguing that, far from being Hollywood's chief competitor, Rank was its agent. They pointed to the financial connections between the Rank Organisation and American companies and emphasised the extent to which Rank, as an exhibitor, was dependent on Hollywood product. 'Why,' asked Mullally, 'if Rank is so determined to cut himself a large slice from Hollywood's cake, are the gentlemen with the funny names over there always so friendly and accommodating to him?'[5] 'It is a curious but an evident fact,' observed Bond, 'that the more cinemas Mr Rank owns the more he is dependent on America to provide films to fill them.'[6] They both argued that the export drive was doomed to failure because, whether or not British films could appeal to the American public, the majors would prevent them reaching a large audience. Mullally also predicted, correctly as it turned out, that Rank would pull back from production when the export drive failed, leaving a vacuum in the British production industry which would give American companies a chance to strengthen their hold on the British market.

Mullally's proposals for action were similar to most earlier proposals in that they revolved round the establishment of an independent authority (he uses the term 'Films Commission') which would perform most of the functions of the tribunal suggested by the Palache report and of the corporation considered by Cripps, with the important difference that this body would not be an addition to existing structures but would replace the Films Council and the Films Department of the Board of Trade. He listed some of the interests which should be represented on it and stressed that 'on no account should the farce of the Cinematograph Films Council be repeated by packing the Commission with representatives of the large-scale production and exhibition interests.'[7] The Bond pamphlet simply backed the recommendations put forward in the Palache report for a finance corporation and a tribunal. Neither pamphlet seriously considered nationalisation as an option. Bond commented that 'nationalisation of the industry does not appear to be practical politics for the time being';[8] and Mullally that 'No one suggests that the state should go into the business of making and exhibiting feature films.'[9] This last remark was not strictly accurate, since Rotha had suggested that there should be a public corporation involved in both production and exhibition. This idea was also taken up by a group of MPs, who made a report recommending the creation of a fourth circuit which, if not run by the state, would nevertheless have to be established by it.

Changes within the trade, however, meant that in certain important respects the pressure for intervention was reduced. In particular there was no longer a vocal independent producers' lobby. This was partly because, in the absence of any other source of finance, many independent producers had gravitated to the Rank Organisation and could no longer be counted as fully independent. Even Michael Balcon, formerly Rank's principal critic, had modified his ideas, and in 1944 entered into an agreement with Rank for the financing and release of Ealing films. Whether Balcon's change of heart was cause or effect of the agreement is unclear; but it was so complete that in 1947, in his contribution to *Twenty Years of British Films*, he was able to say: 'Unquestionably the appearance on the film scene of Mr J. Arthur Rank has contributed in no small measure to the present healthy state of the film industry.'[10] Rank, indeed, was responsible for a certain appearance of health in the industry since, as a result mainly of his extensive investments, most producers were busy and the output of films was rising. The healthy state was more apparent than real because costs had risen far more rapidly than receipts. Even the cheaper films destined for the home market were likely to register losses, while expensive films were budgeted on the assumption of substantial returns from the American market which, as Rank's critics repeatedly complained, they would be unlikely to reach. For the time being, however, the problems were not apparent to everyone, and it is likely that the message which reached Cripps from the industry through informal contacts was that everything was more or less all right.

The Films Council, as the source of official advice, was an important factor and, since 1944, neither independent feature producers nor documentary producers had had a voice on it. The quota committee which was asked to draw up recommendations for the new legislation was, even more than the full council, of a composition likely to favour Rank.[11] There were only two independent members as against seven trade representatives, among whom both producers' representatives, Rank and Korda, were included but at first no employees' representatives – Elvin and O'Brien were later co-opted. To some extent the argument about monopoly was fought out within this committee, although the minority view could only be expressed in notes of dissent. The unions registered strong dissent in relation to a discussion about the proposal for a fourth circuit which was opposed by the rest of the committee; the independent members, Plant and Palache, reaffirmed against the rest of the committee their view that independent arbitration was needed in relation to the practice of barring.

The proposal which was put by Cripps to the Lord President's Committee in 1947 reflects very closely the majority recommendations of the Films Council.[12] The main changes – the adoption of separate quotas for first features and supporting programmes instead of for long and short films, and altering the composition of the Films Council by increasing the representatives of producers and exhibitors and decreasing the number of independent, or lay, members – followed advice given by the Council. The proposal for the fourth circuit was mentioned and rejected. The problem of arbitration was regarded as being still under consideration, and it was noted that 'The exhibitors fear that once new legislation is passed without reference to this subject, the renters' enthusiasm for the joint committee may fade away'.

Doubtless the number of other urgent problems facing Cripps at the time helped influence his decision to accept the advice of the trade and that of his civil servants, which now coincided. But another very considerable constraint was Dalton's refusal to provide the money for the establishment of a finance corporation. Cripps raised this in the Lord President's Committee during the discussion which followed his report, pointing out, in answer to a question about why no plans were being made to establish a state studio, that a studio would only be useful if finance could be made available to produce films in it.[13]

HOLLYWOOD AND THE GENERAL AGREEMENT ON TRADE AND TARIFFS

After the war American competition continued to overshadow all other film problems, and the government's approach to the question remained, as it had been during the war, heavily influenced by general financial and diplomatic considerations. With the war over, the principal constraints were related to the dollar shortage and the national debt. As far as the film trade was concerned, conflict with America was still centred on remittances and the quota.

Although the American industry had successfully maintained its position in Britain, its hold over the world market was rather less secure than it had been before the war. It was apparent that the access of American films to the screens of Eastern Europe would be restricted. There was also some prospect that the same might happen in Western Europe. Europe was short of dollars and needed to limit American imports; and in the case of the major film producing countries – Britain, France and Italy – there had been pressure before the war to strengthen measures to promote national production. Now socialist parties which advocated state aid for culture and state intervention in industry were forming or participating in the post-war governments of these countries. The events of the war had also undermined the view that American dominance of the cinema was inevitable. Much of Europe had been deprived of American films for several years, yet the cinemas had remained open. Despite the difficulties caused by the war and, in France, by enemy occupation, films had been produced. In France, French films had occupied eighty per cent of screen time. Even in Britain, where American films had not been displaced, the great success of a number of British films had shaken the assumption that Hollywood films were necessarily superior to those made elsewhere. The reputation of British films improved so strikingly both with critics and audiences that it is hardly possible to find an article on British films of the time which does not comment on this. The *British Film Yearbook* of 1946 is representative: 'Conversely with the decrease in the number of films there has been a notable and inspiring increase in the general calibre and standard of the home product during the war years.'[14] In a questionnaire conducted by the Granada chain in 1946, 96 per cent of those questioned said that they thought British films had improved whereas only 26 per cent thought that American films had improved.[15] Critical acclaim went hand in hand with box office success and several of the most popular films shown during the war were British. In his account of the Granada cinemas in wartime, Guy Morgan confirms that 'one of the most marked phenomena of the later stages of the war was a genuine unforced interest in British pictures'.[16]

There were even some signs to suggest that the American home market was no longer invulnerable to foreign competition. During the war a number of British films were unusually well reviewed and achieved some popular success in the United States, and this fed the old dream that British films would be able to compete with American ones even on the American home market. The performance of British films in America was, however, frequently exaggerated since they were restricted, in the main, to running in cinemas where they were not competing for the mass market. There were also political reasons during the war for the American industry to be more tolerant than usual of British films. Nevertheless, some of the films, notably *In Which We Serve*, had drawn very good audiences, which slightly dented the myth that American audiences would not tolerate British films. The signs were not strong enough to suggest to anyone except those who needed to believe it that British films were about to gain a commercially significant place in the American market; but, for other reasons, the American companies were not complacent about their future hold on the home market. The anti-trust suit which had been filed against Paramount threatened to lead to the partial break-up of the integrated companies. In this event the producers would no longer be able to guarantee their films screen time, and a foreign competitor might make some headway.

The Motion Picture Association of America was intensely suspicious of any developments which might lead to the emergence of an important centre of film production not under its control. During the war a commercial and diplomatic offensive was launched to prevent this happening. The MPEA (Motion Picture Export Association of America) was formed to enable the MPAA to be even more effective than before in negotiations with foreign governments and with the appropriate American authorities. One of its immediate aims was to secure US government co-operation to enable the film companies to reintroduce American films in the former occupied territories as soon as they were liberated. The British companies also sought government co-operation to this end, but the results were negligible in comparison with those achieved by the Americans. It was widely believed by the trade in Britain that the rapid progress of the American companies was due not only to their superior commercial organisation but to the degree of active government support they were able to call on.

It was no secret that, during the war, American film interests were vigorously promoted by the chief of the film section of the US Bureau of Foreign and Domestic Commerce, Nathan Golden, and by the head of the appropriate section of the War Production Board, Harold Hopper. A report by Nathan Golden pressing the case for free trade was given considerable publicity in the British trade press at the beginning of 1944.[17] The American industry, addressing itself to its own government, often stressed political aspects of the film trade – the extent to which the film industry performed a propaganda and public relations service for the government. For foreign consumption the message was similar, but the role of America as leader of the democratic world was underlined. An article by Jack Alicoate, editor of *Film Daily*, which was circulated to the European press in 1945, justified American intentions along these lines:

> Whether one calls it propaganda or information, it is evident that, as a result of World War II, the motion picture from this day must be regarded as an instrument of public policy as well as a great popular medium of entertainment. This may be, as the late Wendell L. Wilkie believed and wrote, one world but the patterns of thought yet remain to be fused into one. It follows that the screens of the globe, for at least the present, mirror different pictorial concepts. If the dominant note is to be democratic, as it is to be hoped, those industries which are indebted for their growth and progress to the freedom of opportunity in the great democracies, must work together within a framework of friendly and fair co-operation.
>
> The industries of the democratic countries in the post-war period have every reason to stand shoulder to shoulder against the imposition of quota, the creation of cartels and the raising of any and all barriers to the free flow of motion picture commerce.[18]

The film industry was only one of many lobbies putting pressure on the State Department, and the MPEA did not rely on the American government to back up all its demands. Wherever American films had a significant hold over the market, the MPEA was able to exert very considerable pressure in its own right by threatening to impose a boycott. This weapon was used against France in 1945, in response to a law requiring that foreign films should be shown in the original version with subtitles. In Britain, where American films occupied eighty per cent of screen time and where they had never been excluded, the threat was a formidable one.

In the struggle for Europe's screens Britain was of special strategic importance, not only because the British market was the biggest in Europe and, because of language, the most accessible, but because Britain, as one of the principal Allies, would theoretically be able to exert more influence at the negotiating table than the recently defeated powers or the former occupied countries. Since the German film industry had been dismantled, the British industry was also the closest rival to Hollywood in terms of organisation and resources. The main question pending was whether films should be covered by the terms of general trade agreements, and it seemed likely that the other film-producing countries would be influenced by Britain's attitude. If she took a strong line in demanding special treatment for film they would certainly support her; if she took new steps to limit American imports and got away with it, other countries would be encouraged to follow the British example.

During the international trade conferences of 1946 and 1947 the specific issue affecting the film industry was about whether quota regulations would be ruled out by the new trade treaty. They were threatened by a paragraph in the draft treaty which banned 'regulations or requirements affecting sale, transportation, distribution, mixing, processing, exhibiting or other use' of goods. In the course of discussions about how this might apply to films there was a particularly clear case of MPEA influence. The British government argued that films should be among various goods excepted from the ban, and in January 1947 the American government agreed to this in principle. While the details were being worked out, Eric Johnston, President of the MPAA, made a lengthy submission to the State Department outlining the views of the American industry. The points stressed were the value of the British market: 'being virtually as important as all of the other countries of the world and considerably more important than all the seventeen countries with which trade agreement negotiations are to be undertaken'; the potential strength of the British production industry: 'the largest domestic film industry of any country except the United States, and it may be expected that the British film industry will become increasingly important in the immediate future'; and the way in which the quotas affected American interests. Here Johnston made it clear that of the two kinds of quota the MPAA was most anxious to see the exhibitors' quota abolished:

> The renters' Quota is less injurious than the Exhibitors' Quota which diverts a progressively increasing proportion of British screen time from American to British films. As the revenues, i.e. the earning capacity of American films in Britain, must be measured in terms of the screen time available to them the Exhibitors' Quota means a progressively increasing diversion of revenues from American to British films as a result not of the superior quality of the latter or normal competitive trading, but of statutory compulsion. This fact is of vital importance to the American motion picture industry. The British Exhibitors' Quota threatens its established position not only in Great Britain but in other markets as well.[19]

Johnston then paid a visit to Geneva, where this conference was taking place; and soon after his arrival the American negotiators tabled a reservation about the compromise which had provisionally been agreed. Discussions dragged on for some months until a new compromise was reached. The British gained the important objective of retaining the exhibitors' quota but, as a concession to the Americans, agreed on terms which would oblige them to drop the renters' quota.

On this last question, however, there was some disagreement between the Board of Trade and the Foreign Office. The Board of Trade was initially reluctant to agree to the abolition of the renters' quota because of the attitude of the exhibitors. The CEA regarded the two quotas as complementary and maintained that, unless renters were obliged to acquire British films, exhibitors would be unable to obtain the product to fulfil their own quota. Since the Films Act was due for renewal in 1948, the Board of Trade was anxious to avoid alienating the CEA. The Foreign Office, however, was concerned about the reputed power of the American film industry to influence wider international relations. This concern intensified after August 1947 when, in circumstances explained more fully in the following pages, a 75 per cent duty was imposed on American films as a dollar-saving measure, and American film interests responded with a boycott of the British market. The Foreign Office impressed on the Board of Trade the importance of avoiding further conflict with American film interests:

> We feel that this is important because, however justifiable the imposition of the recent 75% tax may be on balance of payments grounds, it does deal a very hard blow to the American industry (the latter commands an immensely powerful propaganda instrument which, if possible, we should prefer not to antagonise).[20]

The Board of Trade's problem was partially resolved when the exhibitors agreed to accept the abolition of the renters' quota on condition that American production plans in Britain would continue. Johnston gave Cripps an assurance on this in October 1947, and the Board of Trade was then reconciled to the new quota arrangements.

BOGART OR BACON

The question of limiting American film remittances was even more sensitive than that of the quota. The quota was vigorously opposed by the MPAA as representing a breach in the principle of free trading, but it had not in the past had much impact on American earnings. The temporary blocking of film revenues during the war, however, had roughly halved the sums reaching America. It was clear that any measure which might have a perceptible effect on the exchange burden was bound to cut substantially the receipts of the parent companies in America. The need to save money on films was also very directly linked with the overall balance of payments problem in Britain, and so could serve as a bargaining counter in the course of more general financial negotiations.

The overall foreign exchange position in 1945 was more serious than it had been during the war, and the cancellation of Lend Lease, just after the defeat of Japan, dashed any hopes of an early recovery. The cost of film imports, like the cost of almost everything, was rising rapidly, and payments made to America in 1945 were more than twice what they had been in 1939. The figures for the war years as a whole were, of course, distorted because of the sums blocked from 1940 to 1942 and released during 1943 (see Table XIX).

TABLE XIX
American remittances 1940–1945

Year ending October	£ million	
1940	4.8	regulated
1941	5.7	,,
1942	8.5	,,
1943	26.5	unregulated
1944	15.6	,,
1945	17.0	,,

(Board of Trade figures)

Film payments represented only about 4 per cent of dollar expenditure but, since a large proportion of the total was spent either on food or on materials needed for industrial reconstruction (that is, on high priority imports), it was natural that all payments for less essential goods should come under critical scrutiny. This particular item became headline news for a time in November 1945 as a result of a parliamentary debate in which the cost of film imports was discussed in relation to the highly emotive subject of the food shortages. The comment which came to symbolise the issue – 'If I am compelled to choose between Bogart and bacon I am bound to choose bacon at the present time' – was made by Robert Boothby, member for East Aberdeen, in the course of a long speech which was otherwise interesting for the way in which it located the problem as a direct consequence of the government's pursuit of American aid:

> If the Government have decided to borrow a very large sum at a considerable rate of interest from the United States, and to go back to the gold standard and multilateral free trade without discrimination as the price, then I suppose the film industry will have to be included in the general 'sell-out' of Great Britain.[21]

The failure to take action on film imports, according to Boothby, was a symptom of a more fundamental defect in government strategy:

> The dilemma which now confronts the Government of this country is inescapable. On the one hand they are trying to build up a planned internal economy in this country. . . . At the same time we know that the Government are under very heavy pressure from the United States of America to revert to an unplanned external economy. You cannot have a planned production and unplanned trade.[22]

As far as film was concerned, Boothby was correct in thinking that the government was inhibited by the desire to obtain from America economic assistance and acceptable trading arrangements, and that this was one reason why nothing was done about American film rentals until the 'Dalton Duty' was imposed in 1947. The year before, when the Treasury was pressing for action, a Board of Trade official referred to the trading negotiations, saying that 'at this particular juncture' he would 'view with alarm any violent battle with United States film interests and their very powerful lobby in that country'.[23] Yet the exigency of the American alliance does not entirely explain why various courses of action were rejected without even considering the possible American response, nor why a form of duty was eventually imposed which did alienate the MPAA without either helping British producers or effectively reducing the dollar drain.

Boothby had launched his attack with a parliamentary question about why dollar expenditure on films had been authorised, to which Dalton's public answer was: 'We must within wide limits meet the public desire for entertainment and it happens that a lot of people go to see these films.'[24] This probably reflected a natural desire on the part of the government to avoid being cast in the role of kill-joy, but it was a very incomplete and somewhat misleading statement since at that very time the Treasury and the Board of Trade were working on a number of proposals for limiting remittances. That round of discussions had, in fact, begun in the spring of 1944 and was to continue until the Anglo-American agreement of 1948 effectively closed the matter.

The problem was not quite the same as the one faced in 1940, when there was an immediate need to throw all possible resources into the war effort. By 1944 it was posed in the context of a long-term task of economic reconstruction. This was recognised to the extent that the Treasury no longer considered that blocking funds was an acceptable solution, even though the Americans had agreed to this before and would probably have preferred it to any other proposal. Nevertheless, although the Treasury was committed to finding a permanent rather than a temporary solution, the discussions were directed towards tackling the cost of the trade's dependence on American films rather than tackling the dependence itself. In this respect it is interesting to look at two courses of action which were suggested from outside the civil service, but which were rejected or ignored by the officials concerned.

One idea, which has already been mentioned in the context of the wartime dollar shortage, involved reducing the number of films needed either by enforcing single-feature programmes or by having weekly, as opposed to half-weekly, runs. In 1941 some support for the introduction of single-feature programmes had come from within the American industry itself. Teddy Carr of United Artists had been reported in *Kine Weekly* as saying: 'To my mind it is nothing short of sacrilege to see a great picture massacred in the public interest by having to associate it with tripe contained in a totally unnecessary second feature.'[25] Even the exhibitors had not been wholly opposed to the idea. The South-East Lancashire branch of the CEA had complained that the double feature was a waste. After the war the idea met with more limited support, mainly from the documentary film-makers, who had a vested interest in abolishing the second feature and making room for more short films. *Documentary News Letter* recommended in 1945 that the new Films Act should prohibit double features. The recommendation was repeated in 1947 after the American companies had announced a boycott of the British market, and the Federation of Documentary Film Units also wrote with the same intent to the Board of Trade.[26] Once the boycott was in force, pressure to adopt measures of this kind became more general. Nicholas Davenport, financial adviser to Korda, wrote to Dalton arguing that the government should promptly ban both second features and the twice-weekly change of programme, and that at the same time they should raise the quota to 50 per cent and consider concentrating cinemas by strategic closures.[27] Shortly after this, the

Labour MP Ben Levy put forward very similar ideas in Parliament.

The other suggestion was that more films should be imported from sources other than the United States. This only became a practicable possibility after the war, but then it also had some relevance to the prospects for increasing British exports. The other European film-producing countries were also short of foreign exchange, and in some of them the earnings of British films were blocked. There was therefore, in theory, more scope for developing mutually advantageous reciprocal trading with Europe than with America. The 1944 notes on industrial reconstruction by the ACT made a broad appeal for co-operation with Europe:

> Foreign markets (particularly European markets) will be a problem demanding the serious attention of the film trade. The Government must concern itself with the problem and must exert such control as is necessary to ensure that foreign markets are not regarded primarily as territory to be exploited. The British film industry must, in fact, co-operate with the allied film industries to revive their own national film industries.[28]

Subsequently, in *Monopoly*, Ralph Bond stressed the desirability of importing from many sources:

> Neither would all foreign imports need to be American. Hollywood would undoubtedly take the largest share, but other countries – France, Czecho-Slovakia, Norway, the Soviet Union etc. – must have the opportunity to send us their best films.[29]

One of the criticisms later made of the 'Dalton Duty' was that it hit all imports equally and therefore hindered the possible expedient of mitigating the film shortage by stepping up imports from Europe. *Documentary News Letter*, for instance, commented:

> It must be remembered that one of the main reasons why European films are not shown more widely here is the determination of the US-influenced section of the Trade that they shall not be shown. Had it been possible to encourage the entry of European films while taxing the entry of US films the general audience in this country – after a period of resistance no doubt – would have benefited a great deal.[30]

The Board of Trade do not appear to have given any consideration to the possibility of encouraging imports from Europe in order to make the trade less dependent on American supplies. Even though the danger of a boycott was mentioned on several occasions alternative sources of films were not discussed. A hint as to the reason for this is provided in a correspondence with the British Embassy in Rome which took place a few years later. The Embassy forwarded to London an Italian proposal for a joint commission to deal with film exports; the Board of Trade replied very negatively, saying that as the British public were 'not interested in dubbed films' they could offer nothing in return.[31] It would seem that the Board of Trade had unquestioningly accepted the trade verdict that dubbed films were unpopular. Yet this theory had never been effectively tested, and there was some counter-evidence in that dubbed American films played to mass audiences in many parts of the world. There was no reason, other than cultural chauvinism perhaps, to assume that the British audience was inherently different in this respect.

The possibility of restricting cinema programmes was not properly investigated, probably because the Board of Trade clung to the conclusions reached in rather different circumstances during the war. In February 1947, when the Lord President's Office made the suggestion, Somervell repeated the objection that dropping the second feature would save only a small proportion – less than a tenth, he calculated – of the cost of importing films, and that other restrictions would reduce takings as a whole.[32] The last argument was also used to dismiss Nicholas Davenport's suggestions about programming restrictions and a higher quota, on the grounds that such restrictions would have a discouraging effect on British production. No effort was made, however, to assess the likely results or to work out ways of minimising the impact on British films. Davenport's scheme, for instance, had the merit that the higher quota would maintain the demand for British films, while the cinemas' total requirements would be reduced to a quarter or less of the existing number of films.[33]

What a film earns, of course, depends on the audience it attracts as well as on the screen time it receives, and the available evidence about the habits of audiences, which came mainly from the Granada survey of 1946,[34] was interpreted by the trade as an indication that changes might be very damaging. This conclusion could, however, be questioned. The pertinent facts from the survey were that about 80 per cent of cinema-goers questioned expressed a preference for the double-feature programme, and that as many as 40 per cent went to the cinema twice a week. Yet the fact that audiences preferred the double feature was not proof that attendances would fall if such programmes were not made available; nor was it clear that weekly programming would alter the habits of the twice-a-week customer, because most cinemas had nearby competitors showing a different film. It could be argued that even those who went to the cinema three times a week would only see half of the three hundred programmes on offer through the year, and that the weekly programmes would concentrate attendances on fewer films which would, even allowing for a slight fall in admissions, benefit the producers of British films.

The Treasury, however, was anxious, for reasons not connected with British production, to avoid a fall in the exhibitors' takings. In this respect, the cost of remittable rentals needs to be seen in perspective. In 1945 gross box office receipts were £115 million, out of which the American companies took £17 million while Entertainment tax took £41 million. The cinema provided 93 per cent of Entertainment tax; besides this, cinema-going was something for people to spend money on at a time when goods were in very short supply and wages relatively high. Both factors interested the Treasury.

While ideas for reducing American imports were hardly discussed, the alternative strategy for redressing the balance of trade – increasing British exports to the United States – was taken very seriously by the Board of Trade. In 1946 Somervell told the Treasury that from his talks with Rank 'I get the impression that they may really have at last got a foot in the door of the American market.'[35] The pursuit of this aim made it progressively more difficult to tackle the trading problem from any other angle because of the premium which was put on good relations with the American industry. This factor also interfered with short-term plans for dealing with the exchange problem.

Three possible methods of reducing the dollar cost of films, apart from blocking funds, competed for official favour in the period between 1944 and 1947.[36] The first, as originally put forward by the Inland Revenue, resembled blocking in that each company would be allowed to export a fixed sum but the excess, instead of being held in a blocked account, would be treated as dividends and therefore taxed at a very high rate. Hugh Gaitskell added the idea that the companies should be able to export, over and above their quota, sums equivalent to receipts gained from British films exploited by them in America. The second method was the *ad valorem* duty eventually adopted. The third was that a state import company should be formed, confusingly referred to as a British Film Institute, which would have sole right to import films and would absorb a proportion of earnings by charging high fees for its service. The last idea, which would have given the government most direct control, was not pushed, partly because of a fear that the Americans would strongly object on principle to the establishment of what would effectively be a state monopoly. The Bank of England also had reservations on the grounds that 'it is surely dangerous for the Government to enter into a field where personal judgment and unpredictable public taste reign supreme'.[37]

The main objection to the import duty was that the customs office would have great difficulty in valuing films since their value was only revealed by exhibition. Import licensing, which was also briefly considered, was rejected on these grounds. In the case of the duty, the difficulty was overcome by the idea of asking for a bond and adjusting the amount eventually paid according to the receipts actually accruing to

NEW FILM STAR

The Dalton Duty. Cartoon by David Low, London *Evening Standard*, 2 July 1947.

each film. Once this was resolved, the duty was favoured as the most straightforward scheme.

The timing of decisions about film imports was much affected by the state of general relations with America. When Lend Lease was cancelled in August 1945, the Treasury immediately activated the machinery for introducing a total ban on film imports. The ban was not introduced because of the fear that it would pre-empt the possibility of reaching agreement with the Americans on one of the less drastic schemes under consideration. By the spring of 1946 plans for an import tax were ready, but the scheme was held back pending the result of the negotiations on the American loan being conducted at the time by John M. Keynes. When the loan was obtained, the plan was temporarily shelved. In the autumn of 1946 the question was raised again by the Treasury, but the Board of Trade advised against action because of the International Trade Organisation conference. In the spring of 1947, as the national debt mounted and the date of convertibility crept closer, the plan was taken off the shelf again.

The advice from the Board of Trade as to the probable reaction from America was that there would be no boycott. A memorandum sent to the

185

Chancellor in May commented:

> The Americans will not like it; but the Board of Trade do not fear that
> they will refuse to supply films. It will not help our films in the US but,
> on a long-term view, the American interests have more to lose from
> open hostilities.[38]

In June, Cripps recommended to the Cabinet the imposition of an *ad
valorem* duty. He thought the Americans would probably not call a
boycott because the British market was too important to them: 'Rather
than do that – especially at the present time when . . . they are already
hard up for cash – the companies would still carry on and make the best
of a bad job.'[39] On 17 June the Cabinet took the decision to include a
clause in the Finance Act to enable the customs to impose such a duty. At
the beginning of August the question was discussed again in the Cabinet.
The MPAA were by then urging the government to consider alternative
proposals for blocking remittances but this idea was rejected:

> The general view of the Cabinet was that an arrangement under
> which American film interests were permitted to build up dollar
> balances in this country would not satisfy public opinion and would
> expose the Government to pressure from the United States to free the
> balances.[40]

Instead, some consideration was given to the suggestion that a complete
ban might be placed on all film imports. At a subsequent meeting,
however, Cripps dissuaded the Cabinet from such a drastic step on the
grounds that it would result in widespread cinema closures.[41] The
outcome of all these discussions was that on 6 August an order was made
under the Import Duties Act of 1932 imposing a 75 per cent duty to come
into effect immediately.

BOYCOTT AND SETTLEMENT

The Board of Trade officials who advised that there would be no boycott
had made an extraordinary miscalculation. Their complacency is the
more surprising given that during the war they took the same threat very
seriously. The threat, it is true, was never carried out, but the British had
never unilaterally taken action to which the Americans were wholeheartedly opposed. The imposition of the duty was precisely an action of
this kind, and the response from America was swift and decisive. Within
a day of the British announcement the members of the MPAA had met
and agreed that they would send no more films to Britain until the duty
was withdrawn. The embargo, which came into effect on 29 August, was
acutely embarrassing for Britain. Cripps and Dalton had apparently

staked everything on the hope that the opinion – and it was only an opinion – of the civil servants would prove well founded. They had not considered what they would do in the event of a boycott and they had not asked for any plans to be made against such a contingency. Proper preparation would have involved decisive measures to assist domestic production and to promote the exhibition of European films. If the government had even begun to take action along such lines it is arguable that the Americans might not have risked an embargo, fearing that they might permanently lose ground against competitors. As it was, neither British nor European producers were able to benefit from the unsolicited period of protection.

The American action not only threatened the future of the exhibition business but also had financial and diplomatic implications which, for the government, were more worrying. The confrontation was likely to produce an unfortunate impression in the United States just when Britain was engaged in the delicate task of trying to renegotiate the terms of American aid. At the same time the boycott had the effect of frustrating the whole purpose of the duty. It had been recognised that the benefits of the duty would be felt only gradually, as new imports began to take the place of films already in the country. But as no new imports arrived, the old films went on running and the revenue from them continued to leave the country untaxed.

Cripps was relieved of the direct responsibility for dealing with the MPAA by his promotion, in October 1947, to Minister for Economic Affairs. The task fell instead to a new and very young President of the Board of Trade, Harold Wilson. Cripps, however, became centrally involved in a new capacity in November when, after Dalton's resignation, he became Chancellor of the Exchequer. Policy aims in this respect were, however, unaffected by the changes in personnel. The overriding consideration behind both the imposition of the duty and the management of the boycott seems to have been not the hope of obtaining some trivial dollar savings on film imports, but the need to bring home to the Americans the serious nature of Britain's economic predicament and to put pressure on them to provide more assistance.

Wilfred Eady, a Second Secretary at the Treasury who was involved in the loan negotiations, wrote a departmental note about the film crisis after a telephone conversation with Eric Johnston at the end of August:

In relation to the present situation we have to remember three things about this industry:
1. It is an extremely powerful lobby in the State Department and capable of very considerable malice.
2. Our primary tactical objective with the United States Administration is to regain early access to the frozen United States credit. It is scarcely conceivable that the United States will release the credit

without making some conditions to meet American interests, e.g. either reduction or repeal of the film tax.

3. Behind all this lies the Marshall Plan and what we may hope to get out of it. Here again one must expect this powerful lobby to be exercised against us in the discussions that will take place on the Marshall Plan.

If we meet the industry and can find some unimportant modification of our present stand and do so by agreement, we have in fact spiked their guns. Even if we can reach no agreement we shall not have acted, so to speak, with unilateral indifference to American interests.[42]

The government was extremely anxious to allay American suspicions that there was a protectionist intent behind the duty, yet at the same time wished to convey the idea that the British industry was ready and willing to take advantage of the unsolicited opportunity afforded by the boycott. In November a Commons debate on the duty provided an opportunity to clarify British aims. The government spokesman, Glenvil Hall, justified the duty in these terms:

I want to make it clear that neither is it intended to obtain additional revenue, nor is it an aggressive act against Hollywood in the interests of our own British film industry. The step had been taken simply and solely because the country cannot afford to allocate the dollars necessary to pay for the exhibition of American films in this country at the present time.[43]

A more defiant tone was struck later in the speech when Hall asserted that:

The best British films are certainly more satisfying than the ones we get from America. . . . The British cinemagoer has not, so far as I know, made any great outcry at the possible risk of losing American films under this duty. That lesson will not, I hope, be lost on the American producers.[44]

When negotiations with the MPAA were renewed in the autumn, the British pursued the course suggested by Eady. Although at the time the Treasury and the Board of Trade had privately agreed that they would not settle for an arrangement based on blocked earnings, they listened politely to proposals of this nature put forward by Fay Allport of the MPAA and avoided any breakdown in the talks until December, when Cripps finally told Allport that his plan did not involve sufficient dollar saving.

The MPAA reacted strongly to the failure of the talks. Eric Johnston

188

issued a press statement to the effect that the British government 'stood firm on the tax and summarily rejected in principle any alternative to it'.[45] Johnston then appealed over the heads of the officials involved and began an all-out campaign to get the issue treated as a major concern of foreign policy. At the beginning of February 1948 he called on the British ambassador in Washington, Lord Inverchaple, and made insinuations about the action that he and his association might take if the British did not adopt a more flexible position. Although his principal criticisms were of the attitude over the duty, he commented as well on internal questions of policy. Inverchaple reported to Ernest Bevin that:

> Mr Johnston then went on to say that he was disturbed particularly by some of the passages in the speech by the President of the Board of Trade made in the House of Commons on the 21st of January when the Cinematograph Films Bill was read a second time. He disclaimed any attempt to influence us with threats about ERP or our position of priority within ERP but he did want us to know that some members of the Motion Picture Association (he mentioned Mr Balaban by name) wanted to placard some extracts from Mr Wilson's speech all over the USA in theatres and in newspapers as evidence of an intention to socialise the film industry. The passages which he mentioned were those which spoke of Government contribution to stability of the industry, the possibility of 'finance by one way or another' and finally the possibility of Government ownership or management of one or more studios. He said that if this school of thought in the Motion Picture industry had its head, great damage would be done and fuel added to the fire of opposition to further aid to Britain under ERP or anything else. He said that he had recently been to the White House and had told the whole story to President Truman. The President had commented that if this films tax procedure persisted and spread to other things and to other countries, the USA and the United Kingdom might as well throw their Havana Charter into the waste paper basket.[46]

With the report was forwarded a copy of Eric Johnston's own summary of the discussion, which did not include such overt references to the European Recovery Programme but noted that: 'A settlement of the film tax controversy has a direct and not unimportant bearing on the settlement of other commercial and economic problems and on the restoration of international trade as a whole.'[47] Johnston's efforts were rewarded. Shortly after this the Treasury backed down over the principle of permitting blocked funds, and at the beginning of March Harold Wilson reopened negotiations on the basis of trying to secure the best possible arrangement based on blocking, rather than taxing, American earnings. The question was not at that stage taken back to the

Cabinet, and it seems that Ernest Bevin was largely responsible for the change in the British position. After the question was settled, George Marshall sent a message to Bevin thanking him for his 'distinctly helpful attitude in making possible an amicable solution to the problem'.[48]

The outcome of the negotiations was an agreement signed on 11 March which allowed the American companies to repatriate 17 million dollars plus a sum equal to the earnings of British films in the United States and some other territories. The remainder of American rentals were to be blocked, but they could be used in Britain for certain specified purposes which included the purchase of the rights to British films and investment in British film production.

The news had a very mixed reception on both sides of the Atlantic. The American trade was divided, although *Variety* reported that the 'most widely held opinion by top execs is that the pact is certainly not all that could be wished for, but is by far the best that could be expected under the circumstances', but that there was considerable criticism on the grounds that the British would be 'using the Americans to build up their industry'.[49] The British trade associations all welcomed the settlement; but whereas the exhibitors were positively jubilant, the BFPA objected that: 'At no time during the recent negotiations was there any consultation with this association on matters included in the agreement which vitally affect the interests of British Film Producers.'[50] The film unions, except for the NATKE, thought the agreement too favourable to America. The press in Britain, both on the left and the right, was highly critical. The *Daily Express* spoke of 'a dark hour in the history of our land'.[51] The *Financial Times* struck a more sardonic note: 'Had the Marx Brothers represented Britain in the negotiations with Mr Eric Johnston they could hardly have produced a more absurd agreement. . . . Surely our innocent economist-socialist President of the Board of Trade should not have been allowed to play poker with the hard-shelled negotiators from Hollywood'.[52] The *Daily Worker* emphasised the danger of the 'continuation of the domination of the screen by the propaganda productions of a State which is avowedly out to bring Britain under the sway of the dollar'.[53] An exception was the *News Chronicle*, which described the agreement as 'a thoroughly good bargain'.[54]

The whole episode of the duty and the agreement is probably the most notorious incident in the history of film industry-government relations. Long afterwards it continued to arouse passionate comment. Contemporary perception of these events was highly coloured by the fact that after the agreement the industry experienced a much publicised crisis. Many people within the industry and outside saw the decline as a direct consequence of the government's handling of the duty, although others thought the industry made the government a scapegoat for its own shortcomings. Two different stories of the events have been handed down, one telling of how the government betrayed the industry, the other of how the industry betrayed the nation. The first version is accepted by Peter Forster in his essay in *The Age of Austerity*,[55] by Rank's biographer Alan Wood, and by George Perry, who says of Wilson in his book *The Great British Picture Show* that 'undoubtedly although unwittingly he was one of the major destroyers of the film industry'.[56] The other version was put most forcefully by some of the trade union leaders. George Elvin of the ACT, for instance, argued in the *Listener* that the film industry had deliberately failed to respond to protection.[57] Both stories have some foundation but both tend to exaggerate the conflict between the government and the trade. Before the duty was imposed the government had, on the whole, followed advice from the trade, and trade and government must therefore share the blame for the failure to formulate an effective policy on the problem of American imports.

Once the duty was in operation and the boycott declared, the exhibitors certainly made little effort to help the government. The CEA wrote at once to the Prime Minister protesting about the duty and predicting that the industry would be destroyed within six months.[58] The NATKE was also highly critical of the duty, and both organisations kept up constant pressure on the government to settle with the Americans. Although individual exhibitors showed initiative in searching for ways of keeping their cinemas open – by offering more live entertainment for instance – the profession collectively adopted a defeatist pose suggesting that there were no alternatives to American films. Instead of criticising the MPAA, which had imposed the embargo, the CEA and the NATKE laid the blame on the government.

The producers, as represented by the BFPA, were also critical but at first expressed some guarded optimism. After an emergency meeting in August the BFPA announced that its members, although not in favour of the duty, would assist the government by raising their output. The case often made later on behalf of the producers was that they did increase production, and that just as this additional supply of films came on to the market the agreement with the Americans was signed, letting in the pick of the previous year's American releases. This unexpected competition caused the British films to flop, thereby triggering off a crisis which nearly extinguished the British industry. Although there is no doubt that the sudden re-entry of American films did do considerable damage to British producers, the story is only partially supported by production statistics (see Table XX overleaf).

The Board of Trade classifies films by length and does not distinguish between first and second features, but it can be assumed that most of the films over 72 minutes would be intended for first-feature release. Both sets of figures therefore suggest that the boycott did not result in a sharp rise in the number of first features produced. The increase between 1947 and 1948 is much the same as between 1946 and 1947, and is not impressive when compared either with pre-war first-feature production,

191

TABLE XX
British feature film production 1945–1950

	1945	1946	1947	1948	1949	1950
Production of first features	28	49	59	63	66	62
No. of films registered over 72 minutes	40	39	48	68	77	74
No. of films registered between 33⅔ and 72 minutes	36	61	58	101	53	59

(Board of Trade figures)

which amounted to 90 films in 1939, or with the best of the war years, 1942, when 60 first features were made. The figures also fail to suggest that there was a severe slump in first-feature production in 1948 and 1949. The figures for shorter features, on the other hand, show a very considerable 'bulge' in 1948 and a marked drop in 1949 and 1950. It may be assumed that some of these were planned as longer films but turned out so badly that, when faced with unexpected American competition, they were cut down and released as second features. Nevertheless, even allowing for this, it would seem that much of any extra effort made by the industry at the time of the boycott was channelled into second-feature production and so cannot easily be attributed to patriotic motives and a worthy desire to help the government, since the main requirement for keeping the cinemas open in the boycott was for first, not second, features.

These figures also pose some questions about the much talked of crisis of 1949. They show that both first-feature production and total production were higher in 1949 and 1950 than in 1947, and that first-feature production was maintained at a more or less constant level. This might suggest that the slump of 1949 was a relatively unimportant affair, a product of the industry shedding some of the surplus capacity used for the abnormally high production of second features undertaken in 1947–8. Much of the evidence of crisis was indeed based on comparisons with that year: the news for instance that in November 1948 thirteen studios and twenty-six stages were idle as compared with six studios and fourteen stages twelve months before.[59] The most striking symptoms of the crisis were studio closures and unemployment. British National closed in April 1948, and early in 1949 Nettlefold and Shepherd's Bush were lost. Employment fell from 7,253 in 1948 to 5,139 in 1949 and 4,104 in 1950. Since there was not a corresponding fall in the total number of films produced, one interpretation might be that these changes were at least partly the result of rationalisation and increased efficiency.

The main reason, however, why the trade press was full of references to a crisis was that, although the output of films had not fallen (except in comparison with 1948) profits were falling to such an extent that it seemed possible that production might soon come to a halt. Owing to the complexity of film finance, however, and the extensive opportunities for manipulating accounts, the reports of losses cannot necessarily be accepted at face value. According to figures submitted later to the government,[60] it would seem that even during the year preceding the levy all films except one or two inexpensive 'hits' were losing money. Yet if these figures are to be taken at face value, it seems surprising that production continued at all. A further reason for treating with caution assertions about the gravity of the crisis is that it was in the interests of everyone in the industry to exaggerate it: the employers were campaigning for a reduction in Entertainments duty, and the employees were urging the government to put public funds into production.

The role played throughout the crisis by Rank requires special mention. The case of Rank is most often cited to substantiate the story of government betrayal. Rank did increase production: in November 1947 the company announced plans to make forty-three films in the following year. The company's financial structure was even reorganised to finance the programme, with Odeon cinemas being given a shareholding in GFD, an arrangement severely criticised in the City. Rank also made serious losses in 1948 and 1949. One of the principal events of the 1949 crisis was the Rank annual report in November disclosing a loss of £4,646,000 on film production. In his report to the shareholders, Rank implied that the losses were the result of the company's response to the boycott and blamed the poor returns partly on a lack of creative talent and partly on the Anglo-American agreement:

> It can now be seen that our plans to meet an unexpected and critical situation were too ambitious, that we made demands on the creative talent of the industry that were beyond its resources and that as a result we spread our production capacity too thin over the films we made. . . .
> Even if all our films had been of the quality we had hoped, this unusually strong competition would have made it difficult to achieve satisfactory results.[61]

Many observers were sceptical about Rank's diagnosis. Paul Rotha questioned the creative judgment shown by the company in its choice of projects and personnel:

> Mr Rank has said that his group made demands on the industry's creative talent that were beyond its resources. It is more accurate to say that available talent has not always been used to the best effect and that other available talent has been neglected.[62]

The authors of the PEP study questioned the financial management of the programme:

> The scale of the effort was not the only explanation of this financial failure. The fact is that part of the expanded programme was carried out by an organisation mainly accustomed to, and adjusted to, high cost production.[63]

The results also reflected the outcome of policies adopted before the crisis of the boycott occurred. Since the war years the company had suffered severe losses on a number of extremely expensive and relatively unsuccessful films, the most notorious being *Caesar and Cleopatra*, released in 1945. The American distribution subsidiary was a further financial burden, since it had failed to show returns by 1949. Some of Rank's defenders attribute this failure also to government policy, suggesting that the duty sabotaged Rank's export drive. Rank himself rather discounted this theory when he reported in January 1948 that:

> The Americans have more than kept the undertaking which they gave me when I visited the US during 1947. They promised then that they would show our films on the five major circuits, and last autumn they began to do this despite the fact that no American films were coming into this country.[64]

It is worth noting that Rank's primary political objective in 1949 was to secure a reduction in Entertainments duty, and to this end his report contained a thinly disguised threat. He announced that in the immediate future production would be reduced and that no plans at all would be made beyond June 1950. Whether production would continue at all would depend on whether the government cut the duty.[65]

Although the trade misrepresented the nature of the 1949 crisis and exaggerated the effects of government action, there can be little doubt that the whole affair of the duty was badly bungled. It seems hardly plausible to argue that the precipitate imposition of the duty was the only, or best, way of persuading the State Department that Britain needed more aid. It would indeed have been reasonable, at a time when most industries were suffering from import restriction, to have asked the film business to take its share of the shortages and to manage with fewer imported films. But the government did not do this. One of the reasons the boycott was so effective was that no realistic attempt had been made before 1947 to reduce the screen time devoted to American films. The most extraordinary aspect of the affair was that Cripps had not considered what to do in the event of a boycott. The fact that he was misled by his officials into thinking a boycott unlikely is not an adequate explanation, since it was recognised that this was a possible outcome.

Once faced by the boycott the government displayed a mixture of intransigence and weakness, hanging on long enough to unsettle the British industry and capitulating just when the Americans had most reason to want to end the dispute. Up to that time America had lost very little revenue but, as the stock of films was nearly exhausted, there was the prospect of falling revenue to be faced at a time when Hollywood was already suffering a crisis for other reasons. The Americans were frightened above all that other countries would follow the British example. They had good reason, since several Commonwealth countries were considering following suit and wrote to the Board of Trade to ask for details. The French were also deeply dissatisfied with the lack of protection against American imports and were following events in Britain with interest. Hollywood, moreover, was not as united as Eric Johnston wished the world to believe. There were sharp disagreements between the majors and the independents, and Morris Ernst, a lawyer acting for the independents, told Wilson that the tax was a sound move and urged him to stand firm against the proposals for blocking funds.[66] Britain, it is true, faced the prospect that the supply of films would run down, but the results were not as catastrophic as the exhibitors suggested. Somervell at the Board of Trade predicted that the main effect on attendances would be that people would not go to the cinema more than once a week but that there would be relatively little fall in once-a-week attendances. There was also no reason to think that the deterioration of cinema programmes would spark off a great wave of opinion against the government.

The press generally came out in favour of the tax, whether for a variety of political reasons or, as *Kinematograph Weekly* insinuated, because the newspaper proprietors would rather see films taxed than suffer further shortages of newsprint. The available evidence suggested that there was popular support for a tough stand. A newspaper poll at the beginning of 1946 had shown that eight out of ten of those questioned thought film imports should be cut before further savings were made on food.[67] In October 1947 a *News Chronicle* poll showed that, in answer to the question 'If the tax on us films means we get no more American pictures . . . should the tax remain or be removed?', 58 per cent thought it should remain against 24 per cent who thought it should be removed.[68]

THE 1948 FILMS ACT AND THE 45 PER CENT QUOTA

The drama surrounding the import duty upstaged the debates on the Quota Bill, which passed through Parliament during the period of the boycott and became law shortly after the signing of the Anglo-American agreement. In comparison with these events the bill aroused little controversy. Its principal critics were the Film Industry Employees' Council (FIEC) and the group of Labour MPs who were advocating a fourth circuit. These groups both engaged in some last-minute lobbying to try to introduce more radical provisions, but their efforts were unsuccessful.

The Act followed closely the proposals originally made by Cripps in 1947 except that, as a consequence of the GATT, provisions for a renters' quota were dropped. The only measures relevant to the control of monopoly were that the arrangements previously made by informal agreement with the circuits were given the force of law, in that the Board of Trade was granted powers to prevent the circuits from acquiring additional cinemas and to require them to show up to six films a year on the recommendation of a Selection Committee. A clause which would have enabled the Board of Trade to fix a higher exhibitors' quota for the circuits was defeated in the Lords. The other main changes effected by the Act concerned the regulations for exhibitors' quota and the composition of the Films Council. Separate quotas for short and long films were replaced by separate quotas for first features and supporting programmes; a cost test of ten shillings per foot labour costs was applied to all films, not, as before, only to long films; the Board of Trade was allowed far more discretion than before in deciding what percentage quota should be required, since the percentage for each quota period was to be established by statutory instrument; regulations were slightly strengthened by a clause requiring cinemas to show their quota films within normal exhibiting hours. In the new Cinematograph Films Council the independent members were reduced from eleven to seven; representatives of exhibitors increased from four to five; representatives of producers increased from two to four; and instead of two representatives of employees in production there were to be four representatives of employees in all branches of the industry. These changes were ostensibly intended to improve the representation of independent producers and exhibitors and of employees. It is arguable, however, that in many respects the influence of the combines and of employers was greater in the new Council. In the old Council the non-trade members who were mostly critical of monopoly had had an overall majority and, in any case, on this issue could rely on support from the employees. In the new Council the non-trade members and the employees together did not constitute a majority.

More conflict was engendered by the Board's subsequent decisions about quota percentage than by the Act itself. In June 1948 the quota for first features was fixed at 45 per cent, to the delight of production interests and the disgust of exhibitors. In this instance the guidance offered to the Board of Trade by the Films Council had been of little use since the divisions in the industry had been faithfully reflected in the deliberations of the Council. The exhibitors had urged a 25 per cent quota while the producers had argued for 50 per cent. The producers won on the basis of a vote but by such a narrow margin – eight votes to six

– that there could be no pretence that the advice represented the views of the industry. The producers, however, had a strong case for some special consideration in the light of the Anglo-American agreement and the sudden intensification of American competition. The signs of approaching recession which were by then all too apparent served as an additional argument for the need to offer incentives for recovery.

The exhibitors did not take their defeat quietly. Alexander King complained that the high quota 'reduces the Cinematograph Films Bill to a farce' and called it 'the most ridiculous thing I've ever heard'.[69] The MPAA was also outraged and threatened to renew the boycott.[70] Johnston himself came over to Britain in August and had talks with Rank, trying to secure Rank's co-operation in pressing for a lower quota in return for the offer of increased American screen time for Rank films. Johnston evidently did not convince Rank, since the following March the producers on the Films Council stood firm in defence of the 45 per cent quota. The Council was completely split again, but this time the producers lost by a narrow margin and a resolution was passed calling for a quota of 33 per cent. The exhibitors complained that 45 per cent was unrealistic, that it left exhibitors with no margin of choice and therefore did not encourage quality production. They pointed out that it had not checked the slump in production. Others, however, argued that this indicated rather that the quota should be higher. The ACT advocated a 60 per cent quota. In practice the 45 per cent quota had not applied to all cinemas. Out of 4,106 halls, relief had been granted to 1,327 and a further 305 had been exempted altogether.[71] The average quota was therefore only 38 per cent. Since most circuit cinemas were among those required to achieve full quota, the effect was similar to that intended by the defeated clause in the bill providing for separate quotas for the circuits. Apart from the impact of relief and exemptions, a large number of defaults had modified the quota actually achieved. For first features there were 1,474 defaults. Nevertheless the quota achieved, 37 per cent, was the highest ever known, and this had been obtained during a year of serious recession.

Faced with conflicting advice and evidence, the Board of Trade adopted a middle course and reduced the quota, but only to 40 per cent. This represented a compromise in relation to the interests which predominated on the Films Council, but was regarded as a defeat by the ACT and others who had hoped for policies to enable national films to occupy at least half the country's screen time. In the year that followed, the major producers abandoned their support for a high quota and the CEA reached agreement with the BFPA to press for a further reduction to 30 per cent. The continuing low profitability of production and the relative importance within the combines of exhibition interests favoured a process of rapprochement. When the question came before the Films Council, the members voted twelve to two in favour of 30 per cent. The

Board of Trade accepted this advice, admitting by implication that the brief attempt to build up the production industry had failed. After 1950, the quota remained at 30 per cent.

10 A Rescue Operation

> It has taken the British Government and its chief Board of Trade, Customs and Treasury advisers approximately five years to discover why film production in this country was such a perilous proposition. It might have taken two if only the film industry had not offered the Administration such an enormous volume of contradictory advice.
>
> Anthony S. Gruner, *Daily Film Renter*, 30 December 1952

THE NATIONAL FILM PRODUCTION COUNCIL

The reluctance shown by Cripps and Wilson to reorganise the industry by compulsory means was in keeping with their approach to the private sector as a whole. The emphasis was on promoting co-operation and encouraging industry to reorganise itself. It was with such aims in view that the Development Councils were set up in 1947 by the Industrial Organisation and Development Act. Explaining his ideas in the House of Commons, Cripps specified the conditions under which planning should take place:

> Firstly advice must come from the industry itself because that is where all the past experience resides; secondly employers and workers should be equally represented because both sides not only have a contribution to make but will also have to carry out any plans that may be decided upon; and thirdly the public and Parliament must be satisfied – whatever the recommendations may be – that they are truly in the public interest and that the two sides of industry have not 'ganged up' against the consumer in their own interest.[1]

Wilson tried to apply these principles to the film industry by setting up the National Film Production Council, a committee of producers and employees in production, presided over by a representative of the Board of Trade. There were seven representatives from each side of the industry. For the employers there were five feature producers from the BFPA, plus Mr Hoare from the Association of Specialised Film Producers and Edgar Anstey from the Federation of Documentary Film Units; for the employees there were three representatives from the NATKE and two each from the ACT and the ETU.

199

The purpose of the committee was to devise ways of increasing efficiency, but it had no powers to enforce any decisions it reached. Wilson, looking back in the 1980s, described it as 'a wonderful talking shop',[2] but it is doubtful whether it was a useful addition to existing bodies. Its membership overlapped considerably with that of the Films Council, since four of the producers – Korda, Rank, Anthony Havelock-Allan and Anstey – were members of the CFC, as were George Elvin for the ACT, Tom O'Brien for the NATKE and Stephens for the ETU. Its composition was similar to that of the Joint Industry Council, an internal industry committee of employers and trade union representatives. The latter, it is true, was bedevilled by internal disputes about representations, particularly between the ACT and the NATKE, and consequently hardly ever met. But the National Film Production Council had problems of its own, and also met very infrequently.

Wilson demonstrated his enthusiasm for the Council by presiding over its first meeting in April 1948. Despite this sign of governmental interest, the initial results were disappointing. At the meeting it was decided that the committee would need some fairly comprehensive information about the costs and earnings of recent productions – information that could be obtained only from the employers, and that had in the past always been treated as highly confidential. The Secretary of the BFPA, Sir Henry French, passed on the request, but the companies dragged their feet. Two months later French admitted to Somervell that the companies were not co-operating: 'I fear their difficulty is the disclosure of figures to Trade Union leaders.'[3] It seemed that the very distrust the Council was supposed to overcome would strangle the experiment at birth. No further meeting was called for six months. When the trade press suggested that the BFPA's refusal to supply figures was the cause of the delay, the BFPA angrily accused the Board of Trade of leaking the story. Eventually the dispute was patched up. Wilson decided to call for a special inquiry into costs, and meanwhile the Board accepted some sample figures. The Council resumed its meetings in October, but the incident was indicative of the main flaw in the system: the real differences of interest between management and workers were simply too great to allow for much co-operation.

THE SELECTION COMMITTEE

Another body set up with good intentions, but in conditions that rendered its work ineffective, was the Selection Committee established under the clause in the 1948 Films Act empowering the Board of Trade to order the circuits to show films they had initially rejected. The procedure was that a producer who considered that his or her film had been discriminated against by the circuit could appeal to the Board of Trade. The film was then shown to the Selection Committee, which considered whether the picture was suitable for circuit release and advised the President of the Board of Trade accordingly. He might then decide to order the circuit to show the film.

This arrangement can be seen as an application of the general theory that gave rise to the Monopolies Act of 1948, and influenced the way it was used. The Act's intention was to discourage abuses resulting from commercial concentration, rather than to discourage concentration itself. By creating the Monopolies Commission the Act provided the means to investigate suspect companies, but it did not introduce obligatory penalties for offenders. The President of the Board of Trade exercised his discretion as to what action to take, and in the few cases that reached this stage a course of minimal intervention was chosen.[4]

The Selection Committee introduced by the Films Act could not be expected to do more than correct specific abuses of the circuit system. In theory, the scheme had the merit of opening up to public scrutiny the question of the way in which programmes were chosen for exhibition. However, even as a means of achieving these limited objectives, the Selection Committee had many drawbacks. One of the obvious problems was that by submitting a film for selection a producer risked antagonising the circuit owners and jeopardising his or her future chances of obtaining favourable deals for other films. In order to take such a risk a producer needed to have confidence that an appeal would be likely to succeed, and that the film would be sufficiently successful to compensate in part for the damage done to future prospects by a confrontation with the combines.

The experience of the voluntary scheme devised by Cripps was disappointing. The Selection Committee promised in March 1946 was not appointed until the following September, and was never convened. The procedure was strengthened when it was given the force of law, but otherwise it was unchanged. The composition of the Committee, clearly a key factor, was almost the same as under the voluntary scheme: there were four independent members, a representative from each of the three circuits and an independent chairman. In the new Committee, the latter position was held by Lord Drogheda, chairman of the Films Council. The presence of the circuit representatives, although conducive to a slightly more co-operative attitude on the part of the combines, inevitably cast doubt on the Committee's impartiality. The fact that films would be judged in part by the very people who had already rejected them lessened the prospect of any appeal succeeding. And since the circuit representatives were the only professional members who could advise from practical experience, they could be expected to exercise considerable influence during the Committee's discussions.

When the Committee started to function in September 1948, it was not besieged by aggrieved producers. Whether this was because complaints against the circuits had been exaggerated, or because producers lacked confidence in the scheme and were afraid of alienating the combines, is open to question. The fact that several films were submitted and later withdrawn before being viewed suggests that applicants were exposed to pressure of some kind.

Only one positive recommendation was made before the Committee was wound up by the Conservative government which took office in 1951, and the case underlines the system's deficiencies. The film was *Chance of a Lifetime*, produced by Del Guidice's company, Pilgrim, and directed by Bernard Miles. The story was, in 1950, an unlikely one for a popular comedy: the owner of a small factory is exasperated by his workers' demands, and challenges them to run the factory themselves. After managing the factory for some time they find that they lack expertise and call back the owner. The circuits rejected this film, primarily on the basis of its content. At the Committee, Sir Philip Warter, representing ABC, 'agreed that the film was of first feature quality but considered that it had no ordinary entertainment value at all and was not, therefore, a commercial proposition'.[5] Discussion centred round the concept of entertainment, although there were suggestions that the circuits were hostile to the political nature of the subject.[6] The Committee's criterion for selection was 'entertainment value', and social or aesthetic judgments were not supposed to intervene. The independent members disagreed with the circuits, and Wilson accepted their advice.

The procedure for enforcing the President's order was cumbersome. First, the owners of the three circuits were called to the Board of Trade, where they drew lots to decide which of them would be burdened with the unwanted film. In this case it fell to Rank, who consequently had to alter existing bookings in order to fit the film in; all the proposed dates had then to be referred back to Board of Trade officials so that they could check that the circuit was not 'cheating' by providing a poor combination of dates and places.

As soon as it was known that a film had been selected, the press showed a great deal of interest. The critics and the public were poised to pass judgment, on the government or on Rank, as soon as the film appeared. An added attraction was that the subject matter was considered very sensitive. Since the film showed an experiment in workers' control, it was regarded by some as being communist-inspired and therefore subversive. The bugbear of a socialist government promoting socialist propaganda was raised again, although in fact the main political reservations came from within the Labour government. George Isaacs, the Minister of Labour, was so worried about the film's message that he raised the matter in a Cabinet meeting, reporting that his advisers 'took the view that this film would be regarded as propaganda for Communism and for workers' control in industry; and it seemed doubtful whether it was expedient that the Government should require an exhibitor to show it.'[7] Fortunately for the government the press liked the film and did not consider it subversive. *The Times* pronounced it 'most adequate entertainment', reassuring the public that 'what propaganda it contains is little more than a message to the effect that the world would be a better place if people got on more amicably together'.[8] Even in Conservative papers there was a grudging approval: 'I am against the Board of Trade putting on a top hat pretending to be a showman,' the *Daily Mail*'s critic wrote. 'In this case, however, I think the action justified.'[9] In the United States the film was quite well received, and the *Motion Picture Herald*, more perceptive than the British trade press, commented: 'the subject matter, being controversial, through proper exploitation, it could prove a box office boon.'[10]

With a different film the results might have been embarrassing for the government. The direct involvement of a member of the Cabinet was a weakness in the Selection Committee mechanism since decisions which would drag the government directly into controversy would inevitably be more cautious. *Chance of a Lifetime* was, from the government's point of view, a perfect example of discrimination, but it was far from typical. Even the circuits did not dispute its technical qualities, and it was excluded mainly because it was out of the ordinary. Films of this kind were rare. It required great ingenuity for even a very well regarded independent producer to raise money for a film the circuits might not show, and any unfamiliar theme was likely to be an extra gamble. Most of the high-cost quality independent films were tailored to suit the circuits, and did secure a release. The issue, therefore, was whether the terms of the release discriminated against the producer. Michael Balcon's *The Overlanders*, for example, was at first refused first-feature billing. Many of the films that failed to get bookings were very ordinary productions, but no worse than many of the combines' films which did secure a release. However, they were squeezed out because the circuit preferred to show the films of its associates. A film entitled *Torment*, viewed at the same time as *Chance of a Lifetime*, was evidently regarded by the Committee as being of this category. No one thought it was good, but some of the independent members considered that it was not as bad as many films shown by the circuits, and argued that the refusal constituted a case of discrimination and the film should be shown. The circuits, however, insisted that it would lose money and, since *Torment* had no strong advocates, the circuits won.[11]

In effect, the Selection Committee was ill-equipped to tackle the complex problem of discrimination against independent producers. The kind of intervention it was able to make was precisely what had happened in the case of *Chance of a Lifetime*: it could step in on the rare occasion an exceptional film was rejected. This might rescue a few good films from oblivion, but could not loosen the grip of the combines. Many believed that the circuits prevented good films from being made in the first place.

Both Cripps and Wilson had indicated that discussions about the need
for further legislation would continue after the Films Act was passed.
One of the main obstacles to introducing new arrangements by
agreement, as Wilson hoped to do, was that conflicts in the industry were
reflected in widely divergent explanations for the unstable and insolvent
condition of the production sector. Wilson's response was to order a
number of public inquiries.

The first of these was conducted by a committee chaired by Sir Henry
Gater, and was concerned with the question of whether an additional
studio should be built and reserved for the use of independent producers.
The Gater Committee was also to consider 'how far it is necessary or
desirable that HM Government should own or control the management
of the aforesaid studio'.[12] The report was published in November 1948,
and added little to what was widely known. By this time the studios
closed during the war had been reopened and renovated. Production was
entering a period of recession, however, and a good deal of studio space
was not being used. The conclusion that there was no shortage of studio
space was therefore predictable, and the Committee considered that the
real problem facing independent producers was lack of finance. The
main positive recommendation relating to independent producers was
that they should form themselves into a co-operative, and in these
circumstances the government might consider buying and owning a
studio:

> Unless free-lance producers form a co-operative production society, it
> would be hazardous for the Government to provide additional space
> in any form. If independent producers formed a co-operative
> organisation the Government would buy and own a studio for it and
> the management of the Government's studio should be entrusted to a
> limited company analogous to the NFFC. . . . In conclusion we feel
> bound to emphasise that in the event of free-lance producers failing to
> achieve an efficient organisation it would be hazardous for the
> Government to embark upon the provision of additional studio space
> in any form.[13]

Sir Henry Gater also chaired the Working Party on Film Production
Costs set up late in 1948 after the November meeting of the National
Film Production Council, largely because Wilson was dissatisfied with
the progress made by that body. A Board of Trade report on the sample
statistics eventually gathered for the Council was used by the inquiry.
The Working Party's brief was 'to examine ways and means of reducing
production costs', but it was dissatisfied with the data made available to
it and reported:

We must . . . frankly admit that neither the Board of Trade report nor the additional figures we obtained later provided a basis on which to form a judgement of the main factors leading to the present high level of production costs and our general survey of the various aspects of cost problems has been based to a much larger extent on written and oral evidence received from both sides of the industry than on detailed analysis of the expenditure of individual companies on particular films.[14]

This to a large extent defeated the purpose of the report. The result was that conflicting opinions were documented, but no firm conclusions were drawn as to which were correct. The fact that the Working Party was itself composed of representatives of the two sides of the industry contributed to its difficulties in this respect. The independent members were W. Coutts Donald and S. C. Roberts; the producers' representatives were H. Boxall of London Film Productions, R. Clarke of ABPC, John Davis of the Rank Organisation, Sir Henry French and F. Hoare. The employees were represented by George Elvin of the ACT, F. Haxell of the ETU, A. Mingaye and Tom O'Brien of the NATKE and Rosamund John of the British Actors' Equity Association.[15] It was hardly surprising to find the report commenting:

Producers tend to attribute present high costs to the increase in the cost of materials; to higher wage rates combined with a shorter working week; to the high level of studio rents; to 'restrictive practices' and to a decline in the team spirit. Studio workers, on the other hand, tend to stress high administration expenses, top-heavy production executive staff (sometimes swollen by the introduction of 'passengers'), high salaries of 'stars', faulty planning, extravagance in sets and properties, and exaggerated standards of perfection.[16]

Although the authors of the report did not decide in favour of one side or the other, their evidence, on balance, gave more credibility to the unions' views than to those of management. They noted, for instance, that while wages had risen since 1939 by between 40 per cent and 110 per cent, the cost of managerial services had increased by 200 per cent.[17] They agreed that there was considerable extravagance and inefficiency, and concluded that 'the most serious deficiency in the industry is the inadequacy of present planning methods'.[18]

The study provided, then, a little new ammunition for the interventionists, but it was too inconclusive to serve as a basis for any kind of consensus about what needed to be done.

A proper examination of the reasons for the industry's low profitability required an analysis of revenues as well as costs. This was the subject of the report on the *Distribution and Exhibition of Cinematograph Films*, the most detailed and thorough of the three reports requested by Wilson. The Committee responsible for this report was, unlike the Working Party, composed entirely of independent persons, although the officers of the trade associations were involved as assessors. It was a conventional Board of Trade Committee, which included a financial expert, a trade unionist, a woman, a person to represent culture, as well as two people who could be expected to have relevant specialist knowledge: J. H. Lawrie, managing director of the recently formed Film Finance Corporation, and Professor Arnold Plant from the Films Council. The chairman was Lord Portal, a man who commanded respect in financial circles and had acquired some knowledge of the industry during his association with Rank, but who no longer had financial interests to disqualify him from the job. In the middle of the inquiry Lord Portal died, and the chair was taken by Professor Plant.

The subject matter of this inquiry was particularly sensitive because of its bearing on the controversy over monopoly and the possible need for a restructuring of the industry. In order to clarify the issues, the Committee set out on a much more thorough fact-finding survey than that conducted by the Palache Committee in 1944. Written evidence was requested from the BFPA, the KRS and the CEA, and oral evidence was taken at twenty-one of the forty-three meetings.

The BFPA submitted a substantial document containing a reasonable amount of statistical data. It argued that Entertainments Tax was the fundamental reason for declining profits:

> The proportion of the total sum taken at cinema box-offices throughout Great Britain which is received by British film producers is quite inadequate. The Exchequer's share, i.e. more than 40 per cent on the average (or 5d in the shilling) of gross box-office receipts is excessive.

Its proposed remedy was that

> the Chancellor of the Exchequer should be recommended to pay 50 per cent of this amount to British producers of all kinds to supplement – and in proportion to – the amount which they will receive from the box-office in 1949–50 and in each future year.[19]

Although by singling out the tax in this way the BFPA were by implication exonerating other sectors of the industry, they did suggest

206

that the Committee might collect audited accounts from a representative sample of different types of cinemas to check whether exhibition was taking a disproportionate share of revenue. This was probably intended primarily to expose to scrutiny independent cinemas, some of which, the BFPA complained, were seeking quota relief and reduced hire terms without providing audited accounts to substantiate their claims. The circuits, on the other hand, were given a clean bill of health: 'We have no complaint as regards the amount paid for film hire by the three major circuits.' The circuits also, the BFPA pointed out, played full quota; and 'it may be said in brief that the three circuits are giving full support to British films'.

Such unconditional praise of the circuits could be seen as evidence of the influence exerted by the combines within the BFPA. It was a view that was certainly contested by the Association of British Independent Film Producers, a recently formed and short-lived grouping of independents.[20] The Association testified that they received worse rentals from the circuits than from independent cinemas. Other charges against the circuits were made by a producer, Jill Craigie of Outlook Films.[21] She provided detailed descriptions of the ways in which, she alleged, the circuits discriminated against independent producers by giving them unfavourable dates, diverting an unjustifiably large share of the rental to the accompanying feature, and block-booking a popular independent film with inferior product so that independents were unwilling to accept the package.

The one aspect of trading practices the BFPA was concerned about was the alleged effort by the CEA to fix rentals with the KRS on behalf of its members. Both the latter associations denied this accusation. The one statement of substance made by the KRS was that 'it has been a cardinal principle of the KRS and one that has been publicly declared many times that the terms for hiring films are a matter of bargaining between individual distributors and their customers'.[22]

The CEA agreed with the BFPA that the Exchequer was the only party taking an excessive share of revenue, but did not want the money handed back to the producers. The CEA asked for a straight tax remission of £6,250,000.

Those who thought that income was not fairly allocated between different sections of the industry singled out for criticism the distributor's rather than the exhibitor's share. The Association of British Independent Film Producers and the ACT both considered that distribution fees were too high. The ACT pointed out that 20 per cent of the distributor's gross was taken for services that excluded publicity, the latter being an extra charge. The BFPA made no comment on the services provided or fees charged by distributors. The KRS also remained silent, and declined the Committee's invitation to submit detailed evidence, simply referring the Committee to the KRS' comments on Palache.

The case for restructuring the industry was made by Equity and the ACT. Both unions stressed their concern about the existing high unemployment. The ACT suggested that the Committee should consider

> whether drastic changes are required in the present structure, to secure by national planning greater stability and a more adequate service to the cinema-going public.[23]

Equity argued:

> It is not enough for the Committee to try and improve the efficiency of distribution and exhibition within the present framework of the industry. It is that framework itself which requires examination and reconstruction upon the basis that the major part of the product will no longer be imported from abroad but will be made at home in British studios.[24]

The NATKE, as usual, stood closer to the employers, agreeing with both the BFPA and the CEA that all that was needed was to lower the tax. No preference was expressed between a subsidy and a rebate.

A major problem encountered by the Committee in trying to assess such conflicting evidence was that it had no powers to force individuals or private companies to disclose confidential information. It was ironic that although the inquiry was intended, to some extent, as a fact-finding operation, the Committee had to rely heavily on statistics provided voluntarily by the trade. In the event the principal sources were the BFPA and the CEA. The Committee's report made a point of drawing attention to the difficulty: 'We have been hampered in our examination of the structure of the industry by the absence of adequate statistics and we consider that an up to date official service of statistics is urgently required.'[25] The Committee was nevertheless able to gather enough information to build up a very much more accurate picture of how the industry functioned than had previously been available to anyone outside the trade. The data showed more clearly than before the extent of the circuits' influence in the market, even though some crucial figures, such as their share of the box-office, were not made available. One advance was that figures for cinema ownership were broken down according to categories of cinema, thus giving substance to the generality that the circuit-owned cinemas were on average much bigger than those owned by other operators. While the circuits' share of all cinemas was only just over 20 per cent, they owned 70.5 per cent of cinemas with a seating capacity of over 1,500; 20 per cent of cinemas with 501 to 1,500 seats; and only 2 per cent of those with less than 500.[26] This placed in perspective information about the bookings a film might obtain. Of the circuits, the Odeon chain was the strongest and could offer up to 354 first-run bookings; the ABC came next with 345; and the Gaumont last with 301. Total bookings obtained by a successful film might be as many as 2,500; at the other end of the scale, a film receiving less than 1,500 bookings would lose money.[27]

Distribution of receipts was not broken down as between circuits and others, nor by size of cinema. However, a breakdown was given according to type of settlement (see Table XXI). Since it could be assumed that larger cinemas were situated mainly in big cities and it was known that the circuits were particularly strong in the London area, this breakdown offered some clue about the proportion of receipts obtained from a circuit booking.[28]

TABLE XXI
Box office receipts in terms of population size

	% of receipts
London general release	19.6
Provincial towns with population of 100,000 and over	32.8
Provincial towns with population of 50,000–100,000	10.8
Smaller towns and villages (under 50,000)	36.8

An important point revealed in the evidence, although not included in the report, was that Rank and the American majors between them completely controlled the opening of films in London prior to general release. Out of eight West End first-run solo cinemas CMA (Rank) owned three, Paramount owned two and MGM, Warners and United Artists one each. A further four first-run concurrent halls were all owned by CMA.

On the question of the share of total receipts taken by the different sectors of the industry, information was again patchy. The CEA provided a breakdown of the total box-office (see Table XXII).[29] According to a BFPA estimate, British features took £10 million of the £25 million; out of this the distributors took £2.5 million, leaving £7.5 million to be paid to producers of British films.

The CEA also provided detailed information about the distribution of exhibitors' gross and net takings for different categories of cinema. Figures were given for 1938–9 as well as for 1947–8. This data provided support for the view that the exhibitors were already paying high enough rentals. For all categories of cinema, profits accounted for a smaller percentage of takings in 1947–8 than in 1938–9. Taking the average for all types of cinema, the only item with a larger share of gross takings was Entertainments Tax, which had increased from 11.5 per cent to nearly 36 per cent. Looking only at net takings, film hire accounted for a slightly higher percentage in 1947–8: 39.3 per cent as against 37.8 per cent in 1938–9. Wages and salaries accounted for 20 per cent as opposed to 15 per cent, and profits were down from 15.2 per cent to 12.7 per cent.

TABLE XXII
Box office receipts: a breakdown

	£ million
Gross box-office	109
Entertainments Tax	39
Net box-office	70
Exhibitors' gross	42.5
Distributors' gross	27.5
Payment for supporting programme	2.5
Receipts for first features	25.0

On the vexed question of the distributor's share and the expenses of distribution, no details were made available. The silence of the KRS and its members thwarted further investigation, but did not dispel the suspicion that the charges against them might have some foundation. The Committee was apparently of this view, since it made a series of recommendations about the contractual arrangements with the intention of checking abuses if they existed. Particularly important was the suggestion that the producer of a film should have the right to examine the distributor's books relating to that film.

On the subject of revenue the Committee reached the conclusion that Entertainments Tax was too high, but rejected the BFPA proposal for a subsidy. Instead the Committee recommended that the level of tax should be lowered, and that various restrictive practices should be abolished so that 'the operation of ordinary market forces may be relied on to distribute appropriately throughout all sections of the trade' the benefits of the tax reduction.[31]

Of possible methods for tackling restrictive practices the Committee rejected the two most radical options – divorcement or state control:

> While we share the conviction that the creation of more competitive conditions is urgently necessary throughout the industry, we are unanimously of the view that a precipitate change, such as compulsory divorcement would involve, is not in present circumstances a practicable means of attaining that end.[32]

Its reasoning was that divorcement would endanger British production interests, firstly because the American companies might buy up cinemas or studios put on the market as a result of a sale order, and secondly because a major source of production finance would dry up – the loans raised by the combines against their other assets. The Committee admitted, however, that 'it might be argued that both these difficulties would be met by the state itself entering the field of both production and exhibition of entertainment films', but found this solution unacceptable:

> For our part we are unanimously of the view that film production which requires the free exercise and development of individual enterprise, skill and craftsmanship is among the businesses least appropriate for state ownership and operation.[33]

This statement constituted an ideological position rather than an argument, although at the end of the paragraph the substantive objection was made 'that the government might find itself under strong pressure for fear of unemployment to take over properties for which suitable buyers were not immediately forthcoming'.[34]

In offering positive recommendations, the Committee concentrated on specifying the changes in trading practices it considered necessary. The main suggestions were that the release pattern should be more flexible; bars should be relaxed; competitive bidding introduced; conditional booking abolished;[35] and that the system of paying rentals as a percentage, on a sliding scale, of box-office takings should be more widely used in place of fixed-rate terms.

The Committee did not discuss in detail how such reforms would be carried out, but stressed, in line with the Palache Committee, that government action would be needed since the trade could not be relied upon to implement them itself. 'It would hardly be reasonable,' the Committee commented in the context of barring clauses, 'to expect a purely trade body to deal with wider questions of public interest.'[36] The concrete proposal it made was that an independent authority should be established. This body would not have extensive powers to coerce the trade. Its functions would be to seek proposals from the trade for implementing government policy; to consider such proposals; to supervise the work of the existing trade committee of exhibitors and distributors; and, when necessary, to act as an appeal tribunal.

THE NATIONAL FILM FINANCE CORPORATION AND THE GROUP PRODUCTION SCHEME

By the time the Films Bill was passing through Parliament early in 1948, Wilson had reached one conclusion about the various outstanding issues. This was that special arrangements were needed to increase the finance available for independent production. In March 1948 he announced that plans to this effect were being prepared. He was not, however, at that stage thinking in terms of using state funds for the purpose – a step still opposed by the Treasury, even though Cripps, who had previously advocated this, was now Chancellor. Nor was Wilson interested in the proposals outlined in the Palache report, in Rotha's memorandum and in the submissions of the FIEC for a public corporation with quite wide powers that would compete in certain areas with private enterprise. Wilson's aim was rather to find a way of channelling private capital into the weakest sector of the industry to try to create more competitive conditions within the existing framework.

With this end in view, Wilson turned to two institutions that had been set up just after the war to act as instruments of the Labour government's industrial development policy – the Finance Corporation for Industry (FCI) and the Industrial and Commercial Finance Corporation (ICFC). The purpose of the former was to provide loans for rehabilitating industry, while the latter was designed to aid small and medium-size businesses by providing capital for expansion and development. Both were funded by the Bank of England and major private banks.

The theory associated with these institutions owed much to the ideas canvassed by a circle of Labour intellectuals identified with the XYD club, formed in the 1930s to bring Labour politicians together with economists and Labour supporters in the City. Two of the financial experts who were to play an important part in the plans for film finance were members of this group. One was James Lawrie, at that time general manager of the ICFC; the other was Nicholas Davenport, who was employed as financial and political adviser by Alexander Korda.[37] Davenport had worked for Gabriel Pascal for a time during the war and had been involved in the attempts to persuade the government to rescue *Major Barbara*.[38] He had also published articles and corresponded with the Board of Trade about how the films bank, under consideration at that time, should be organised. He was drawn into the new round of discussions in the first instance because the future of Korda's company, British Lion, was linked with the government's plans.

British Lion was an independent distributing company acquired by Korda in 1946 through London Film Productions as a step towards re-establishing a powerful presence in the British industry. Subsequently British Lion purchased a controlling interest in the British Lion Studio company, owner of Shepperton Studios. In this way Korda created a semi-integrated organisation that lacked only an exhibition arm. By 1948 an impressive array of distinguished producers and directors were associated with it, including Carol Reed, Herbert Wilcox, Anthony Asquith, Anthony Havelock-Allan, Emeric Pressburger and Michael Powell. British Lion was the only serious competitor to the combines, the only other British distributor or financier of importance. Korda was, however, experiencing difficulty raising finance for the planned production programme, and in February 1948 British Lion applied to the FCI for a medium-term loan of £1 million. The request was turned down.

The Board of Trade and the Treasury had been following developments with concern, since the failure of this group would both jeopardise plans for increasing the output of British films and remove from the field the main existing support for independent producers. A plan then took shape whereby the Board of Trade and the Treasury would use their influence to secure the support of the FCI or the ICFC on the understanding that British Lion would undertake to finance all suitable independent producers. Since neither finance corporation was equipped to deal with applications in respect of individual films, some kind of intermediary organisation would be needed to channel the money to small producers; and it was in keeping with the aim of reforming the industry under its existing management that the chosen instrument should be the biggest existing independent company.

The idea of privileging British Lion in this way naturally encountered criticism within the industry, especially from independents who were not anxious to work with Korda. A small drama developed around the fate of another leading producer, Del Guidice. After a long association between his company, Two Cities, and the Rank Organisation, Del Guidice had broken with Rank and, with the backing of a Birmingham industrialist, had set up a new company called Pilgrim, a name apparently chosen because of the religious leanings of Sir Stafford Cripps, with whom Del Guidice was on friendly terms. Del Guidice's first independent venture, an expensive film called *The Guinea Pig*, was begun in association with Korda, but the producers had quarrelled and the connection was severed. Del Guidice then had great difficulty raising finance for Pilgrim's future productions, largely, according to Somervell, 'owing to the fantastic sums at which he values his own personal services'.[39] When a Treasury official suggested that Del Guidice should again work with British Lion his backer protested, enclosing by way of explanation copies of the impassioned correspondence with Korda that had been occasioned by the dispute. Thus, as negotiations with British Lion continued, officials found themselves acting as peacemakers as well as fund-raisers.

The scheme foundered eventually not because it proved impossible to patch over the differences between British Lion and other groups, but because the FCI and the ICFC both refused to have anything to do with film finance. Even when the Treasury agreed to guarantee half of any losses incurred, they still withheld their co-operation. In July 1948 the hope of reaching agreement was abandoned, but by then the need for finance was more acute than ever. The 45 per cent quota introduced in June would prove unworkable unless the supply of British films was increased or at least maintained. Yet there was every sign that production would fall. The settlement with the Americans had not resulted in a sudden renewal of confidence. The position of independents, and of British Lion and Pilgrim in particular, was more precarious than ever. Faced with this situation, Wilson asked for a Treasury loan to set up a specialised film finance corporation. According to Wilson's own account, the Treasury officials were still unwilling to provide funds, and the loan was authorised only because Cripps intervened to overrule the objections of his officials after his attention had been drawn to the problem by news of Del Guidice's difficulties:

> One morning, Stafford telephoned me to say that Del was having to pay off his workers. He couldn't get on with his film and I said 'Look Stafford, there is nothing I can do. I haven't got any money at all. The Treasury are refusing. My officials are knocking on their door every day'.
> So he said, 'You shall have it.' . . . So I got my permanent secretary to phone theirs and we were able to make a start.[40]

Before the end of July, Wilson was able to announce the decision to set up a film fund with £5 million provided by the Treasury.[41] While the necessary legislation was being prepared, as an interim measure a company was formed under the existing Finance Acts to administer an advance of £2.5 million. J. H. Lawrie was appointed managing director and Nicholas Davenport was brought on to the Board after resigning his position with Korda. The other three Board members were all businessmen.

With the constitution of a specialist body of this kind, one of the principal reasons for assigning a special role to the British Lion group became inoperative. Nevertheless, when the company started work in September, its first move was to make an immediate advance to British Lion of £1 million with a promise of a further £2 million in the future.[42]

This decision, which was to have such serious repercussions on the future of the film finance corporation, was taken in the face of evidence that the company's finances were unsound. The Board of Trade had in its possession a document indicating both that the company's calculations were unrealistic and that the real prospects were unpromising. This was a list of recently completed films and productions in progress showing estimated costs and receipts. The figures showed a net profit of £651,000 on a capital outlay of £3,919,000, but this result was achieved by writing in very optimistic estimates, including foreign revenue for one film of £250,000, for pictures not yet released. There was also no evidence to suggest that the performance of British films abroad was improving dramatically.[43] The Board of Trade needed to monitor earnings in America because of the terms of the Anglo-American agreement, so it must have been aware that the position in the American market was far from sound. For the six months from June to December 1948 net British earnings for all films amounted to only just over $1 million.

There is no record, however, that at this stage the officials involved sounded a warning. Indeed, Nicholas Davenport suggests in his memoirs that Wilfred Eady was promoting the cause of British Lion, while he himself, despite his recent connection with Korda, was the principal critic of the scheme. Referring to his own appointment to the finance company, he recalled:

> What I did not know at the time was that Sir Wilfred Eady at the Treasury had persuaded Wilson that British Lion . . . was the proper instrument for channelling public money into the film production industry. 'Good heavens', I thought, 'did they know that British Lion was controlled by Alexander Korda and was already in financial trouble?'[44]

Davenport, of course, did know about the earlier plan for feeding money from the FCI through British Lion. He had even helped Korda prepare a lengthy memorandum on the subject for the Board of Trade. Yet it appears that he changed his mind even before joining the finance company, since he wrote to the Board of Trade in June saying that he had reservations about the idea under discussion because he was afraid that the money might get 'swallowed up' in British Lion.[45] In the light of this, his story of the loan seems plausible. According to Davenport, by the time he joined the Board Lawrie and Eady had already decided to allow British Lion £1 million. With his inside knowledge of the company Davenport was worried about 'what was tacked on to the film budgets by way of Korda's family overheads',[46] and he persuaded Korda to agree to hand over a controlling interest in the company to a public trust as long as public money was being used. When he put the idea to Eady, he recalled, 'I was sharply told to forget it'.[47]

Nevertheless, some conditions were attached to the loan. A new managing director was appointed (H. C. Drayton, described as a 'new star' in the City[48]) and a report on the company was commissioned. The report confirmed the doubts expressed by Davenport and indicated that either the company would have to be liquidated or a further investment made.

Korda's high reputation and his personal standing with the politicians and officials concerned no doubt influenced the decision to back his company so heavily,[49] but another important factor was that the policy of which the bank was to be an instrument did not allow for a coherent alternative strategy. When the initial plans for the bank were made at a meeting between Eady, Somervell and Wilson in July, the decision was made that the bank should lend to renters, not to producers. Three reasons were given: that in this way the government would supplement, rather than compete with, private capital; that a less elaborate organisation would be needed; and that the choice of individual projects would not be made by a public body and so would not be the subject of Parliamentary questions. The first point was the most fundamental: the bank was not to compete with private enterprise. Thus although Wilson

215

had opted for a state bank, he had not opted for the bank envisaged by the FIEC. He had no intention of laying the foundations of a permanent state organisation to counter the growth of private monopoly. Yet one of the functions of the bank was precisely to check the growth of monopoly, but by promoting such private enterprise as there was outside the orbit of the two combines. Since there was very little that was not linked in some way with British Lion, it was hardly possible to pursue such a policy and bypass British Lion.

Not surprisingly the plans for the bank were criticised both from the left and the right. Some Labour MPs and the ACT continued to press for the creation of a distribution department attached to the finance corporation. All the unions, including the NATKE, argued that it should be allowed to lend directly to producers. The Conservatives questioned the use of taxpayers' money for such a purpose, and sounded a warning about state control and possible political interference with the content of films.

The Act, the Cinematograph Film Production (Special Loans) Act, was passed in March 1949, and the National Film Finance Corporation (NFFC) was constituted in April after taking over the assets and liabilities of the former company. The directors of the Corporation were the same as those of the company, except for Davenport, who had resigned in January. Lawrie remained as managing director. Lord Reith was appointed as chairman, a choice that suggested that the Corporation was intended at that stage to exercise cultural as well as financial influence. Lord Reith certainly approached his task from this standpoint, as he made clear in a memorandum addressed to Wilson in February:

> Let us be clear as to the issues at stake. . . . The most compelling are of the moral order – evidenced in the influence which the industry can exercise over so considerable a proportion of the population – interests, outlook and behaviour; in the projection of England and the English way of life to the Dominions and foreign countries; in the enhancement of the prestige and worth of England.[50]

The Corporation's influence of any kind was, however, curtailed from the start, first by the commitment to British Lion, and secondly by the conditions under which it had to operate. It was initially granted a revolving fund of £5 million, increased to £6 million to July 1950. In December of that year the NFFC was, for the first time, empowered to lend money for certain films that did not include a financial contribution from the producer. The PEP report of 1952 calculated that by the end of March 1951 the NFFC had approved loans of £5,539,404, but £5,211,222 of this had already been drawn.[51] In 1952 the NFFC's borrowing powers increased by a further £2 million. In all, the total amount lent to British

216

Lion was £3 million, but by 1954, after the company announced a loss of £150,330 for 1952–3, the government called in the loan and a receiver was appointed.[52]

When the Treasury decided, in the spring of 1950, to grant the NFFC an additional £1 million, Sir Wilfred Eady proposed that some of the new money (about £250,000) could be used by a new company to be formed with the aim of encouraging new talent to make low-budget films and 'to break through some of the present glooms and incidentally to see whether we can find a way of maintaining British production without having to subsidise it any further beyond the £6 million in the FFC'.[53] At the time Rank was contemplating cutting back production, and it was felt that British Lion was the only company producing good films. After consultation with the NFFC, Lawrie and Balcon suggested a more ambitious scheme, and Reith elaborated this in a memorandum submitted to the Treasury and the Board of Trade in November 1950. This proposed the formation of three new production groups. Two of these were to be organised, for distribution purposes, in conjunction with the major combines, Rank and ABPC, and were to be made up of existing first-feature producers. The third, based on Eady's plan, was to be led by John Grierson, and would offer chances for new talent. The overall aim was 'to provide a programme of sufficient size to enable losses and profits on individual films to be evened out, thus ensuring a reasonable measure of stability for the production company'.[54] The scheme required the provision of an additional £4 million for the NFFC, and a considerable widening of the latter's functions, so that it could, for example, take shares in a limited company.

The Board of Trade and the Treasury were reluctant to endorse Reith's scheme because of the implications of extending the NFFC's powers and resources, and because of the inevitable criticism that would be voiced of the links between two of the groups and the combines. Eady was against the NFFC becoming more involved in first-feature production, and was only in favour of the Grierson group. Golt, a Board of Trade official, could not see an alternative arrangement without circuit participation:

So long as the present set-up in the film industry exists, there is no doubt that in one way or another producers must work through Rank and ABC distribution organisations, and any lasting settlement of production problems must either recognise this fact or set out on some much more drastic measure – which might have to include a distribution organisation controlled either by the State or NFFC and even a state-controlled or NFFC-controlled circuit of cinemas. Whether we like it or not GFD and ABC are, with British Lion, the dominant distributors, and their ownership of the circuits makes it impossible to disregard them.[55]

Harold Wilson's main objection to the Reith plan was that it would mean an expansion of the NFFC's brief and resources. Wilson met Reith on 11 December 1950 and tried to persuade him that the Grierson group might be established first.[56] Wilson was reluctant to agree to the NFFC being granted an additional £4 million before the 'second dose' of the Eady plan had been implemented, and before the trade made a move towards reforming itself in accordance with some of the recommendations of the Plant report. He was, like Eady, agreeable to the plan that the Grierson group should be announced, and pointed out to Reith that, with only £1 million in new funds, if all three groups were launched very little money would reach the independents. Reith defended his scheme the next day in a letter to Wilson:

> We are not driving the producers to the big organisations. We are carrying out your orders not to replace bank finance but to supplement it. Banks only lend against guarantees from distributors strong enough to satisfy them; the best risks are the two big organisations. The independents must therefore look to them for support, whether we like it or not.[57]

In the end a compromise was reached: the three groups were launched, but strictly within the NFFC's existing powers and resources. In January 1951 Wilson approved the Reith scheme. The first group was formed in association with Rank, and a holding company was formed called British Film Makers Ltd.[58] The usual pattern in this case was for GFD to provide a distribution guarantee so that a bank loan could be obtained, with the rest of the money (30 per cent) coming from the NFFC. Production was at Pinewood studios, and the NFFC had a controlling interest in the share capital of the holding company. Producers associated with the group included Anthony Asquith, Betty Box, Thorold Dickinson and Anthony Havelock-Allan. The second group was linked with ABPC and Elstree studios, but this time no formal holding company was established. Group 3, as it was called, was different in that it was supposed to 'encourage, and to provide facilities, both technical and financial, for the producer who is not yet established in the main feature industry'.[59] Many of those involved, however, were experienced in making 'shorts' and second features – Grierson and John Baxter, for example.

None of the groups fared well. Group 3 was wound up in 1955 after completing twenty-two features budgeted at an average cost of £50,000. By 1954 group one had produced fourteen films, and it collapsed after only two years in operation. Group two managed to complete only five films.[60] Nevertheless, the episode confirmed the Board of Trade's stance towards reforming the industry's structure, as the PEP report commented:

It is obvious that the question of the group production scheme raises a fundamental issue about the policy which the Government should adopt towards the industry. Should it accept the existing structure and co-operate with the main powers in order to create a stable production industry, or should it re-fashion the present structure?[61]

The Board of Trade adopted the former course. As Nicholas Davenport wrote in his memoirs of Wilson and the NFFC: 'If he had been a real socialist, he would, of course, have nationalised or municipalised the two great circuits which were later shown up by the Monopolies Commission in 1966 to be riddled with restrictive and monopolistic practices'.[62]

POLICY AFTER THE PLANT REPORT

During the year that the Plant Committee was pursuing its investigation, the production industry reached the worst phase of the crisis. Neither the 45 per cent quota nor the loans made by the NFFC had reversed the trend. The decision to lower the quota indicated a lack of confidence in existing measures. In March 1949 the matter was raised at a Cabinet meeting and the outcome of the discussion was that the Cabinet

> invited the President of the Board of Trade on receipt of the report of the Portal Committee on the structure of the film industry to submit a full factual report on the industry to the Cabinet with recommendations on the action which the government should take to increase the efficiency of the industry and to secure any necessary measures of control.[63]

Wilson accordingly set out his ideas in a lengthy memorandum to Somervell. The document shows that he was convinced by this time that the central problem was the monopolistic control over exhibition exercised by the combines; and despite a reluctance to trespass on the rights of shareholders, he had decided to seek new radical powers of intervention. He wrote:

> The time has come when we cannot allow national film policy economically, morally or artistically to be dictated by these two Oriental potentates. The power of the circuits must be broken or at least severely limited. This is not an undue interference with private enterprise or the rights of shareholders. . . . Once a private undertaking has reached the size of these organisations and has assumed power of a quasi-monopolistic character, it is quite appropriate that that power, if the State permits it to be continued to be exercised, should be circumscribed by such safeguards for the public interest as the State may decide.

The lesson of all this is that the decision of what films are made should be transferred from the shoulders of the two gentlemen in question, to some authority in whom the public and, so far as possible, individual producers themselves, can have confidence.[64]

Wilson was prepared to contemplate restructuring but only in the distant future:

One possible and radical solution would be to bust up the circuits. This may come in the fullness of time; I hope it will, but I do not consider it a likely development in the immediate future and although I think we should keep it in our minds as a long-term objective I am not sure that we ought to pursue it as national policy in the months that lie immediately ahead.[65]

Nevertheless, the memorandum did constitute a clear directive to the administration to evolve proposals for legislation which would curtail the power of the circuits in some way. Yet by the time the Labour government was voted out of office, no progress had been made. The events which followed Wilson's memorandum provide a revealing case-history of the way in which administrative procedures can frustrate a politician's intention, although it is also arguable that the brief was defective.

Wilson did not advocate nationalising any part of the industry, but envisaged a degree of public control over the detailed decisions of management which could otherwise only be achieved through quite complex administrative machinery. His idea about safeguarding the public interest in the short term involved elaborate regulations for imposing a new kind of quota responsibility on the circuits. The plan was that films would be scheduled for quota at the script stage by a panel consisting, probably, of independent persons and industry experts. The circuits would be obliged to show a high proportion, possibly all, of such quota films so that projects which the panel approved would effectively be guaranteed a circuit release before they went into production. It would have been a cumbersome arrangement and would have required revision to the existing legislation banning advanced booking. These were not the principal objections raised by civil servants, but they were obstacles in the way of preparing detailed workable proposals.

Somervell's answer to Wilson betrays a deep-seated hostility to the idea of the state directly or indirectly managing the film industry:

As I understand it the proposal . . . would in effect place the whole of British first feature production under the control of a body appointed by the Government. One must ask whether the risk of abuse is really such as plainly to justify so drastic a remedy.[66]

Somervell plays down the risk of abuse, suggesting that the criticisms about the selection procedures of the circuits were much exaggerated and that the only producers likely to suffer were freelance producers whom he characterised as 'the weakest and least satisfactory element in the industry'. He was sceptical that even a freelance would run a risk of being rejected by both circuits 'if his reputation and his project are really good'. It is possible to see a connection between Somervell's attitude to state control and his dislike of the freelance producer, in that both stem from a tendency, discernible in previous Board of Trade documents, to regard the business side of film production as very much more important than the creative or technical side; a 'good' producer must therefore be a 'man of substance' and the idea, implicit in the case made by the unions, that creative and technical teams could make competent films without the guidance of such men was regarded as absurd. Given such a view of the industry Somervell was unsympathetic to Wilson's general intention, and it was natural that he should emphasise the drawbacks attached to the specific suggestions rather than elaborate alternative proposals for achieving the desired result. Somervell's final remarks to Wilson are characteristic:

> The production industry still has very difficult problems to solve and their solution will require the co-operation of all those engaged in production and indeed of all sections of the industry. The industry has got to do this work for itself. The Government can only sit on one side and watch for opportunities to remove friction or to exercise discreet pressure on the obstinate. NFFC will continue its positive task of seeing that competent producers are organised and equipped in such a way as to give them the best chance of success. The calmer the atmosphere and the less limelight (Parliamentary or otherwise) for the prima donnas concerned the better the chance of some solid achievements.[67]

The Plant Committee potentially constituted an alternative source of advice. Its terms of reference certainly enabled it to make recommendations relating to monopolistic practices. But here too the Board of Trade officials exercised considerable influence because they proposed the members of the Committee and were also responsible for producing specific proposals based on its recommendations. As far as the membership of the inquiries is concerned, Michael Foot made the sweeping criticism that 'on most of these inquiries the Government appoint many of the people who are responsible for having got the industry into this mess'.[68] Looking back some thirty years later, Wilson remarked about the two chairmen responsible for the Plant Report that Portal was 'a wrong choice for the thing . . . he was in part in the film industry but he was a tycoon and a monopolist in his own area', while

Plant 'was a laissez-faire economist. This was a chap the Department of the Board of Trade would choose . . . his prejudices were certainly for less state intervention'.[69] It is clear from the memorandum that Wilson was worried about this at the time, and had been talking to Plant in the hope of preventing the Committee from making firm recommendations against action. He wrote:

> I very much hope that we shall ensure that Plant leaves the door open one way or the other or we shall be acutely embarrassed if we attempt to introduce a more radical policy. But you will recall that we are under commitment to bring before the Cabinet, as soon as the Plant report is in, our views on the ultimate objective and immediate methods of film policy, with particular reference to any proposals that Plant may make. It is now clear that the Plant proposals will be very limited in character and therefore I think we must give immediate consideration to the problem I have set out above and to the means, whether as in my proposals or by some other method, of dealing with it.[70]

In the event, the Plant Report was rather more favourable, from Wilson's point of view, than had been expected, since the recommendation for an independent authority prepared the way for a considerable extension of public control. It was, moreover, couched in conveniently vague terms which left the government to determine more precisely what power the authority might have. The trade certainly regarded the proposal as a potential threat and, when consulted on the Report, all the employers' associations strongly opposed it. On this point the KRS was the most outspoken and asked indignantly:

> On what ground did the Plant Committee presume, with no vestige of supporting evidence, to assert that a lay body, however well intentioned, would be more competent to direct the affairs of a large and highly complicated industry than those who have made it their life's work and who are responsible for the success it has achieved?[71]

The Board of Trade official responsible for summarising the results of consultation with the industry gave the impression that no one dissented from the KRS view. His comment read:

> Every organisation is strongly opposed to this recommendation, believing that adequate machinery already exists in the trade itself to deal with any problems and that nothing but harm could come from interference by an outside body with insufficient technical knowledge.[72]

Although it was true that none of the organisations consulted had

222

expressed support for the proposal as it stood, the above comments were a flagrant misrepresentation of the views of most of the film unions. The ETU had not opposed an authority, but had stipulated that it should not be composed entirely of lay members. Both the ETU and Equity had made it clear that their general criticism of the Plant recommendations was that they were inadequate, so it could hardly be supposed that they considered existing arrangements satisfactory.[73] The ACT did not consider it necessary to outline its criticisms of the report, since in November 1949 a mass meeting of the union had passed a resolution reaffirming support for the ACT's own much more radical recommendations for extending the powers of the NFFC, setting up a state-owned distributor and a fourth circuit, and imposing a higher quota.[74] George Elvin clarified his union's position by publicly dissenting from the report of the trade committee of the CFC on the Plant proposals. This report, while accepting Plant's general contention that trading practices were too rigid, had rejected not only the proposal for a tribunal but most of the minor practical recommendations for increasing competition. In his note of dissent, Elvin wrote:

> I hold that the time has come to stop trying to make minor improvements here and there. Both the mild proposals of the Plant Report and the still milder proposals of the Committee of Trade members may result in a little benefit to the producer but will completely fail to put either the production industry or the British film industry as a whole on a healthy basis.
>
> Neither I personally, nor my trade union, has ever advocated nationalisation of the British film industry. I do not do so now, but I fail to see how the industry can be put on a satisfactory basis unless some organisation emerges with such strength as can act as an effective competitor to the existing combines, and particularly will pay prime regard to the interest of the producer and not have its production policy dominated by exhibition and distribution interests. In my view only the State is in a strong enough position to do this.[75]

The establishment of an independent authority would certainly not have satisfied the unions, but it was clearly misleading to suggest that they were opposed to the idea in the same way as the employers. By presenting the views of the industry in this way, the civil servants gave the impression that such an authority would be universally unpopular, a prospect which was clearly discouraging and cast doubts even on whether such a body would be able to command sufficient co-operation to function at all. Whether Wilson accepted the view of the officials, or was simply too preoccupied with other problems to contest it, is not clear; but no steps were taken to establish either the authority or a panel of the kind outlined in the memorandum.

The action which was eventually taken to assist producers was in line with recommendations from the trade to the extent that it involved a reduction in Entertainments duty. Tax relief was, however, linked with an agreement on the part of the exhibitors to contribute a proportion of their takings to a fund from which payments were made to boost the receipts of British films. The effect was to adjust the distribution of takings in favour of producers, which was roughly what the BFPA had suggested in its proposal to the Plant Committee.

At the time it seemed as if a marked shift in government thinking had taken place between the end of 1949, when Wilson had referred critically to the 'unaccustomed and sinister unanimity of all sections of the trade' in the campaign against Entertainments tax,[76] and the middle of 1950 when the scheme was announced. This received some comment in the study of the industry done by Political and Economic Planning, which suggested that the government was influenced by the 'constructive' approach to the Plant report of the Cinematograph Films Council trade committee. The trade committee's submission was described as 'one of the most astute acts of "government relations" that the industry ever carried out'.[77] The strategy of the trade after publication of the Plant report was certainly skilful, involving on the one hand intractable opposition to certain of the recommendations, and on the other hand the provision of detailed comments and suggestions relating to other recommendations. But the trade committee's own report can hardly have been a major influence since, by the time it was presented in June 1950, the scheme had already been prepared after months of interdepartmental consultation.

As early as February 1949, Wilson was aware that the NFFC alone would probably not solve the shortage of production finance, and he raised with the Bank of England the problem that, although the NFFC was providing end money, the banks were still hesitating to put up front money. Over the next year the Board of Trade also obtained figures on the costs and earnings of films, which indicated that all the major producers were failing to recoup their costs. In November 1949 Wilson indicated that further financial aid was under consideration, but that no decision would be taken until the Plant and Gater reports were published. Meanwhile Board of Trade officials were seeking information about the subsidies recently introduced in France and Italy, and looking into the question of whether a subsidy would contravene the GATT, in particular Article 4, which confined internal quantitative restrictions relating to films to screen quotas.

Consideration for the terms of the GATT was not the only reason the government was anxious to avoid providing a direct subsidy. The Treasury was opposed to a subsidy paid out of box office receipts because of a general dislike of parafiscal aids and an attachment to the principle that special taxes, like the road tax, should be treated as a general revenue. There was also a danger that any form of subsidy would encourage other industries to clamour for similar favours. Officials were effectively searching for something which worked like a subsidy but which would not be seen to be subsidy. The solution was the Eady Levy, named after Sir Wilfred Eady, the Treasury official concerned. The plan involved reductions in Entertainments duty and certain increases in cinema seat prices which were expected to have the combined effect of increasing the industry's annual income by £3 million. Half this was to be retained by the exhibitors; the other half was to be paid by voluntary agreement into a fund for producers of British films. Payments made to producers would be based on the box office earnings of their films. Thus, despite government protestations to the contrary, the Eady Levy was very like an automatic subsidy.

Board of Trade officials were encouraged by the precedent set by France and Italy, but they did not follow closely the example of either country. The British system was simpler and was designed for one purpose only, to increase the proportion of the industry's takings accruing to one section of the industry. The differences in the character of the subsidies no doubt reflect different administrative traditions. Whereas the British officials favoured a policy of minimal interference and had confidence in the operation of market forces, their continental counterparts had a more *dirigiste* approach. The subsidy in France and Italy was used as an instrument of policy to encourage certain developments in the industry.

The French aid was first introduced in September 1948 and, like the Eady Levy, was intended as a temporary expedient. Redistribution of revenue was achieved by an additional tax on the box office which went to a fund, the *Fonds d'aide*, from which payments were made to producers in proportion to their receipts. These payments, however, were different from normal receipts in that they had to be reinvested in future films and so served to encourage continuity of production. Also, in calculating a company's entitlement to aid, foreign receipts were not only taken into account but were treated as twice the value of domestic earnings, so that there was a built-in incentive to producers to produce for export. Exhibitors received no compensating tax rebate in this scheme, but they were entitled to aid to repair or modernise their cinemas. In the Italian case, the incentives were designed to encourage a certain kind of production. A law was passed at the end of 1949 which gave producers a subsidy of 10 per cent on their receipts but allowed for an additional 8 per cent to be paid in the case of films of particular artistic value. The principle of using aid as a means of directing private enterprise was elaborated later in both countries. France began to experiment with measures which discriminated in favour of work designated as of artistic merit, first in the form of cash prizes and later through the much more complex arrangements associated with the policy of *Arts et Essai*.[78]

The British officials took note of the arrangements already existing in France and Italy, but they did not put forward the possibility of following a similar path and using aid as a means of control. As it was, if anything the levy reinforced the existing trade structure. Producers received payments in proportion to the box office earnings of their films, so those who benefited most were those already favoured by the system of distribution and exhibition. No precedent was established for discriminatory payments of any kind, and this left the trade in a strong position to resist suggestions, which were made later, to adopt some of the principles involved in the French system which make it possible to encourage the production of 'art films'.

The Board of Trade officials were primarily preoccupied with the problem of how to gain trade co-operation for the Eady Levy and avoid a new confrontation with the Americans. From this point of view, the less interventionist the arrangement was the better. The exhibitors were expected to constitute the principal source of opposition but, in the event, the CEA General Council accepted the scheme, apparently because they thought – mistakenly – that it would be blocked by the KRS.[79] The government was therefore able to go ahead and introduce into the Finance Bill the necessary changes in Entertainments tax on 3 July 1950.

The scheme was presented to the trade as a temporary measure to last a year only, but in 1951 the government again used the Entertainments tax as a bargaining counter and succeeded in gaining a three-year extension. The scheme became statutory in 1957, although the government held to the view that the levy did not constitute a subsidy.

11 In Search of a Policy

> If the public considers it desirable for political, cultural or
> economic reasons that British films should be produced, then
> it must be prepared for the Government not only to protect
> the industry indefinitely, but also to aid it financially for as
> far ahead as can be seen.
>
> Political and Economic Planning,
> *The British Film Industry*, 1952

Financial aid for British production, in the form of the Eady Levy and
the NFFC, was introduced just when the film industry was on the brink of
the long period of decline and adjustment associated with the spread of
television. The BBC reintroduced its television service in 1947, and two
years later cinema admissions began to fall. In the mid-1950s, when
commercial television was on the air, this downward slide continued,
and it was soon aggravated by a spate of cinema closures. By 1960 the
cinema had lost two-thirds of its 1950 audience; in the next decade it lost
half of what remained.[1]

The drop in revenue was not as severe as the fall in attendances
because admission prices were rising steeply. Gross revenue nevertheless
fell by about a half between 1953 and 1963.[2] Such a severe contraction of
the home market naturally had far-reaching effects on the strategy
pursued by the trade. Producers began to look increasingly to revenue
from exports and sales to television.

While the industry was adapting in a variety of ways to the new
circumstances, official policy scarcely changed. After a prolonged trade
campaign Entertainments Tax was eventually reduced and was finally
abolished in 1960. No other help was offered to exhibitors. In relation to
production, the main shift in government thinking was that financial
assistance, originally conceived as a temporary expedient, came to be
regarded as a long-term requirement. The assistance continued to be
offered in the form of an automatic subsidy and quasi-commercial loans.
Acts in 1960, 1967 and 1970 prolonged the life of the Eady Levy and the
NFFC, and also perpetuated the exhibitors' quota.

The new and crucial problem of regulating relations between the
cinema and television was left to the trade.[3] Exhibitors and producers

were, as usual, too divided to adopt a coherent strategy, but confrontation gradually gave way to collaboration. The CEA at first tried to minimise the impact of television on its members by restricting the showing of cinema films on the small screen. In 1952 a boycott was instituted, first against companies that sold films to television, and later just against the films concerned. However, the CEA was unable to prevent the other trade associations signing an agreement with the BBC for the sale of films in 1956. The following year ABC Television started to show a series of Alexander Korda's films, and the BBC announced the acquisition of the television rights for seven years to one hundred RKO features. By 1958 the two channels between them were showing 150 films per year.[4] The trade united again briefly to form the Film Industry Defence Organisation (FIDO), a body financed to acquire the rights to films to prevent them from being sold to television. The arrangement only partly succeeded, and after six years FIDO ceased trading.

By this time links were growing between the film industry and television, or more specifically between the film industry and Independent Television. Film companies benefited from the new market by making material for television and by acquiring interests in the broadcasting business. One of the most long-lasting links between cinema and television was forged when Sidney Bernstein's Granada group was given the television franchise for northern England. The major producers also attempted to enter the field. ABPC acquired a controlling interest in Thames Television in the mid-1960s; British Lion joined an unsuccessful group to bid for the franchise for Yorkshire Television in 1967; and Rank acquired a 38 per cent interest in Southern Television in 1972.

The long-standing problem of monopoly in the film trade, which had been shelved after the Plant Report, remained a live issue. However, despite continuing criticism successive governments declined to reopen the matter. Meanwhile, competition for a shrinking audience accentuated the old conflicts between the circuit owners and independents. In exhibition, the conditions of decline directly favoured an extension of monopoly. As admissions fell, the independents were caught in a vicious circle: as their takings decreased they became less able to modernise their cinemas, which became less attractive so that takings decreased still further. The circuit owners, and to a lesser extent the owners of chains, were in a better position to use the capital assets which their cinemas represented. By selling off or redeveloping some of their halls they could afford to modernise the remainder. Some critics accused the circuits of adopting a policy in relation to closures that was designed to inflict maximum damage on their competitors by, for instance, hesitating to close a hall when there was a rival in the area, and closing others too readily where there was no alternative. It was even alleged that in some instances Rank closed a viable cinema and refused to lease or sell it to an independent.[5]

There were also complaints that the restrictive trading practices which put the independents at a disadvantage were increasing. Changes in the release pattern and more frequent use of extended runs made traditional barring arrangements more irksome, but in some cases the circuits also started to impose time and distance bars in excess of those normally agreed between distributor and exhibitor. One of the most extreme examples, frequently cited at the time, was the case of the Glasgow circuit that introduced 70mm projection and proceeded to extend its bars to cover the whole of Scotland. The trading practices of the distributors' association were also considered to be increasingly unreasonable. In addition to suffering from the KRS ban on co-operative booking, independents had to contend with a ban on the use of their premises for other purposes, such as bingo.

Whether by fair competition or through such practices, it is clear that during the 1950s and 1960s Rank and ABPC consolidated their hold over exhibition. In 1944 they owned between them 22 per cent of halls; by 1965 they owned 29 per cent. Calculated in terms of cinema seats, this figure rises to 44 per cent. The quality of the cinemas was high, enabling the circuits to increase admission prices and modernise their premises. The circuits owned the majority of London cinemas, giving them a powerful position in the exhibition sphere but also considerable influence over production, as explained by Vicki Eves in 1970:

> Their ownership of the majority of London cinemas adds extra power to their exhibition chains, because, when booking a film for London, they book it for all their suitable first-run houses elsewhere. Many other independent and minor circuit houses, in areas where one or both of the two majors have no cinemas, will automatically take the film up and lesser houses will take the film on its second run. . . . Thus, without any extensive activity in the production field, Rank and ABPC are able to influence the kind of films made. Few distributors, other than British Lion, will back films that they consider to be unacceptable to the two combines and British Lion may be avoided by a British producer because of the distribution disadvantages and for this reason films that step outside the requirements of Rank and ABPC may never be made.[6]

The independent producer was even more disadvantaged than before. Following reorganisation by the Rank group, one of the circuits eventually disappeared. This development took place in two phases. First, in 1958 Rank amalgamated its best Odeons and Gaumonts to form the 'Rank Release' circuit, and linked the inferior ones with some independents to form a new third circuit, the 'National Release'. The latter was a very inferior affair, both for the distributor and for the cinema audience. It became progressively less attractive as its cinemas dwindled in numbers, and in 1963 it was abandoned. Fewer films could be accommodated on the two remaining circuits at a time when they represented an ever increasing share of the market.[7]

Trade politics at this time were marked by an attempt by some independents to organise themselves in opposition to the combines. The Association of Independent Cinemas (AIC) was formed in 1953. This organisation, still in existence, has campaigned vigorously if unsuccessfully for anti-monopoly measures. In 1957 independent producers from inside and outside the BFPA joined together to set up the Federation of British Film Makers (FBFM). Eventually the two associations merged to form the Film Producers Association. In the late 1950s both the AIC and the FBFM played an important part in keeping the question of monopoly before the public and in lobbying the government to take further action.

In the early 1960s the President of the Board of Trade, Edward Heath, eventually responded to the pressure by referring the industry to the Monopolies Commission. This decision, however, was not welcomed by the critics of the combines because the Commission would take at least two years to deliver its report, and the move appeared to be a means of postponing action. George Elvin, General Secretary of the ACTT, commented at the union's 1965 Annual Conference: 'Why, in two years there may be hardly any independent producers left to raise even a feeble squeak of protest when, after the near elephantine period of gestation, the Monopolies Commission finally give birth to their report.'[8] Decisions were postponed for even longer than two years because, when the report was finally issued in October 1966, very little time was left to consider its findings before the films legislation was due to expire in 1967. Acting on advice from the industry, the government simply passed an Act extending existing legislation until 1970.

The report,[9] based on the most comprehensive survey of the industry conducted since the 1952 and 1958 studies by PEP, substantiated most of the criticisms of the combines, but did not support any of the remedies suggested. The Commission found that a monopoly situation, as defined by the 1948 Act,[10] did exist in that 'more than one third by value (as measured by licence fees paid by exhibitor to distributor) of the films supplied for exhibition in Great Britain' were supplied in circumstances that restricted competition.[11] The circumstances named were Rank's share of the supply of films; the lack of competition between Rank and ABC; the practices of barring and of conditional booking; the KRS ban on co-operative booking by independents, and its ban on the use of cinema premises for purposes other than showing films. The Commission found that 'these conditions operate and can be expected to operate against the public interest'.[12]

Despite this indictment of the industry, the Commission recommended only a few minor changes, such as the relaxation of bars; the introduction of more flexible booking policies; an element of competitive bidding; and

230

the abolition of the KRS' two restrictive practices. Referring to more radical suggestions, the Commission commented: 'Given the situation as it now exists we are impressed by the formidable and probably expensive practical problems in the way of adopting any of the proposals.'[13] Even those measures suggested were to be implemented not by an independent body, but by the trade itself. As an editorial in *Film and TV Technician* put it: 'In broad terms they ask the poachers to turn gamekeeper and voluntarily ameliorate some of their own shortcomings'.[14]

In the years following the inquiry the trend towards monopoly continued. By 1972 the circuits between them accounted for 32 per cent of cinemas, 52 per cent of admissions and 52 per cent of takings. In 1978, after an extensive programme of doubling and tripling of halls, they accounted for 37 per cent of all cinema screens.[15]

A new factor was that while the circuit owners were increasing their share of the film business, film interests were decreasing in importance in relation to other company activities. In the case of Rank, this came about through the company's own efforts to expand and diversify. The most important venture outside films was the acquisition of interests in Xerox, later transformed into a major share-holding in a separate company. ABPC branched out into television and other leisure activities in the 1960s, but did not develop on the same scale as Rank. In 1969, however, the company was taken over by EMI, with its extensive music interests; ten years later EMI was swallowed up by Thorn, becoming Thorn-EMI.

While little was done at any stage to help the independent exhibitor, the establishment of the NFFC had been justified partly on the grounds that it would help to sustain an independent element in distribution and production. As we have seen, however, the Corporation's ability to help producers was limited from the start, since it had no powers over distribution and exhibition. And since its main function was to provide risk money on terms a private investor would not consider, it was almost inevitable that it should suffer regular losses. Its capital was slowly eroded, and its influence, such as it was, diminished. A summary of the NFFC's activities up to 1972 shows that in this period it received £7 million from the Treasury; advanced £28 million to assist 731 long films and 173 'shorts'; and lost £6.2 million but had also paid £2.9 million to the Treasury as interest. However, these dealings were not spread evenly throughout the Corporation's career. 1964 can be seen as a turning point. Up to then it had supported 640 long films, the lowest number backed in any one year being 27 and the highest 63. The sums advanced per year ranged from just under £1 million to just under £2 million. In 1964 there was a sharp drop in investment – only 18 films were supported, and less than £500,000 was advanced. Late in 1966 normal lending was suspended because the revolving fund was exhausted, and it was not resumed until the middle of 1967. The 1970 Films Act, intended to give the Corporation a new lease of life, was nullified by the decision of the incoming Conservative government not to advance funds made available under the Act.

Although the NFFC was not empowered to act as a distributor, it was intended that it should promote the development of a private renter with no links with either circuit, to handle the products of independent producers. In the short term this arrangement proved extremely damaging to the Corporation in that the bankruptcy of the chosen agent, British Lion, caused it to lose over half its initial allocation of capital. The crisis and its sequel also showed up the contradictions inherent in the NFFC's brief. In order to maintain a third force in distribution it took over the bankrupt company, but with a clear commitment to return it to the private sector as soon as possible. In its subsequent dealings with British Lion the NFFC was consistently the loser.

In 1957 David Kingsley, formerly managing director of the NFFC, became managing director of British Lion and brought on to the Board the film producers John and Roy Boulting, Frank Launder and Sidney Gilliat. Kingsley and the four directors were allowed to acquire shares in the company, each paying the modest sum of £1,800 for their holding. During the following years the fortunes of the company improved and in 1962, for the first time, a dividend was paid. The NFFC report of 1964 gives four reasons for the improvement: reduction in overheads; increased exploitation of the film library; profits from Launder and Gilliat and Boulting Brothers' films; and an increasingly 'discriminating' use of funds. Ironically, this increasing discrimination was partly achieved at the expense of the NFFC, which had backed a number of unprofitable films made by satellite companies attached to but not funded by British Lion. Conversely, the NFFC had not been asked to participate in the more successful films financed by British Lion.

In its next transaction with the company the NFFC again ended up arranging a poor deal for itself. In 1963 it bought back the shares belonging to the directors in preparation for the long intended sale to private interests, and paid out £158,735 for these holdings acquired six years previously for £9,000. The intended sale was strongly opposed by most independent producers, and criticism mounted when it leaked out that the prospective purchaser was Sidney Box, a producer who had close links with Rank. In the FBFM report of 1964 the suggestion was made that the circuit owners had influenced the decision:

> The independent status of British Lion had been preserved partly because of the personalities in control and partly because of the psychological effect of the Government having a 50 per cent holding. It is significant that the monopolies' increasing pressure on British Lion in 1963 coincided with the growth of reports that the NFFC was a somewhat unhappy and reluctant partner in the fight to maintain the independence of the company.[16]

Following numerous letters to the press and a lively debate in Parliament, the government agreed to postpone the sale and to introduce into the terms of sale certain safeguards. The Corporation was to retain one special preference share, entitling it to receive the benefit of the tax loss carried forward from the old British Lion losses, and also conferring on it the right to veto any future sale of the company or of its subsidiary, Shepperton Studios. These safeguards, however, proved to have relatively little influence on the course of events. The initial purchaser was a group headed by Michael Balcon; but only two years later Balcon resigned, and after that the character of the Board changed. General business interests came to predominate over specific film interests. In 1968 the company went public and a sale was permitted to Hambros Bank. The company was now valued at £3 million, nearly twice the 1963 valuation. Shortly afterwards profits began to fall, and in 1972 a new sale was planned to Barclay Securities, a company which had acquired some notoriety as an asset stripper. The film unions strongly resisted the sale, but in 1973 British Lion eventually passed to another property company interested in developing the land occupied by Shepperton Studios. An agreement permitted the sale of 40 out of 60 acres, on condition that the remaining studio facilities were retained and modernised. The distributing and financing side of the business was discontinued.

A HOLLYWOOD COLONY?

The eclipse of the NFFC and of British Lion was related to the changing role of American interests in the industry, as well as to the growing power of the circuits. During the 1950s the American companies became far more willing to invest in British production and to distribute British films. By the 1960s American capital was flowing into the industry on an unprecedented scale. As the Americans became more involved in film finance, there was a corresponding decline in the part played by British finance and British renters. Over a period of twenty years, the American share of British distribution increased from 10 per cent to 60 per cent (see Table XXIII).[17] American involvement reached its peak in the late 1960s when, according to NFFC figures, some 80–90 per cent of films made in Britain had American backing (see Tables XXIV[18] and XXV[19]).

The encouragement of American finance for British films had been an aim of the British Treasury since the 1930s: the triple quota clause in the 1938 Films Act, the wartime financial arrangements with America, the monetary quota system, and the Anglo-American Film Agreements of the 1940s and early 1950s all sought to entice dollars. However, it was not until after 1950 that investment occurred on a large scale; and this was less a result of British films policy than the outcome of changes in the American industry that made the prospect of overseas investment more tempting. Even so, once the Americans decided to come to Britain, the

TABLE XXIII
us majors' share of British distribution

	1950	1958	1970
Total films distributed	400	360	235
Total British films distributed	72	84	74
% of total films distributed by us majors	68%	65%	75%
% of British films distributed by us majors	10%	42%	60%

TABLE XXIV
British first features shown on the two major circuits 1962–71

Year	No. of films	% wholly or partly us-financed
1962	46	43
1963	50	46
1964	56	59
1965	48	64
1966	51	71
1967	50	72
1968	49	88
1969	45	78
1970	44	66
1971	50	50

TABLE XXV
American finance in British production

Year	No. of films	% us finance
1965	69	75
1966	70	75
1967	68	90

weakness of the legislation ostensibly designed to protect the British film industry from American competition influenced the scale of American penetration.

The Paramount anti-trust case of 1948 was only one factor in the shift away from Hollywood-based mass production.[20] But it meant that the American majors, forced to relinquish their exhibition interests, had to protect their traditional dominance of the American and overseas markets by adopting new distribution strategies. Exhibitors were also concerned about the decline in the number of films released. In 1937 the majors released 408 features, a figure that remained more or less constant until the early 1950s; but by 1955 the number had fallen to 215, and by 1960 to 151.[21] For the first time American exhibitors were interested in solving the product shortage by showing foreign films, and the majors were determined that some of these films had American financial participation. As Thomas Guback wrote in 1967:

> This represents an interesting reversal of policy for the American majors. Until the series of anti-trust suits which culminated around 1950, the self-interest of Hollywood producers dictated that foreign films be kept out of the US so that company-owned theatres could exhibit company-made films. When vertical integration was dissolved, and with runaway production becoming important, the self-interest of the major companies dictated that foreign films (in which they had investments) be brought into the foreign market so that investments in them could be amortised.[22]

'Runaway production' was the term used to describe co-productions and productions partly or wholly American-financed, initially because of the Film Agreements and the need to utilise blocked earnings in accordance with 'permitted uses', which included producing films in Britain. These were distributed in the US, but usually more money left Britain than returned.

The contribution of the Eady Levy to the influx of American capital in the 1950s and 1960s is difficult to assess. Guback has argued that the rate and character of the subsidy was a crucial inducement for the US majors and independents to establish British subsidiaries. The Monopolies Commission report also emphasised the point: 'Production in Britain is economically attractive to United States film companies both because of the lower production costs and because of the subsidy provided by the British Film Fund Agency.'[23] During the 1960s American films financed abroad rose from 35 per cent to 60 per cent of the total output of American producers.[24] The Eady Levy, based on box-office takings, was a high rate of subsidy compared with its European counterparts, and also, as Guback commented:

> American companies avail themselves of the British subsidy by adhering to the legal criteria of what constitutes a 'British' film as defined in the Films Act. . . . The Films Act says nothing about the nationalities of the stockholders or where the overall control of the company is exercised, nor does the law set requirements for the source of the production money. Thus, in organising a British subsidiary, an American parent can incorporate the company under British laws and appoint a majority of British subjects to the board of directors. The result is a British company whose affairs are conducted by directors predominantly British but which is owned by, and has its overall policies set by, the American parent.[25]

Some American companies drew large sums from the Fund. *Goldfinger* and *Tom Jones* – 'British' films made with American participation – each retained over a million dollars. *Variety*, the American trade paper, claimed that *Thunderball* took $2.1 million, or 15 per cent of the Fund, and quoted a British producer in 1966 as saying: 'We have a thriving film production industry in this country which is virtually owned, lock, stock and barrel, by Hollywood.'[26] It seemed that the Production Fund, originally intended to aid British producers, was more remunerative to the Americans. The irony of the situation was pointed out by Alexander Walker in his study of the British film industry in the 1960s:

> One had to be successful to qualify. If one was, one didn't need it. If one wasn't, one didn't get it. In this lay a 'Catch-22' situation for the independent British film makers. What the levy did was make the rich man richer still. Successful American companies with tied relationships to the cinema circuits were in better shape to profit from the levy than their wholly British counterparts. So not only was the home market inadequate to give milk to keep the local producers happy, but also its very cream went to keep the foreigners fat.[27]

Despite this, not all American companies considered the Levy as the major incentive for production in Britain, and as Vincent Porter has argued, it was perhaps only one factor among many which enticed dollars:

> The factors which attract foreign investment are many and complex, including the nature of the subject, the suitability of British locations, the availability of studio space and creative and technical personnel, the exchange rate of the pound, and thus the dollar costs of technical labour, of hiring lights, equipment and post-production facilities, as well as the attractions of the Eady Levy. It is only if all the other factors are equal that the Eady incentive will tip the scales in Britain's favour.[28]

Indeed, in the 1970s, despite the existence of the Levy, American investment in British production declined. And so it appears that in the 1950s and 1960s it was a combination of inducements, rather than just the existence of the Eady money, that explains the high levels of American participation in British film-making.

The other inducements were economic and cultural. The exchange rate favoured the dollar, making production in Britain an attractive financial proposition. Studio facilities and labour costs were cheaper in Britain than in Hollywood, and there was an exodus of directors and stars from the US after the anti-Communist purge by the House Committee on Un-American Activities. In the Spring 1966 issue of *Sight and Sound*, Penelope Houston wrote an article entitled 'England, their

England' about why Britain had become a popular production centre: her list of comparative newcomers included Truffaut, Kubrick, Antonioni, Joseph Losey and Dick Lester. The presence of American finance was noted:

> MGM money backs Kubrick and Antonioni; MCA backs Truffaut; Fox money backs Losey. British crews make the pictures, which means that they qualify for quota and Eady money here; and once they get outside British territorial waters . . . they can always haul up the Stars and Stripes.[29]

Another reason for the proliferation of American finance was the emergence, in the late 1950s, of new styles and themes in British cinema. In the early 1950s American companies showed little enthusiasm for backing films that looked 'British'. Instead American productions in Britain, and co-productions with British companies, were often Hollywood-style films made on location. In 1957 Sam Spiegel, an American, made *The Bridge on the River Kwai*, technically a British film but essentially a 'mid-Atlantic' production geared to the international market. This sort of collaboration was useful in the sense that expertise and finance backed British production, but the trend did little to promote films that were characteristically British.

Although the emergence of the New Cinema in Britain – with films like *Look Back in Anger, Room at the Top, The Entertainer, Saturday Night and Sunday Morning, A Taste of Honey, A Kind of Loving* and *Billy Liar* – coincided with the influx of American capital, the relationship between the two is complex. Many of the films were made by independent British companies, but the finance did not always come from British sources, and by the mid-1960s it was hard to find British films without some form of American participation. However, the breakthrough of the New Cinema owed much to developments outside the film industry, like the revival of British theatre heralded by the production in 1956 of John Osborne's *Look Back in Anger*. Many new writers had their works adapted for the screen.

Three main British independent film companies were associated with the New Cinema – Bryanston, Woodfall and Allied Film Makers. Bryanston was started in 1959 by several established producers who had previously worked with Ealing or Rank. It was linked with British Lion and Shepperton studios and, under the influence of its chairman, Michael Balcon, set out to make inexpensive films designed primarily for the British market. The company suffered a major setback, however, when the backing of *Tom Jones* was lost to United Artists in 1962.[30] Woodfall was set up by Tony Richardson and John Osborne. Richardson, along with other future feature directors such as Lindsay Anderson and Karel Reisz, had been associated with the Free Cinema movement – a group of film enthusiasts who were active in the mid-1950s writing film criticism and making their first short films, some of them aided by the BFI's Experimental Film Fund.[31] Allied Film Makers, formed in 1959 and linked with Rank for distribution purposes, included the production team set up by Richard Attenborough and the actor and screenwriter Bryan Forbes. This partnership had made a reputation with *The Angry Silence*, and went on to make some of the more successful of the company's films, like *The League of Gentlemen*.

It is clear that the early phase of 'runaway production' indirectly helped the British industry by encouraging higher technical standards and bringing in finance for modernisation. However, with the exception of Warners' backing for Woodfall's first film, *Look Back in Anger*, American companies did little to promote this kind of cinema during the initial, most risky period when its actors and directors were virtually unknown. American money followed rather than precipitated the new-found success of British films abroad. Karel Reisz's *Saturday Night and Sunday Morning*, a joint venture by Bryanston and Woodfall released in 1960, made £500,000 for the two companies. It was the popularity and success of the New Cinema which attracted American investment; and after 1961 it became increasingly difficult to define any part of the industry as British rather than Anglo-American. There was too much working against the British independent companies: the monopolistic structure of the industry; the lack of alternative sources of finance; the weakness of the NFFC; and the willingness of British producers to accept American backing.

During the 50s and 60s, the attitude of British film interests to the American companies was naturally more complex than at the time when American influence was perceived in terms of the domination of the screen by American imports. Although American control was arguably more complete than when exerted indirectly, the finance provided new opportunities for producers and more work for technicians. Independent producers found American assistance far more effective than the NFFC or British Lion. American finance was usually in the form of a 100 per cent guarantee, whereas British guarantees were seldom more than 70 per cent. American sponsorship made independents less susceptible to the domination of Rank and ABPC, and they actively defended the American majors in the face of complaints from the British combines that too much of the aid intended for British producers was being taken by subsidiaries of American companies. One of the reasons for the formation of the Federation of British Film Makers was

> the feeling that an important body of makers of British films had been isolated because they had American finance or distribution. With a membership that includes representatives of some of the major Anglo-American organisations the Federation has helped greatly to

238

influence the climate of opinion and to reduce the old suspicions and hostility.[32]

During the deliberations about the 1960 Films Act, the FBFM successfully resisted an attempt to introduce into the new Act a more stringent definition of 'British' that would have prevented many American-backed films from benefiting from quota and levy.[33]

In February 1966, the House of Lords debated the question of American finance in the British film industry. Lord Willis, President of the Writers' Guild and director of two small independent film companies, spelt out the link between the legislation and American domination:

> These three measures [quota, NFFC and the Eady Levy] . . . were all intended to help British film production, and were mainly directed to the task of preventing our own native film industry from being swallowed up and dominated by the immensely powerful American industry. . . . By a strange paradox, most of our film legislation has had an effect which is the precise opposite of its intentions. Far from giving British film producers greater independence and finance, it has weakened them. And far from preventing American domination of the British film industry, American domination was never so complete and overwhelming as it is today.[34]

It would appear that the Treasury's aim of encouraging American finance had been fulfilled. In the long term, however, the price paid was the continuation of inadequate protective measures, and the consolidation of the monopolistic structure of the British film industry.[35]

INTO THE 70S

In the early 1970s American investment in British films declined dramatically. In 1968 the American majors imported £31.3 million for production by their British subsidiaries, but by 1974 this had fallen to £2.9 million (see Table XXVI).[36] The majors had suffered catastrophic losses between 1969 and 1971 – MGM showed a loss of $53 million in 1969, for instance – and were forced to retrench, though by 1972 they were beginning to recover.[37]

Towards the end of the 1960s many British films backed by American finance failed to do well, especially overseas. Alexander Walker has argued that there were cultural as well as economic reasons for the withdrawal of American capital: the 'British' films sponsored by American companies began to appeal less and less to American audiences, as the early films of the 'New American Cinema' like *In the Heat of the Night*, *The Graduate* and *Easy Rider* created a demand for more

239

TABLE XXVI
Imported capital for film production by British subsidiaries of the major American film companies (total receipts by UK subsidiaries)

Year	£ millions	Year	£ millions
1965	14.9	1973	4.8
1966	18.0	1974	2.9
1967	22.8	1975	4.2
1968	31.3	1976	4.8
1969	20.9	1977	5.3
1970	12.8	1978	7.9
1971	18.6	1979	6.0
1972	14.0		

indigenous themes that reflected social changes in America.[38] While this is partly true, the main reason the majors reduced financial commitment abroad was economic rather than cultural or social. The companies had overspent and overstocked with films. The market (domestic, foreign and sales from television distribution) could support an investment of about $500 million, but in 1968 the total investment in films for current release was a staggering $1.2 billion.[39] The 'back to Hollywood' movement was also encouraged by changes in American tax law, making it possible for producers to deduct 7 per cent of a film's production cost from their tax bill. And as an ACTT report explained in 1973:

> The US Export-Import Bank can now finance up to 80 per cent of the foreign rights of a domestically produced film. . . . Income tax can also be deferred on a film's foreign earnings if the money is re-invested in another domestically made film which can be exported. On a wider front, the US Government is using GATT negotiations to force countries to lift restrictions on the importation of US films, and finally the two successive devaluations of the dollar will raise the American film industry's foreign earnings while at the same time considerably reducing the financial attraction of overseas production.[40]

After a series of management reshuffles, the majors had recovered by the mid-1970s and began to invest more in Britain, but not on the scale of the 1960s. The Hollywood companies were powerful mainly because of their hold over distribution and its tendency to be the cornerstone of production finance. In the 1970s the dominant film culture was the 'big-budget' movie; and once again Hollywood called the tune by expanding the market and inflating production costs.[41]

The American model of the blockbuster film was followed by the British majors in the 1970s – EMI, Lord Grade's Associated Communications Corporation (ACC) and Rank (although Rank considerably reduced production in this period). These companies financed and co-financed films like *Close Encounters of the Third Kind* (financed by EMI and Columbia), and produced overseas – *Convoy*, *The Driver* and *The Deer Hunter* (EMI); *The Boys from Brazil*, *Capricorn One* and *Love and Bullets* (ACC). EMI provided all the finance for *Death on the Nile* and *Murder on the Orient Express*, both films with 'international appeal'. The results of this type of production from the point of view of Britain's balance of payments were very encouraging, as Table XXVII illustrates.[42]

By the end of the decade, however, it was clear that the British majors were less successful from a cultural point of view. New directors went to Hollywood for backing, rather than to EMI or ACC.[43] The latter were reluctant to use promising but untried talent on international pictures because of the high risk involved. The tax situation in Britain, and the greater variety of finance available in America, encouraged a 'talent drain' from Britain. In 1980, the American director Norman Jewison was reported to have asked: 'How is it that the hot group of directors in Hollywood right now are all British, and yet there are virtually no British pictures? Why don't EMI and Lew Grade finance the local talent? Whatever happened to fifty years of British film-making experience?'[44]

In 1970 the Labour government intended to inject £5 million into the NFFC, but the incoming Conservative government reduced this figure to £1.5 million and promised a further £1 million on condition that the NFFC could attract £3 million from private sources. In 1972 John Terry, a solicitor who had joined the NFFC in 1949 and who became its managing director in 1958, set up a Consortium with private investors. £1 million was duly advanced by the government, and ten groups in the private sector contributed £750,000. But the record was poor: in its first six years the Consortium financed the production of only nineteen features, one short and a television series. By 1978 the original capital of £1.75 million had earned only £464,000 in interest and profits.[45] In the 1970s the NFFC's role in financing British production was unspectacular: from 1973 to 1981 it loaned £4 million for the production of thirty-one features and six shorts. The two major handicaps continued to be inadequate capital resources and the constraint of having to function strictly on commercial lines 'at the riskiest end of a high risk industry'.[46] However, a significant achievement was the establishment of the National Film Development Fund in 1976. This was designed to provide finance for films at early stages of production and has since proved to be a crucial lifeline for some independents.

In January 1979, when John Terry retired, the Labour 'Films Minister', Michael Meacher, appointed Mamoun Hassan, a former head of the BFI Production Board, as managing director of the NFFC. Many hoped that this would herald the beginning of better prospects for the NFFC and the industry as a whole, particularly since at the same time Colin Young, the first principal of the National Film School, and Romaine Hart, an independent exhibitor and distributor, were made

241

TABLE XXVII

Net receipts from overseas for the performance and production of films, 1965–79

	Performances of films			Production of films			Total receipts		
	United Kingdom subsidiaries of major American companies (£ millions)	Other companies	All companies	United Kingdom subsidiaries of major American companies	Other companies	All companies	United Kingdom subsidiaries of major American companies	Other companies	All companies
1965	(10.4)	3.7	(6.7)	12.6	0.3	12.9	2.2	4.0	6.2
1966	(10.2)	4.6	(5.6)	13.0	1.3	14.3	2.8	5.9	8.7
1967	(6.2)	3.5	(2.7)	17.3	9.5	26.8	11.1	13.0	24.1
1968	(8.9)	3.2	(5.7)	26.4	2.4	28.8	17.5	5.6	23.1
1969	(8.5)	4.0	(4.5)	13.1	5.2	18.3	4.6	9.2	13.8
1970	(6.6)	2.9	(3.7)	11.9	3.2	15.1	5.3	6.1	11.4
1971	(7.9)	4.8	(3.1)	15.3	2.4	17.7	7.4	7.2	14.6
1972	(11.6)	3.6	(8.0)	13.8	2.6	16.4	2.2	6.2	8.4
1973	(8.0)	3.4	(4.6)	3.8	2.7	6.5	(4.2)	6.1	1.9
1974	(9.4)	7.2	(2.2)	2.6	6.1	8.7	(6.8)	13.3	6.5
1975	(10.4)	17.4	7.0	3.3	6.1	9.4	(7.1)	23.5	16.4
1976	(11.1)	17.5	6.4	4.3	8.8	13.1	(6.8)	26.3	19.5
1977	(14.5)	24.2	9.7	4.9	15.8	20.7	(9.6)	40.0	30.4
1978	(21.3)	34.7	13.4	3.9	25.2	29.1	(17.4)	59.9	42.5
1979	(24.7)	33.2	8.5	2.0	24.1	26.1	(22.7)	57.3	34.6

The statistics are those issued by the Department of Trade.

In the 1979 inquiry, revisions were made to the figures to allow for smaller film companies not adequately covered in previous inquiries. In this table, the revised figures have been used from 1974 onwards.

Figures in brackets: negative – i.e. represent a net overseas expenditure.

board members. When Hassan replaced Terry, he remarked optimistically: 'The last three managing directors . . . have been an accountant, a banker and a lawyer, so to appoint a film-maker is certainly curious, unless it means that the government has accepted that the situation has changed so drastically that it calls for a new approach'.[47] Shortly before Hassan took up his new appointment the NFFC had already started to support projects that were less 'trans-Atlantic', like James Ivory's *The Europeans*, Ken Loach's *Black Jack* and Franco Rosso's *Babylon*. Films like Bill Forsyth's *Gregory's Girl* obtained backing from the NFFC even though there were no major stars in the cast. The NFFC became vitally important in the financing of films unlikely to attract alternative backing and budgeted at a relatively modest level.

Some activity survived outside the orbit of the majors. However, neither the growth of a new independent sector nor the continued existence of more conventional forms of 'independent' production owed much to assistance provided under the Department of Trade.[48] An important factor was the determination of film-makers to find a means to work whatever the odds. 'Independent' film-making in the radical sense was based initially on unpaid labour and otherwise financed by small private loans and by grants from charities and political organisations. A few of the film-makers made a living working in commercial film, but many had no links with the industry and gained their introduction to film either through voluntary work in workshops and co-operatives or via training on a film course. In the commercial sphere new companies and production teams vigorously, although usually unsuccessfully, pursued new sources of finance. In this case, the existence of a pool of people with the ideas and experience to promote plausible feature projects was due as much to training and opportunities provided by television as to those offered in the film industry.

In the mid-1970s two associations were formed corresponding to the two concepts of 'independence'. The Association of Independent Producers (AIP), formed in 1976, drew its membership from producers, directors, writers and senior technicians working in the film and television industries. The principal aim of this association was to 'stimulate a new area of production – the low to modest budget commercial film – for cinema and television audiences'. The Independent Film-makers' Association (IFA), formed in 1974, brought together disparate individuals and groups engaged in various kinds of non-commercial film-making, and aimed to promote the production, distribution and exhibition of films outside the structure of mainstream cinema and television.

Both associations campaigned on issues relating to film and broadcasting policy, and to some extent were instrumental in opening up new opportunities for their members. They were active participants in the debate about the fourth television channel, lobbying for a structure favourable to independents. The IFA fought vigorously for a requirement that the new channel should be 'innovative'. Although most of their specific proposals, especially those of the IFA, were ignored, Channel Four, once established, did prove an important source of support for independent production. The policy associated with 'Film on Four' led to a modest revival in low budget feature production, and IFA members benefited from the new channel's appointment of a commissioning editor sympathetic to their aims. Cultural funding for film through the BFI Production Board and the Regional Arts Associations increased considerably in the late 1970s and early 1980s. This was partly due to pressure from the IFA and – before Channel Four money became available – had already transformed the basis for the kind of work advocated by the IFA. Increasingly film workshops were able to obtain capital grants for equipment; and, with funds available for production, wages could be paid.[49]

A CULTURAL POLICY FOR FILM?

> What should be the object of government policy for films? To stimulate an industry for the normal economic reasons – to create employment, encourage productive investment and increase exports? Or to aid an art form? Or to encourage the making of films which reflect British life? We believe that all three objects are valid. We also believe that the barriers between industry and art in relation to film are largely artificial and subjective, and that government policy should cater for films as a whole.
>
> Interim Action Committee, 1979.[50]

In the mid-1970s it became increasingly obvious that film policy needed to be rethought, and a number of official reports began to stress the benefits of a more cultural policy. In August 1975 Prime Minister Harold Wilson set up a Working Party, chaired by John Terry, to consider 'the requirements of a viable and prosperous British film industry over the next decade'. Its report was published in January 1976, and the preamble stated the problem clearly:

> Britain, though it owes much to the enterprise and example of the US film industry, has for too long been an economic and cultural colony of Hollywood. In economic terms, many of the greatest successes of British film talent have assisted the US economy far more than they have helped the British. In cultural terms, the continuing dominance of the British film industry by Hollywood has militated against the development of a characteristically British cinema.[51]

The report's main recommendations concerned finance and regulation.

244

The Working Party calculated that total investment in film production should be a minimum of £40 million a year, but that current levels were only £25 million – £16 million of this being American capital. The report argued that an additional £5 million a year of British finance was needed, which it was hoped would attract further support. A new film fund was recommended, with initial 'equity' – or interest-free capital – of £5 million from the government. The money for the fund was to be collected from the excess profits tax payments of the commercial television companies, in line with the report's general aim to encourage television companies to invest more in film production. The fund was to have the right to call on additional amounts up to £5 million a year for three years, and the Eady fund was to contribute £1 million a year. The BBC also informed the Working Party that it was prepared to put £250,000 into ten projects a year, and to pay another £25,000 for a showing on television once the initial investment had been recouped.

Another proposal was that the industry's voluntary agreement not to show films on television until five years after release should be replaced by a statutory three-year ban. The most important recommendation, however, was that a British Film Authority should be established to co-ordinate in a single body the activities of the Department of Education and Science, the Department of Trade, the NFFC and the British Film Fund Agency. A later report by the Interim Action Committee, set up after the Working Party's report was published to work out some of the details of the proposals, elaborated the functions and composition of the British Film Authority (BFA).[52] It was to be responsible to one Minister so that 'responsibility for film-as-an-industry and film-as-an-art should be unified'. Its powers were to be wide, including supervising and deploying the financial resources available to the fund recommended by the Working Party. An important and promising proposal was that the BFA should promote schemes to provide finance for short films and films of outstanding merit and to support specialised cinemas.

The Interim Action Committee's (IAC) second report dealt with finance, and recognised that the Eady Levy had to be operated more selectively if it was going to help the industry. Previously Eady money was distributed on an automatic basis, but the report recommended that greater benefit would result from half the money being used in a discretionary way by the BFA for film production and, to a lesser extent, to support cinemas. The report's conclusion suggested the beginnings of a more cultural policy:

> The major problem in the British film industry is that so few films, especially those of character and originality, see the light of projection. Thus the means of support for the film industry should be adapted to help bring about a significant improvement in the situation of feature film production in this country.[53]

It is not clear, however, that the IAC's proposals would have brought about major changes, and some have argued that this is because they were not sufficiently interventionist. The reports envisaged that only half the Eady money would go to the film fund and thus private sources would have to supplement state funding. The experience of the NFFC and the Consortium showed that the combination of state support and private enterprise discouraged experiment, and in the end films of the high-budget category were backed, such as *The Man Who Fell to Earth* and *The Duellists*. As Vincent Porter has commented:

> It is difficult to avoid the conclusion that the marriage of financial probity and national culture proposed for the NFFC is an impossible mix to achieve without substantially modifying the commercial relations between the Corporation and the exhibiting sector . . . and in particular to maximise the returns from the UK box office.[54]

Mamoun Hassan feared that the BFA might be too centralised, so that 'non-conformist elements could find it very difficult to get access to the money'.[55] However, there were some indications that the Labour government intended to broaden the IAC's proposals by allowing the BFA public funds for its cultural functions, and by making it a condition of licensing cinemas for public exhibition that a quota of films registered by the BFA as British, rather than Anglo-American 'British', should be shown. The initiative was lost when Labour lost the general election of 1979. In the 1980s the very survival of state support for the film industry became the focus of debate.

In 1981 the NFFC was restructured and government funding in its previous form was ended. Instead the NFFC was given £1 million and was to be allowed to borrow up to £5 million at any one time on commercial lines. £1.5 million, or 20 per cent of the gross receipts from the Eady Levy, whichever was the greater, was to supplement this, with the result that the NFFC's fate became inextricably bound up with that of the Levy.

Many argued that since cinema attendances had fallen from a peak of 1.6 billion in 1946 to 64 million in 1982, a levy on cinema takings was increasingly inappropriate as a fund to support production. In 1984 it was calculated that out of a total fund of £4.5 million a year, only £2,375,000 was available to producers in the normal way after the deduction of £500,000, £125,000 and £1.5 million a year respectively to the National Film and Television School, the BFI Production Board and the NFFC.[56] In recognition of the problems of allocating the fund purely on box-office success, a ceiling was established in 1980 of £500,000 for features and £50,000 for shorts. Even so, as the practice of pre-selling films to distributors became widespread, the Levy was criticised for failing to benefit those it was originally intended to help – British producers. And, as we have seen, the inducement of money from the Eady fund was not necessarily a decisive factor in attracting foreign investment to British film-making.

Although Eady was clearly malfunctioning, there was a case to be made for retaining the Levy but in a restructured form. Eady payments to the National Film and Television School, the BFI Production Board and the NFFC had, after all, become crucial. One proposal by the AIP was that the yield from the Levy should be increased from £4.5 million a year to £35 million. This was to be achieved by lowering the contribution from cinemas, but supplementing it with payments from other relevant but previously untapped sources – charges for film broadcasts on television or cable and on blank video-cassettes. The AIP envisaged that the fund should be distributed in the following way: £12.5 million to British films in relation to box-office success; £17.5 million to the NFFC; £3.5 million for cinema improvement grants; and £1.75 million as a training allocation.[57]

In January 1983 the quota was suspended, in line with the Conservative government's aim to dismantle state support for the industry. When Iain Sproat, Parliamentary Under-Secretary at the Department of Trade, announced this decision to the Commons in July 1982, he referred to the quota as 'a formidable and unnecessary administrative burden'. The decision to suspend the quota had been put off, and in January 1982 it had been reduced from 30 per cent for features and 25 per cent for shorts to 15 per cent for all parts of the programme. The Cinematograph Films Council and the IAC had expressed doubts about the quota's effectiveness. And it was clear that it was insufficient protection against American domination, that it did not prevent the British majors from investing abroad, and that it was riddled with an elaborate system of exemptions and relief for small cinemas.

WHITE PAPER: BLACK FUTURE?

The film debate now focused on the combined fate of Eady and the NFFC. However, before the publication of the government's long-awaited White Paper in July 1984, the industry suffered yet another setback when the Chancellor of the Exchequer announced that a crucial tax-shelter device from which producers had benefited since 1979 was to be discontinued.[58]

The White Paper by Kenneth Baker, Minister for Information and Technology, announced that the Eady Levy, the NFFC and the Cinematograph Films Council were to be abolished.[59] The AIP's proposal for restructuring the source and allocation of the fund was rejected on the grounds that a charge on television film purchases would increase broadcasting costs and licence fees, and that this was an unwise strategy when Channel Four planned to invest £8 million a year in film-making. The major circuits have apparently given 'assurances' that 'they will not simply absorb the benefits within their organisation but seek to deploy the savings to the benefit of the cinema-going public'.[60] The issue of monopoly has, significantly, been shelved once again, as it was by the Monopolies Commission's report of May 1983.[61] This is hardly surprising, since the government's new proposals depend largely on finance from the combines.

The 'film policy' outlined in the White Paper hands over the major responsibility of film financing to the private sector. The government is prepared to contribute a total of £2.5 million to be allocated in the following way: £1.5 million a year for five years to a new private company to replace the NFFC in 1985 and to be co-financed for three years by annual contributions from Thorn-EMI, Rank, Channel Four, the British Videogram Association and from past royalties from NFFC projects with an estimated annual yield of £200,000; £500,000 a year for five years for the National Film Development Fund; £250,000 for the television faculty of the National Film and Television School for 1985–6; and finally £250,000 as a contribution towards the 'Year of the British film' announced by the industry for 1985–6. The replacement advisory body for the Cinematograph Films Council is not outlined in any detail, but the White Paper states that the IAC is to be its nucleus.

The withdrawal of state support will leave the industry exposed to market forces almost as much as it was sixty years ago. This will not make for a fundamental change in direction. Finance and profit have always been the main factors in deciding what films are made and shown in Britain. The system of state aid was not designed to replace or to compete with commercial finance, and it failed to reverse the long-standing trends towards monopoly and American control. Nevertheless, it represented a commitment to the maintenance of a production base in Britain, and this implied a need to modify some of the consequences of those trends. Aid has done this. It has influenced the opportunities open to film-makers and the product offered to the audience. Even the modest funds available to the NFFC and the BFI Production Board have enabled a few films to be made which would probably never have been scripted if the initiative had been left entirely with the dominant media groups. The change of policy will therefore almost certainly lead to a decline in all film activity not promoted by major commercial interests. It will also mean that in future there will be nothing to prevent these commercial interests from choosing to supply their captive market entirely with imports. Against these odds British film production may finally lose its protracted but tenacious struggle for survival.

Notes

PRO = Public Record Office
CAB = Cabinet Office
FO = Foreign Office
BT = Board of Trade
DO = Dominions Office
LAB = Ministry of Labour
INF = Ministry of Information
T = Treasury
SMT = Securities Management Trust, Bank of England

Introduction

1. *Report of the Committee on Cinematograph Films*, London, HMSO, 1936. Cmd. 5320, p. 4.

2. *Film Business is Big Business, An Investigation into Film Production Finance*, London, Association of Cine-Technicians, 1939.

3. Simon Rowson, 'Statistical Survey of the Cinema Industry in Great Britain in 1934' in *Journal of the Royal Statistical Society*, 99 (1936), pp. 67–129.

4. Asa Briggs, *The History of Broadcasting*, vol. 1, Oxford, Oxford University Press, 1961, p. 8.

5. Rachael Low, *The History of the British Film*, London, Allen and Unwin. Several volumes covering the years 1896–1939.

6. James Curran and Vincent Porter (eds.), *British Cinema History*, London, Weidenfeld and Nicolson, 1983. For an excellent survey of the literature on the film industry see the 'Select Bibliography' compiled for the book by Susan Daws.

7. Tino Balio, *United Artists*, Madison, University of Wisconsin Press, 1976. And see also Tino Balio (ed.), *The American Film Industry*, Madison, University of Wisconsin Press, 1976.

1   A Quota for the Film Industry?

1. *Parliamentary Debates* (Lords), vol. 69 (1927), col. 272, and Rachael Low, *The History of the British Film 1918–29*, London, Allen and Unwin, 1971, p. 156.

2. W. A. Lewis, 'International competition in manufactures' in *American Economic Review*, Papers and Proceedings, XLVII (1957), p. 579, and S. Pollard, *The Development of the British Economy, 1914–80*, 3rd edition, London, Arnold, 1983, p. 116.

3. See Tony Aldgate, 'Comedy, Class and Containment: The British Domestic Cinema of the 1930s' in James Curran and Vincent Porter (eds.), *British Cinema History*, London, Weidenfeld and Nicolson, 1983. Aldgate questions the argument that the BBFC ensured that 'all cinema-goers got was harmless, escapist amusement' by suggesting that there were opportunities for film-makers to thwart the BBFC's rules. The 'content control' argument is put forward by

Jeffrey Richards in his article 'The BBFC and content control in the 1930s' in *Historical Journal of Film, Radio and Television*, vol. 1, no. 2, 1981, and by Nicholas Pronay, 'The First Reality: Film censorship in Liberal England' in K. R. M. Short (ed.), *Feature Films as History*, London, Croom Helm, 1981.

4. Nicholas Pronay, 'The Political Censorship of Films in Britain' in N. Pronay and D. Spring (eds.), *Propaganda, Politics and Film*, 1918–45, London, Macmillan, 1982, p. 122.

5. Figures for 1916 are from the *Kine Year Book* 1917, p. 57. Those for 1920 and 1924 are from Low, *The History of the British Film 1918–29*, pp. 48–9.

6. Cinematograph Exhibitors' Diary, 1928.

7. Rachael Low, *The History of the British Film 1906–14*, London, Allen and Unwin, 1949, p. 133.

8. *Kine Year Book*, 1919, p. 67.

9. S. R. Kent, 'Distributing the Product' in J. P. Kennedy (ed.), *The Story of the Films*, New York, 1927, p. 266.

10. US Department of Commerce data. Figures for British imports are from *Kine Year Books*.

11. Simon Rowson, *Kinematograph Weekly*, 2 July 1925, p. 41.

12. Cinematograph Exhibitors' Diary, 1928.

13. *The British Film Industry*, London, Political and Economic Planning, 1952, pp. 41–2.

14. B. B. Hampton, *The American Film Industry*, New York, Dover, 1970, p. 357. The figures are taken from *Variety*. Statistics for the period before the Board of Trade began registering films for the quota legislation vary considerably.

15. *The Times*, 3 February 1927.

16. Will H. Hays, *Memoirs*, New York, 1955, pp. 505–6.

17. Low, *The History of the British Film 1918–29*, p. 156.

18. Ibid., pp. 40–1.

19. *Kinematograph Weekly*, 12 February 1925, p. 45.

20. Low, *The History of the British Film 1918–29*, p. 89.

21. Paul Rotha, *The Film Till Now*, quoted in Low (1918–29), p. 90.

22. Lord Swinton, *I Remember*, London, Hutchinson, 1959, p 36.

23. *Parliamentary Debates* (Lords), vol. 61, 14 May 1925, col. 273.

24. PRO: CAB 32/59 (Imperial Conference 1926), and see *Parliamentary Debates* (Commons), vol. 203, col. 2040, 16 March 1927.

25. *The Times*, 27 September 1926.

26. *Parliamentary Debates* (Lords), vol. 61, col. 277.

27. Ibid., col. 278.

28. *Imperial Educational Conference, Report of the Committee on the Use of the Cinematograph in Education*, London, HMSO, 1924, p. 19, quoted in D. J. Wenden, *The Birth of the Movies*, London, Macdonald, 1974, p. 147.

29. T. J. Hollins, 'The Conservative Party and film propaganda between the wars', *English Historical Review*, vol. 96 (1981), p. 363.

30. *Parliamentary Debates* (Lords), vol. 61, col. 282.

31. *Kinematograph Weekly*, 14 May 1925, p. 46.

32. C. Tennyson, *Stars and Markets*, London, Chatto & Windus, 1957, p. 161.

33. PRO: CAB 27, 198, CU 752, memorandum from Tennyson, 28 May 1925.

34. Paul Swann, 'The British Documentary Movement, 1926–46', University of Leeds Ph.D., p. 35.

35. *Parliamentary Debates* (Commons), vol. 185, col. 2084, 29 June 1925.
36. Ibid., col. 2017.
37. PRO: FO 371/10651, A 3269/25, minute by A. Willert.
38. Tennyson, op. cit., p. 162.
39. Swinton, op. cit., p. 51.
40. Ibid., p. 37.
41. *Kinematograph Weekly*, 16 December 1937, p. 1.
42. *Kinematograph Weekly*, 6 August 1925, pp. 30–1.
43. *The Times*, 25 February 1926.
44. *Kinematograph Weekly*, 12 November 1925, p. 54.
45. *Kinematograph Weekly*, 19 November 1925, p. 33.
46. *Kinematograph Weekly*, 26 November 1925, p. 39.
47. PRO: CAB 24/178, CP 69, BT memorandum 16 February 1926.
48. *The Times*, 23 March 1926.
49. *Kinematograph Weekly*, 17 June 1926, p. 51.
50. Ibid.
51. *Kinematograph Weekly*, 5 August 1926, p. 32.
52. Ibid.
53. H. Butler to C. J. North, 19 January 1926. National Archives, Washington D.C. Record Group 151, Bureau of Foreign and Domestic Commerce, General Records, Motion Pictures, 281, UK.
54. *Variety*, 20 January 1926, p. 26. Ufa also received a loan of $275,000 from Universal and agreed to distribute its films in Germany. However, in 1927 Ufa was reorganised and the leader of the National Conservative Party (DNVP), Hugenberg, bought out the American interests. See Julian Petley, *Capital and Culture: German Cinema 1933–45*, London, BFI, 1979, pp. 36–7.
55. National Archives, Washington D.C. Record Group 151, General Records, Motion Pictures. North to Canty, 14 April 1927.
56. *Kinematograph Weekly*, 5 August 1926, p. 31.
57. *The Times*, 3 October 1926.
58. *Kinematograph Weekly*, 22 April 1926, p. 42.
59. P. M. Taylor, *The Projection of Britain: British Overseas Publicity and Propaganda, 1919–39*, Cambridge, Cambridge University Press, 1981, from the EMB Annual Report, 1928–9 (HMSO, 1929).
60. L. S. Amery, *My Political Life*, vol. 2, London, Hutchinson, 1953, p. 346.
61. Ibid.
62. J. A. Cross, *Lord Swinton*, Oxford, Oxford University Press, 1982, p. 69.
63. Amery, *My Political Life*, p. 354.
64. PRO: DO 35/203 (A).
65. Rosaleen Smyth, 'Movies and Mandarins: the Official Film and British Colonial Africa' in Curran and Porter (eds.), *British Cinema History*.
66. PRO: CAB 32/59, E (E) 48. General Economic Sub-Committee, 13th Report, 18 November 1926.
67. Ibid.
68. *Daily Express*, 18 March 1927.
69. *Parliamentary Debates* (Commons), vol. 203, col. 2058, 16 March 1927.
70. *Kinematograph Weekly*, 24 March 1927, p. 38.
71. *The Times*, 8 February 1926.
72. *Parliamentary Debates* (Commons), vol. 204, col. 245, 22 March 1927.

2 Adjusting to Protection

1. *The British Film Industry*, London, Political and Economic Planning, 1952, p. 56.
2. M. L. Sanders, 'British film propaganda in Russia, 1916–18', *Historical Journal of Film, Radio and Television*, vol. 3, no. 2, 1983.
3. *Kinematograph Weekly*, 5 January 1928, p. 38.
4. PEP, *The British Film Industry*, p. 49.
5. US Department of Commerce, *European Motion Picture Industry*, reports by the Motion Picture Division of the Bureau of Foreign and Domestic Commerce, 1927–32.
6. Ibid., 1930, p. 13.
7. Upton Sinclair, *Upton Sinclair presents William Fox*, Los Angeles, 1933, p. 78. See also Simon Hartog, 'L'Histoire exemplaire de la Gaumont-British' in *Film Exchange*, no. 13, 1981.
8. National Archives, Washington D.C. 841.4061 MP/474, memo. on Fox, Loews and Gaumont-British, 1943, p. 1. (US State Department files, RG 59).
9. Sinclair, op. cit., p. 79.
10. National Archives, Washington D.C. 841.4061 MP/474, pp. 4–5.
11. PRO: BT 64, 86/6267/31. Lawrance, Messer and Co. to President of BT, 22 May 1931.
12. Ibid., Minute, 3 June 1931.
13. Table from F. D. Klingender and S. Legg, *Money Behind the Screen*, London, Lawrence and Wishart, 1937, p. 53.
14. *Economist*, 14 July 1928, pp. 74–5.
15. *Economist*, 20 April 1929, pp. 859–60.
16. *Economist*, 30 November 1929, p. 1027.
17. *Economist*, 15 August 1931, p. 314.
18. *Parliamentary Debates* (Commons), vol. 241, col. 1949, 22 July 1930.
19. Adrian Brunel, *Nice Work*, London, Forbes Robertson, 1949, p. 166.
20. Ibid.
21. US Department of Commerce reports, 1927–35. In the late 1920s Britain imported films also from Germany and to a lesser extent from France.
22. Ibid., report for 1932, p. 1.
23. National Archives, Washington D.C. US Department of Commerce, Bureau of Foreign and Domestic Commerce, RG 151, special report by Coldwell S. Johnson, 2 November 1937.
24. Douglas Gomery, 'Economic Struggle and Hollywood Imperialism: Europe converts to sound' in *Yale French Studies*, no. 60, 1980, p. 82.
25. US Department of Commerce reports.
26. *Economist*, 31 December 1932, p. 1234.
27. US Department of Commerce report, 1930.
28. National Archives, Washington D.C. 841.4061 Movietone/2.
29. *Kinematograph Weekly*, 4 April 1929, p. 21.
30. *Kinematograph Weekly*, 5 September 1929, p. 21.
31. Minutes of evidence of the Committee on Cinematograph Films, HMSO, 1936. CEA evidence, p. 88.
32. US Department of Commerce reports, 1929 and 1930.
33. US Department of Commerce report, 1932, p. 39.

34. US Department of Commerce report, 1931, p. 8.
35. Tony Aldgate, 'Comedy, Class and Containment: The British Domestic Cinema of the 1930s' in James Curran and Vincent Porter (eds.), *British Cinema History*, London, Weidenfeld and Nicolson, 1983.
36. *Parliamentary Debates* (Commons), vol. 241, cols. 1949–50, 22 July 1930.
37. PRO: BT 56/28/CIA/1428/30.
38. Ibid.
39. London School of Economics, *New Survey of London Life and Labour*, 1930, p. 295.
40. Report of the Colonial Films Committee, Cmd. 3630 (HMSO 1930), p. 23.
41. *The Film in National Life*, report of an enquiry by the Commission on Educational and Cultural Films, London, Allen and Unwin, 1932, p. 143.
42. Ibid., pp. 155–6.
43. *Parliamentary Debates* (Commons), vol. 266, col. 740, 27 May 1932.
44. Ibid., col. 741.
45. PRO: BT 64 86/8227/32, Samuel to Baldwin, 4 June 1932.
46. *The Times*, 10 June 1932.
47. Rachael Low, *The History of the British Film 1929–39: Documentary and Educational Films of the 1930s*, London, Allen and Unwin, 1979, pp. 16–17.
48. PRO: BT 64 87/6503/34.
49. *The Times*, 4 August 1932.
50. *The Times*, 9 August 1932.
51. Walter Ashley, *The Cinema and the Public*, London, Nicolson and Watson, 1934, p. 7.
52. Ibid.
53. R. S. Lambert, *Ariel and all his Quality*, London, Gollancz, 1940, p. 197.
54. PRO: BT 64 87/6503/34, minute, 6 February 1934.

3 Reviewing the Films Act

1. *Report of a Committee appointed by the Board of Trade to consider the position of British films* (HMSO, 1936), Cmd. 5320, p. 4.
2. PRO: BT 64 97/7749/33. Minute, 20 October 1933.
3. Ibid. Fennelly's memorandum, November 1934.
4. PRO: BT 64 88/7411/35.
5. Ibid.
6. Ibid.
7. Lord Kennet, a director of the Equity and Law Life Assurance Society, which supported film production, was offered and refused the chairmanship before Moyne's appointment.
8. R. Griffiths, *Fellow Travellers of the Right: British enthusiasts for Nazi Germany, 1933–39*, London, Constable, 1980, pp. 158–62.
9. Cmd. 5320, p. 11, para. 25.
10. Ibid., p. 37.
11. *Minutes of Evidence to the Committee on Cinematograph Films* (HMSO, 1936), 5 May 1936, p. 5, para. 39.
12. PRO: BT 64 92/6757/38. 10th meeting of the Moyne Committee, 20 July 1936.
13. Ibid.

14. F. D. Klingender and S. Legg, *Money Behind the Screen*, London, Lawrence and Wishart, 1937, and 'Secrets of British Film Finance' in *World Film News*, January 1937.

15. *Money Behind the Screen*, pp. 15–17.

16. Tino Balio, *United Artists*, Madison, University of Wisconsin Press, 1976, p. 129.

17. *The British Film Industry*, London, Political and Economic Planning, 1952, p. 62.

18. *Money Behind the Screen*, pp. 19–20.

19. Cmd. 5320, p. 37.

20. Ibid., p. 12.

21. PRO: BT 64 92/6757/38.

22. Simon Rowson, *Minutes of Evidence*, 30 June 1936, p. 115.

23. Ibid., p. 120, para. 1233.

24. *Money Behind the Screen*, p. 48.

25. Ibid., pp. 49–50.

26. Ibid., p. 54.

27. 13th meeting of the Moyne Committee, 13 October 1936.

28. 11th meeting of the Moyne Committee, 21 July 1936.

29. *Minutes of Evidence*, Fennelly, p. 5; Simon Rowson, 'A Statistical Survey of the Cinema Industry in Great Britain in 1934' in *Journal of the Royal Statistical Society*, vol. XCIX, 1936 p. 103.

30. Rowson, 'Statistical Survey', p. 133, para. 27.

31. 10th meeting of the Moyne Committee.

32. Cmd. 5320, p. 14.

33. 10th meeting of the Moyne Committee.

34. Cmd. 5320, p. 37, rec. iv.

35. *Minutes of Evidence*, Paul Rotha, 19 May 1936.

36. Ibid., John Grierson, 30 June 1936, pp. 33–4.

37. PRO: BT 64 4501/1687, CFC (5) 14.

38. *Minutes of Evidence*, Fligelstone, 26 May 1936, p. 89.

39. Cmd. 5320, p. 20.

40. Minutes of Evidence, Fennelly, p. 8, Table E, and Simon Rowson, 'Statistical Survey', p. 110.

41. Tony Aldgate, 'Comedy, Class and Containment: The British Domestic Cinema in the 1930s' in James Curran and Vincent Porter (eds.), *British Cinema History*, London, Weidenfeld and Nicolson, 1983, p. 262.

42. *Minutes of Evidence*, Fennelly, p. 10.

43. Ibid., p. 9.

44. Ibid., Eckman, pp. 105–6.

45. Ibid., CEA, p. 81.

46. Rowson, 'Statistical Survey', pp. 88 and 110.

47. Balio, *United Artists*, p. 134.

48. *Minutes of Evidence*, FBI, p. 38.

49. Ibid., CEA, p. 167.

50. Cmd. 5320, p. 21.

51. Ibid., pp. 35–6.

52. PRO: BT 64/92/6757/38, 6th meeting, 23 June 1936.

53. Ibid., 11th meeting, 21 July 1936.

54. Ibid., 12th meeting, 6 October 1936.
55. Ibid., 13th meeting, 13 October 1936.
56. *Minutes of Evidence*, FBI, p. 40.
57. Ibid.
58. Cmd. 5320, p. 36, rec. xvii.
59. Ibid., p. 29.
60. Ivor Montagu, 'The Moyne Report' in *Sight and Sound*, vol. 5, no. 20, Winter 1936–7, pp. 120–2.
61. PRO: BT 64 89/6551/37, FBI memorandum, 28 January 1937.
62. Ibid., CEA memorandum, 13 January 1937.
63. National Archives, Washington D.C. Bureau of Foreign and Domestic Commerce (RG 151). Report by H. Stebbins, 2 August 1937, including extract from Hays memorandum.

4   Film Finance in the 1930s

1. *The British Film Industry*, London, Political and Economic Planning, 1952, p. 67.
2. Alan Wood, *Mr Rank*, London, Hodder and Stoughton, 1952, p. 91, and *Kinematograph Weekly*, 13 January 1938, p. 139.
3. William Marston Seabury, *The Public and the Motion Picture Industry* (New York, 1926), p. 195, quoted in Thomas H. Guback, 'Hollywood's International Market' in Tino Balio (ed.), *The American Film Industry*, Madison, University of Wisconsin Press, 1976, p. 391.
4. Ernest Betts, *Inside Pictures*, London, Cresset Press, 1960, p. 6.
5. Robert Murphy, 'Rank's Attempt on the American Market, 1944–9' in James Curran and Vincent Porter (eds.), *British Cinema History*, London, Weidenfeld and Nicolson, 1983.
6. Tino Balio, *United Artists*, Madison, University of Wisconsin Press, 1976, p. 145.
7. *World Film News*, vol. 1, no. 3, June 1936.
8. *Morning Post*, 15 January 1937.
9. Karol Kulik, *Alexander Korda: The Man Who Could Work Miracles*, London, W. H. Allen, 1975, p. 170.
10. *The British Film Industry*, p. 70.
11. *Financial Times*, 13 July 1937.
12. *Financial Times*, 14 July 1937. See also *Kinematograph Weekly*, 14 January 1937, p. 13. This article estimated that the producer paid, on average, a premium of 4½ per cent to the insurance company, as well as interest to the bank at 4½ per cent.
13. F. D. Klingender and S. Legg, *Money Behind the Screen*, London, Lawrence and Wishart, 1937, p. 55.
14. *World Film News*, January 1937.
15. Betts, *Inside Pictures*, pp. 11 and 13.
16. Ibid., p. 8.
17. *Kinematograph Weekly*, 11 May 1939, p. 17.
18. *The Times*, 2 May 1939.
19. Ibid.

20. *The British Film Industry*, pp. 70–1.
21. Bank of England, SMT2/33, 34, 35.
22. R. S. Sayers, *The Bank of England, 1891–1944*, Cambridge, Cambridge University Press, 1976, vol. 2, p. 550. For the Portal/Norman story see Herbert Wilcox, *Twenty-Five Thousand Sunsets*, London, Bodley Head, 1967, p. 107.
23. SMT2/33, doc. 7, Lever's memorandum sent by Munro to Norman, 18 March 1937.
24. Ibid.
25. SMT2/33, doc. 45, Munro's draft scheme, 16 April 1937.
26. Ibid., doc. 60.
27. Ibid.
28. Ibid., doc. 71.
29. Ibid., 'A policy for films' by Simon Rowson, 30 April 1937.
30. SMT2/34, doc. 86, Bunbury's minute.
31. Balio, *United Artists*, p. 146.
32. SMT2/34, doc. 97.
33. Ibid., doc. 104.
34. Ibid., doc. 123.
35. SMT2/35, doc. 147.
36. Ibid., doc. 147, Bunbury to Norman, 1 June 1937.
37. Ibid., doc. 154, Norman, 7 June 1937.

5 American Diplomacy and the Films Act

1. PRO: BT 64 89/6551/37.
2. A. Plummer, *New British Industries in the Twentieth Century*, London, Pitman, 1937, p. 300.
3. *Kinematograph Weekly*, 11 March 1937, p. 36.
4. *Kinematograph Weekly*, 9 January 1936, p. 34.
5. *Kinematograph Weekly*, 5 March 1936, p. 11.
6. James Curran and Vincent Porter (eds.), *British Cinema History*, London, Weidenfeld and Nicolson, 1983. Appendix by Patricia Perilli, 'Statistical Survey of the British Cinema Industry', p. 372.
7. *World Film News*, November 1937.
8. *Kinematograph Weekly*, 5 March 1936, p. 11.
9. *Kinematograph Weekly*, 29 April 1937, p. 7.
10. PRO: BT 64 89/6551/37, Kearney to Fennelly, 5 May 1937.
11. Ibid., Kearney to BT, 25 May 1937.
12. Basil Dean Special Collection, BFI Library. See also US State Department document (National Archives, Washington D.C.) 841.4061/Motion Pictures 127, correspondence between Lord Strabolgi and Fay Allport, March 1938. On 8 March Strabolgi wrote to Allport: 'I have been trying to work out an amendment . . . to give the reciprocity advantage you speak of, but I can't quite see how to do it. If you would like to do it yourself, I will put it into Parliamentary language.' Allport wrote to Major Herron of the Hays Office the next day: 'This is the first time . . . that we have been invited to write British film legislation.'
13. PRO: BT 64 89/6551/37, Fennelly's minute.
14. PRO: CAB 24/270, CP 181 (37).

15. PRO: BT 64 90/7323/37, Allport to BT, 29 October 1937.

16. Nathan D. Golden, *Review of Foreign Film Markets*, 1938, US Department of Commerce, 1939, p. i.

17. Sarah Street, 'The Hays Office and the defence of the British market in the 1930s', to be published in *Historical Journal of Film, Radio and Television*, vol. 5, no. 1, 1985.

18. US State Department doc. 841.4061/MP 42, Hull to US Embassy, London, 16 March 1937.

19. PRO: BT 64 90/7323/37, Fennelly to Somervell, 7 October 1937.

20. PRO: LAB 8/75.

21. PRO: BT 64 90/7880/37, TUC memorandum for BT.

22. *Parliamentary Debates* (Commons), vol. 328, col. 1173, 4 November 1937.

23. *Parliamentary Debates* (Commons), vol. 332, cols. 395–6, 23 February 1938.

24. John Grierson, 'The fate of British films', *The Fortnightly*, July 1937.

25. *The Times*, 18 November 1937, and see also the Basil Dean Special Collection, BFI Library.

26. PRO: BT 64 90/7863/37.

27. PRO: FO 371 21530/ A 791.

28. US State Department, 841.4061/MP/114, Kennedy to Hull, 14 March 1938.

29. PRO: FO 371 21530/A 175, minute by Beith, 10 January 1938.

30. PRO: BT 64 91/6181/38, Williamson to Palmer, 10 May 1938, and note by Fennelly, 13 May 1938.

31. *Kinematograph Weekly*, 5 May 1938, p. 29.

32. *The British Film Industry*, London, Political and Economic Planning, 1952, p. 65.

33. SMT2/44, doc. 15.

34. Ibid., doc. 22a.

35. *The British Film Industry*, pp. 94–5.

36. *Report of a Committee appointed by the Board of Trade to consider the position of British films* (HMSO, 1936), Cmd. 5320, p. 4.

6 Adaptation to War

1. PRO: INF 1/194.

2. *Parliamentary Debates* (Commons), vol. 351, col. 1504, 28 September 1939.

3. *Parliamentary Debates* (Lords), vol. 114, col. 1219, 3 October 1939.

4. *Kinematograph Weekly*, 5 October 1939, p. 5.

5. *Kinematograph Weekly*, 26 October 1939, p. 5.

6. Cinematograph Films Council Annual Report for the year ended March 31st 1939, p. 4, para. 17.

7. Alfred Duff Cooper, Viscount Norwich, *Old Men Forget: The Autobiography of Duff Cooper*, London, Hart-Davis, 1957.

8. Andrew Boyle, *Poor Dear Brendan*, London, Hutchinson, 1974; Edward Lysagt, *Brendan Bracken*, London, Allen Lane, 1979.

9. Adrian Brunel, for instance, cited the state aid given to film production in Italy and the large sums spent by Goebbels on propaganda, in a memorandum about film production sent by him both to the MOI and to Sir Andrew Duncan, President of the Board of Trade, in the summer of 1940. PRO: BT 64 60/8982.

10. *Parliamentary Debates* (Commons), vol. 371, col. 338, 29 April 1941.

11. *Parliamentary Debates* (Lords), vol. 114, col. 1220, 3 October 1939.

12. Guy Morgan, *Red Roses Every Night*, London, Quality Press, 1948, p. 31.

13. PRO: BT 64 70, 10 July 1941.

14. Muriel Box, who started to direct documentary films during the war, relates in her autobiography, *Odd Woman Out* (London, Leslie Frewin, 1974), how Arthur Elton, who was then working for the MOI, refused to accept her as the director of *Road Safety for Children* because he said it was not a suitable film for a woman to direct (p. 163). After the war, when she was offered her first feature film, Michael Balcon objected on the grounds that a woman could not control a large feature crew (p. 205).

15. PRO: BT 64 1378.

16. Policy-making was further complicated by the wartime cabinet arrangements. The war cabinet had far fewer members than a normal cabinet, and neither the President of the Board of Trade nor the Home Secretary were members of it. Civilian government was organised initially by five separate committees co-ordinated by the Lord President of the Council. After Sir John Anderton became Lord President in October 1940, his committee assumed greater responsibility and functioned almost as a cabinet for civilian affairs.

17. PRO: INF 1/194 and INF 1/196.

18. PRO: BT 64 58/4660.

19. There were also rumours that Korda had been asked by Churchill to undertake intelligence work in the United States. Karol Kulik discusses both versions of Korda's wartime activities in her biography, *Alexander Korda* (London, Allen and Unwin, 1975), pp. 254–7. Nigel West mentions Korda's supposed espionage activities in *M.I.6: British Intelligence Service Operations 1909–1945*, London, Weidenfeld and Nicolson, 1983, pp. 68, 69 and 84.

20. PRO: BT 64 60/10742/40.

21. PRO: BT 64 61/14026.

22. *Parliamentary Debates* (Commons), vol. 351, col. 1129, 26 September 1939.

23. Ian Maclane, *Ministry of Morale*, London, Allen and Unwin, 1979, p. 3 and pp. 39–42.

24. Frances Thorpe and Nicholas Pronay, *British Official Films in the Second World War*, Oxford, Clio Press, 1980, p. 23.

25. Paul Rotha, 'The British Case (2) 1941' in *Rotha on the Film*, London, Faber and Faber, 1958, p. 224.

26. Kenneth Clark, *The Other Half*, London, John Murray, 1977, p. 11.

27. Thorpe and Pronay, *British Official Films*, p. 34.

28. Only nine films were released in 1939, and five of these were made by the GPO unit.

29. Clark, *The Other Half*, pp. 11 and 12.

30. Thirteenth Report from the Select Committee on National Expenditure, HMSO, 21 August 1940, p. 4, para. 5.

31. Kevin Gough-Yates, *Michael Powell: in collaboration with Emeric Pressburger*, London, British Film Institute, 1970.

32. Select Committee on National Expenditure, 1940, p. 5, para. 6.

33. PRO: CAB 65/27.

34. PRO: BT 64 60/10742.

35. Paul Rotha, 'Documentary is neither short nor long' in *Rotha on the Film*, p. 234.

36. *Kinematograph Weekly*, 5 December 1940, p. 3.
37. PRO: BT 64 94/5740.
38. There was a series of complaints in the autumn of 1940. See *Kinematograph Weekly*, 24 October 1940, pp. 3 and 17; 7 November 1940, pp. 3 and 5.
39. *Kinematograph Weekly*, 21 November 1940, p. 7.
40. PRO: BT 64 95/2974, 1943.
41. PRO: INF 1/75.

7   A Wartime Policy for British Films?

1. PRO: BT 64 94/7303, 21 October 1939.
2. US State Department, 841.4061/MP/184, telegram no. 1975, Kennedy to Hull, 9 October 1939.
3. PRO: BT 64 94/7303, 8 October 1939.
4. The British community in Hollywood was naturally a target for such criticism. Korda was subpoenaed to appear before the Senate Foreign Relations Committee in November 1941, but the case was dropped after the Americans entered the war.
5. *Documentary News Letter*, vol. 1, no. 8, August 1940, p. 2.
6. PRO: BT 64 61/12979, 25 September 1940.
7. Ibid., 23 October 1940.
8. SMT2/43, doc. 48, 23 December 1941.
9. PRO: BT 64 95/4967, 13 April 1943.
10. SMT2/35, doc. 235a, 17 November 1939.
11. In a letter to Joseph Ball at the MOI, reported in *Kinematograph Weekly*, 12 October 1939.
12. SMT2/35, doc. 227, 24 October 1939.
13. PRO: BT 64 61/17793, 1940.
14. Ibid., p. 5.
15. Ibid., p. 8.
16. Ibid., p. 6.
17. SMT2/35, doc. 254.
18. Two other partners in this firm were at different times called on to advise on film industry affairs. Munro worked on the 1937 report; Sir Nigel Campbell was asked, in 1941, to report on the Bank proposal.
19. SMT2/40, doc. 3.
20. Ibid.
21. Ibid.
22. Ibid., 5 April 1940.
23. PRO: BT 64 58/4660.
24. PRO: BT 64 58/4660, correspondence on the subject.
25. Gabriel Pascal's production of *Major Barbara* ran out of money in the summer of 1940. Nicholas Davenport, who was then working as Pascal's financial adviser, wrote to the Board of Trade asking them to find £25,000 completion money and threatening that if the money could not be found, they would go to United Artists and take the picture to America for completion. The Bank of England officials consulted on the case expressed concern that the departure of such a big production might result in pressures to set up a films bank without

adequate preparation. In the event, the National Provincial Bank advanced the necessary capital.

26. SMT2/43, doc. 2, 11 December 1940, Lyttleton to Governor.
27. *Daily Film Renter*, 12 February 1941, p. 2.
28. *Daily Film Renter*, 20 February 1941, pp. 1 and 14 for text of joint letter by Ostrer and Parish written in response to Balcon's championship of the proposed Films Commission published in *Daily Film Renter*, 17 February 1941, pp. 1 and 29.
29. PRO: BT 64 95/2974.
30. SMT2/43, doc. 40b, 10 October 1941, Skinner's note.
31. PRO: CAB 71/9.
32. PRO: CAB 71/7.
33. PRO: CAB 71/12, 20 February 1943.
34. PRO: BT 64 95/2974, 8 December 1943.
35. PRO: CAB 71/12, 20 February 1943.
36. Detailed accounts of the growth of the Rank interests are given in Alan Wood, *A Study of J. Arthur Rank and British Films*, London, Hodder and Stoughton, 1952, and in *The British Film Industry*, London, PEP, 1952.
37. Michael Balcon's views had changed since the 1930s, when he had spoken of 'internationalisation' and the need to penetrate foreign markets.
38. ACT, 1939.
39. *Film and Television Technician*, May–June 1941, p. 62.
40. Michael Balcon, *Michael Balcon Presents . . . A Lifetime in Films*, London, Hutchinson, 1969, p. 152.
41. Cinematograph Films Council, Fifth Report, 1943, Postscript, p. 4.
42. Board of Trade, *Tendencies to Monopoly in the Cinematograph Industry*, HMSO, 1944, p. 5, para. 1.
43. Ibid., p. 5, para. 3.
44. Ibid., p. 19, para. 60.
45. Ibid., p. 20, para. 65.
46. Ibid., p. 21, para. 73.
47. Ibid., p. 23, para. 81.
48. Ibid., p. 6, para. 7.
49. Ibid., p. 30, para. 108.
50. Ibid., p. 32, para. 112.
51. *Manchester Guardian*, 3 August 1944.
52. *Daily Telegraph*, 3 August 1944.
53. Cinematograph Films Council, Seventh Report, 1945, p. 2, para. 4.
54. *News Chronicle*, 10 August 1944.
55. PRO: BT 64 96/4085, 1944.
56. Ibid.
57. All the examples of advice quoted are contained in a report for the President of the Board of Trade. PRO: BT 64 96/4085, 1944.

8   A New Scenario?

1. *Let Us Face the Future, a declaration of Labour Policy for the Consideration of the Nation*, Labour Party, 1945, in F. W. S. Craig (ed.), *British General Election Manifestos 1900–1964*, London, Macmillan, 1975, p. 129.

2. Ibid., p. 123.
3. *Kinematograph Weekly*, 9 December 1948, p. 11.
4. *Parliamentary Debates* (Commons), vol. 476, col. 2541, 29 June 1950.
5. According to statistics from the Wartime Social Survey for the MOI in J. P. Mayer, *British Cinemas and Their Audiences*, London, Dennis Dobson, 1948, pp. 257–60 and 263.
6. *Documentary News Letter*, vol. 3, no. 8, August 1942, p. 109.
7. *Parliamentary Debates* (Commons), vol. 464, col. 1395, 6 May 1949.
8. Dallas Bower in Peter Noble (ed.), *The British Film Yearbook*, 1946, p. 93.
9. *Parliamentary Debates* (Commons), vol. 444, col. 1484, 3 November 1947.
10. *Parliamentary Debates* (Commons), vol. 406, col. 1823, 20 December 1944.
11. For example see 'Information Please', *Documentary News Letter*, vol. 6, no. 56, April–May 1947.
12. The British Film Institute, 12th Annual Report, 1945.
13. *Documentary News Letter*, vol. 6, no. 60, November–December 1947, p. 156.
14. *Documentary News Letter*, vol. 6, no. 58, August–September 1947, p. 117.
15. PRO: BT 64 4468, 1949.
16. *American Outlook*, 15 August 1947.
17. *Parliamentary Debates* (Commons), vol. 406, col. 1839, 20 December 1944.
18. *Parliamentary Debates* (Commons), vol. 454, col. 592, 22 July 1948.
19. PRO: BT 64 95/4934.
20. Ibid., 14 February 1944.
21. Ibid.
22. This trend is described in Robert Hewison, *In Anger: Culture in the Cold War 1945–1960*, London, Weidenfeld and Nicolson, 1981, and in David Pryce-Jones, 'Towards the Cocktail Party' in Michael Sissons and Philip French (eds.), *Age of Austerity*, Harmondsworth, Penguin, 1964.
23. Allen and Unwin, 1948, 2nd edition 1963.
24. Harmondsworth, Penguin, 1944.
25. Ibid., p. 20.
26. Ibid., p. 12.
27. Mayer, *British Cinemas and Their Audiences*, p. 246.
28. Ibid., p. 244.
29. *Report of the Departmental Committee on Children and the Cinema*, Cmd. 7945, 1950, p. 47, para. 132.
30. *The Factual Film*, The Arts Enquiry, interim draft 1945, p. iv of digest and recommendations.
31. PRO: BT 64 2236, report from the Minister of Education.
32. Ibid.
33. *The Factual Film in Great Britain*, London, PEP, 1947, p. 32.
34. Ibid., p. 36.
35. British Film Academy, April 1948.
36. *Report of the Committee on the British Film Institute*, Cmd. 7361, April 1948, p. 3.
37. Ibid., p. 5, para. 11.
38. Ibid., p. 5, para. 13.
39. Interview with Basil Wright in Elizabeth Sussex, *The Rise and Fall of British Documentary*, London, University of California Press, 1975, p. 163.
40. Paul Rotha, 'Information Services and Documentary Film Makers', privately circulated memorandum, 1947, reprinted in *Rotha on the Film*, London,

Faber and Faber, 1958, p. 238.

41. Ibid., p. 240.

42. Interview with Basil Wright in Eva Orbanz, *Journey to a Legend and Back*, Berlin, Verlag Volker Spiess, 1977, p. 139.

43. Paul Rotha, 'Documentary is neither short nor long' in *Rotha on the Film*, pp. 228–9.

44. *Documentary News Letter*, vol. 5, no. 49, September 1945, p. 86.

45. PRO: CAB 124/1013.

46. Ibid.

47. Paul Rotha, 'The Government and the Film Industry' in *Rotha on the Film*, pp. 261–75.

9   Conflicts and Crises 1945–1949

1. PRO: BT 64 2188.

2. Paul Rotha, 'The Government and the Film Industry' in *Rotha on the Film*, London, Faber and Faber, 1958, p. 273.

3. PRO: CAB 132/2, LP (46) 57, 7 March 1946, memorandum by the President of the Board of Trade, p. 1, para. 3.

4. PRO: CAB 132/8, LP (47) 99, 12 June 1947.

5. Frederick Mullally, *Films, An Alternative to Rank*, London, Socialist Book Centre, 1946, p. 2.

6. Ralph Bond, *Monopoly, the Future of British Films*, London, ACT, 1946, p. 18.

7. Mullally, *Films*, p. 28.

8. Bond, *Monopoly*, p. 27.

9. Mullally, *Films*, p. 25.

10. Michael Balcon and others, *Twenty Years of British Films*, London, Falcon, 1947, p. 9.

11. *Recommendations of the Cinematograph Films Council for New Legislation on Cinematograph Films*, HMSO, 1947.

12. PRO: CAB 132/8, LP (47) 99, 12 June 1947.

13. PRO: CAB 132/6, LP (47) 18, 20 June 1947.

14. Peter Noble (ed.), *The British Film Yearbook*, 1946, p. 72.

15. Guy Morgan, *Red Roses Every Night*, London, Quality Press, 1948, p. 98.

16. Ibid., p. 72.

17. See for example *Kinematograph Weekly*, 6 January 1944, p. 3.

18. Jack Alicoate, 'The Cinema and Public Policy', *Cinématographie Française*, 29 December 1945, p. 87.

19. PRO: BT 64 2229.

20. PRO: FO 371/62315/8543, 17 September 1947.

21. *Parliamentary Debates* (Commons), vol. 415, col. 2539, 6 November 1945.

22. Ibid.

23. PRO: BT 64 204, 12 September 1946.

24. *Parliamentary Debates* (Commons), vol. 415, col. 1085, 6 November 1945.

25. *Kinematograph Weekly*, 9 January 1941, p. 32.

26. PRO: BT 64 2283, 21 August 1947.

27. PRO: BT 64 2284, 31 October 1947.

28. PRO: BT 64 95/4934.

29. Bond, *Monopoly*, p. 28.
30. *Documentary News Letter*, vol. 6, no. 59, October 1947, p. 110.
31. PRO: BT 64 4511, 5 January 1950.
32. PRO: BT 64 2283.
33. The three circuits would require only about 150 films altogether, running weekly single-feature programmes, whereas the requirement for half-weekly double-feature programmes was nearer 600 films.
34. Quoted in Morgan, *Red Roses Every Night*, pp. 100–01.
35. PRO: BT 64 204.
36. Ibid.
37. Ibid.
38. PRO: BT 64 2283.
39. PRO: CAB 129/19, CP (47) 174, 9 June 1947.
40. PRO: CAB 128/10, CM 67 (47) 2, 1 August 1947.
41. PRO: CAB 128/10, CM 69 (47) 2, 5 August 1947.
42. PRO: BT 64 2283, 29 August 1947.
43. *Parliamentary Debates* (Commons), vol. 443, col. 1464, 3 November 1947.
44. Ibid., cols. 1469 and 1470.
45. PRO: BT 64 2284.
46. PRO: BT 64 2370, 10 February 1948.
47. Ibid.
48. PRO: BT 64 2374.
49. *Variety*, 17 March 1948.
50. PRO: BT 64 2284.
51. *Daily Express*, 12 March 1948.
52. *Financial Times*, 15 March 1948.
53. *Daily Worker*, 12 March 1948.
54. *News Chronicle*, 12 March 1948.
55. Peter Forster, 'J. Arthur Rank and the Shrinking Screen' in Michael Sissons and Philip French (eds.), *Age of Austerity*, Harmondsworth, Penguin, 1964, pp. 294–6.
56. George Perry, *The Great British Picture Show*, London, Hart-Davis, MacGibbon, 1974, p. 137.
57. *The Listener*, 1 April 1948.
58. *Kinematograph Weekly*, 14 August 1947, p. 3.
59. *Kinematograph Weekly*, 18 November 1948, p. 4.
60. PRO: BT 64 4490, 4491 and 4492.
61. *Financial Times*, 8 November 1949.
62. *Manchester Guardian*, 2 December 1949.
63. *The British Film Industry*, PEP, 1952, p. 109.
64. *Sunday Times*, 25 January 1948.
65. *Financial Times*, 8 November 1949.
66. PRO: BT 64 2284.
67. *Kinematograph Weekly*, 14 February 1946, p. 7.
68. *Kinematograph Weekly*, 2 October 1947, p. 4.
69. *Kinematograph Weekly*, 17 June 1948, p. 11.
70. *Kinematograph Weekly*, 24 June 1948, p. 3.
71. *Kinematograph Weekly*, 16 December 1948, p. 177.

10   A Rescue Operation

1. Colin Cook, *Richard Stafford Cripps*, London, Hodder and Stoughton, 1957, p. 336.
2. *Screen*, vol. 22, no. 3, 1981. Interview with Sir Harold Wilson by Simon Hartog and Margaret Dickinson.
3. PRO: BT 64 2372, 23 January 1948.
4. Paul Foot, *The Politics of Harold Wilson*, Harmondsworth, Penguin, 1968, pp. 67–9.
5. PRO: BT 64 4466, minute of meeting, 7 February 1950.
6. Bernard Miles in *Film and Television Technician*, February 1981, p. 8.
7. PRO: CAB 128/17.
8. *The Times*, 1 May 1950.
9. *Daily Mail*, 28 March 1950.
10. *Motion Picture Herald*, 3 February 1951.
11. PRO: BT 64 4466.
12. See *The British Film Industry*, PEP, 1952, p. 106.
13. *Kinematograph Weekly*, 25 November 1948, p. 18.
14. *Report of the Working Party on Film Production Costs*, HMSO 1949, p. 17, para. 40.
15. *Kinematograph Weekly*, 1 December 1949, p. 7. Some idea of the attitudes of the civil servants involved may be conveyed by the remarks made by White about one of the names put forward by Equity, actress Rosamund John: 'Miss John, in my humble opinion, is a very charming and talented actress but from what I have seen of her screen personality (not perhaps a very good test but I am not privileged to be otherwise acquainted with her) I should not expect her to contribute much to the Working Party's deliberations.' PRO: BT 64 2435.
16. *Report of the Working Party on Film Production Costs*, p. 7, para. 11.
17. *Kinematograph Weekly*, 1 December 1949, p. 7, reprint of report.
18. Ibid.
19. PRO: BT 64 2426, BFPA memorandum.
20. PRO: BT 64 2372.
21. Later married to Michael Foot.
22. PRO: BT 64 2426.
23. Ibid.
24. Ibid.
25. *Report of the Committee of Inquiry on the Distribution and Exhibition of Cinematograph Films*, Cmd. 7837, HMSO 1949, p. 61, para. 22 of summary.
26. Ibid., p. 13, paras. 27–8.
27. Ibid., p. 15, para 33, and p. 17, paras. 38–9.
28. See PRO: BT 64 2426.
29. *Report*, Cmd. 7837, p. 19, paras. 40–2.
30. PRO: BT 64 2426, CEA memorandum, and *Report*, Cmd. 7837, p. 46, para. 114.
31. *Kinematograph Weekly*, 8 December 1949, p. 10.
32. *Report*, Cmd. 7837, p. 37, para. 87.
33. Ibid., p. 38, para. 90.
34. Ibid.
35. Lawrie had reservations about the report and commented: 'I have been less impressed than some of my colleagues with the desirability of maximising the producer's share on successful films at the expense of the less successful.' See

Kinematograph Weekly, 8 December 1949, p. 41.
36. *Report*, Cmd. 7837, p. 43, para. 108.
37. Nicholas Davenport, *Memoirs of a City Radical*, London, Weidenfeld and Nicolson, 1974, pp. 137 and 163.
38. Ibid., pp. 123–4.
39. PRO: BT 64 2366, Somervell, 2 April 1948.
40. *Screen*, no. 3, 1981, interview with Sir Harold Wilson.
41. *Kinematograph Weekly*, 22 July 1948, p. 3, and 29 July 1948, p. 3.
42. Davenport, *Memoirs*, p. 165.
43. PRO: BT 64 2366.
44. Davenport, *Memoirs*, p. 164.
45. PRO: BT 64 2366.
46. Davenport, *Memoirs*, p. 165.
47. Ibid.
48. PRO: BT 64 2366.
49. Karol Kulik, *Alexander Korda*, London, Allen and Unwin, 1975, p. 324. David Eady, Sir Wilfred's son, made two short films for London Films.
50. PRO: BT 64 4519.
51. *The British Film Industry*, PEP, 1952, p. 259.
52. Kulik, *Alexander Korda*, p. 325.
53. PRO: T 228/273, Eady's note, 31 May 1950.
54. Ibid., Reith's memorandum, 3 November 1950.
55. PRO: BT 64 4521, meeting between Wilson, Golt and Calder at the Board of Trade, 27 November 1950.
56. PRO: T 228/273.
57. Ibid., Reith to Wilson, 15 December 1950.
58. *The British Film Industry*, PEP, 1952, pp. 260–9 for following details.
59. Ibid., p. 262.
60. Richard Dyer McCann, *Sight and Sound*, vol. 46, no. 3, Summer 1977, p. 168.
61. *The British Film Industry*, PEP, 1952, p. 263.
62. Davenport, *Memoirs*, p. 166.
63. PRO: CAB 128/15.
64. PRO: BT 64 4515, 25 September 1949.
65. Ibid.
66. PRO: BT 64 4515, 4 October 1949.
67. Ibid.
68. *Parliamentary Debates* (Commons), vol. 476, col. 2545, 29 June 1950.
69. *Screen*, no. 3, 1981, interview with Sir Harold Wilson.
70. PRO: BT 64 4515, 25 September 1949.
71. PRO: BT 64 4468.
72. Ibid.
73. Ibid., ETU submission 30 January 1950 and Equity submission 31 January 1950.
74. ACT, 'The Film Crisis', resolution passed unanimously at a mass meeting on 20 November 1949.
75. Cinematograph Films Council, *Distribution and Exhibition of Cinematograph Films*, Recommendations to the President of the Board of Trade on the Report of the Committee of Enquiry, Report of the Committee of Trade Members, Board of Trade, HMSO 1950, p. 12.

76. *Parliamentary Debates* (Commons), vol. 470, col. 2694, 1 December 1949.

77. *The British Film Industry*, PEP, 1952, p. 127.

78. See Paul Leglise (ed.), *Le Cinéma d'Art et d'Essai*, Notes et études documentaires, no. 3839, 30 November 1971.

79. Anthony S. Gruner, *Daily Film Renter*, 30 December 1952, p. 15.

11   In Search of a Policy

1. A detailed analysis of the causes of the decline in cinema-going can be found in John Spraos, *The Decline of the Cinema*, London, Allen and Unwin, 1962. Spraos suggests that cinema closures considerably accelerated the trend, and that when a cinema closed 75 per cent of its audience was lost permanently.

2. See Patricia Perilli, 'Statistical Survey of the British Cinema Industry' in James Curran and Vincent Porter (eds.), *British Cinema History*, London, Weidenfeld and Nicolson, 1983, p. 382.

3. See Michael Jackson, 'Cinema versus Television', *Sight and Sound*, vol. 49, no. 3, Summer 1980.

4. Political and Economic Planning, 'The British Film Industry' in *Planning*, 1958, p. 141, and see Jackson, 'Cinema versus Television', p. 180.

5. Terence Kelly et al., *A Competitive Cinema*, London, Institute of Economic Affairs, 1966, pp. 56–7.

6. Vicki Eves, 'The Structure of the British Film Industry', *Screen*, vol. 11, no. 2, 1970, pp. 48–9.

7. Monopolies Commission, *Report on the supply of films for exhibition in cinemas*, HMSO, 1966, p. 59, para. 176.

8. *Film and Television Technician*, April 1965, p. 68.

9. Monopolies Commission, *Report*, op. cit.

10. *Monopolies and Restrictive Practices (Inquiry and Control)*, HMSO, 1948.

11. Monopolies Commission, *Report*, p. 87, para. 262.

12. Ibid.

13. Ibid., p. 80, para. 246.

14. *Film and Television Technician*, November 1966, p. 496.

15. Economic Intelligence Unit, *Retail Business*, 177, November 1972.

16. Vickers da Costa, *Entertainment Catering and Leisure Quarterly Review*, March 1979.

17. 1950 and 1958 figures are from PEP reports 1952 and 1958. 1970 figures are from ACTT, *Nationalising the Film Industry*, 1973, p. 12, para. 43, and Appendix IIIF, p. 43.

18. NFFC, 1972, Cmnd. 5080, p. 4, para. 16.

19. NFFC, 1970, Cmnd. 4402, p. 5, para. 17.

20. Janet Staiger, 'Individualism versus Collectivism', *Screen*, vol. 24, no. 4–5, July–October 1983.

21. Staiger, 'Individualism versus Collectivism', p. 71, and Jean-Claude Batz, *A propos de la crise de l'industrie du cinéma*, 1963, p. 14.

22. Thomas H. Guback, 'American Interests in the British Film Industry' in *Quarterly Review of Economics and Business*, 7, Summer 1967, p. 19.

23. Thomas H. Guback, 'Hollywood's International Market' in Tino Balio (ed.), *The American Film Industry*, Madison, University of Wisconsin Press, 1976, p. 401.

266

24. Monopolies Commission, *Report*, p. 73.

25. Guback, 'American Interests', pp. 15–16.

26. Ibid., p. 17, quoted from *Variety*, 4 May 1966.

27. Alexander Walker, *Hollywood England: The British Film Industry in the 1960s*, London, Michael Joseph, 1974, pp. 460–1.

28. Vincent Porter, 'Film Policy for the '80s: Industry or Culture?', *Sight and Sound*, vol. 48, no. 4, Autumn 1979, p. 222.

29. Penelope Houston, 'England, their England', *Sight and Sound*, vol. 35, no. 2, Spring 1966, p. 55.

30. Walker, *Hollywood England*, pp. 72–5 and 133–52.

31. Ibid., pp. 26-37.

32. Federation of British Film Makers, Annual Report, 1959, p. 4.

33. See Thomas H. Guback, *The International Film Industry*, Bloomington, Indiana University Press, 1969, pp. 118–20.

34. *Parliamentary Debates* (Lords), vol. 272, col. 372, 2 February 1966.

35. See Eves, 'The Structure of the British Film Industry', op. cit.

36. Perilli, 'Statistical Survey', Table 7, p. 378.

37. *Economist*, 4 November 1978, p. 86.

38. Walker, *Hollywood England*, pp. 444–50.

39. David Gordon, 'Why the Movie Majors are Major' in Balio (ed.), *The American Film Industry*, p. 464.

40. ACTT report, 1973, p. 20.

41. David Gordon, 'The Movie Majors', *Sight and Sound*, vol. 48, no. 3, Summer 1979.

42. Perilli, 'Statistical Survey', Table 8, p. 379.

43. Simon Perry, 'Finance for Local Talent', *Sight and Sound*, vol. 49, no. 3, Summer 1980.

44. Ibid.

45. Porter, 'Film Policy for the '80s', p. 223.

46. Penelope Houston in *Sight and Sound*, vol. 40, no. 4, Autumn 1971, p. 191.

47. *Sight and Sound*, vol. 48, no. 2, Spring 1979, p. 70.

48. For details of these developments see Simon Blanchard and Sylvia Harvey, 'The Post-war Independent Cinema – Structure and Organisation' in Curran and Porter (eds.), *British Cinema History*.

49. For the implications of Channel 4 see *Stills*, vol. 1, no. 5, and for a review of 'Film on 4' see Chris Auty, *Stills*, September–October 1983.

50. Interim Action Committee, *The Financing of the British Film Industry*, Cmnd. 7597, London, HMSO, 1979.

51. *The Future of the British Film Industry*, Report of the Prime Minister's Working Party, Cmnd. 6372, London, HMSO, 1976, p. 4.

52. Interim Action Committee, *Proposals for the setting up of a British Film Authority*, Cmnd. 7071, London, HMSO, 1978.

53. *The Financing of the British Film Industry*, p. 10.

54. Porter, 'Film Policy for the '80s', p. 266.

55. *Sight and Sound*, vol. 48, no. 2, Spring 1979, p. 73.

56. *Film Policy*, Cmnd. 9319, London, HMSO, 1984, p. 10.

57. *Sunday Times*, 8 April 1984, p. 34.

58. See Alan Stanbrook, 'When the lease runs out', *Sight and Sound*, vol. 53, no. 3, Summer 1984, pp. 172–3 for full details of the phasing out of capital allowances.

59. *Film Policy*, 1984.
60. Ibid., p. 12.
61. This report recommended that barring should be abolished and that the length of exclusive first-runs outside London's West End should be restricted. Ian Christie commented on these proposals as 'two sensible though perhaps largely symbolic measures which may prove as impractical as they will be ineffective in substantially helping independent exhibitors, without a government-backed development policy to help the cinema find its place in the multi-media future.' *(Sight and Sound*, vol. 52, no. 3, Summer 1983, p. 152).

Select Bibliography

1. Unpublished archival sources and special collections

Public Record Office, Kew Gardens, London: Board of Trade, Cabinet Office, Dominions Office, Foreign Office, Ministry of Labour, Ministry of Information and Treasury records.
Bank of England: Securities Management Trust records.
National Archives, Washington D.C.: US State Department, US Department of Commerce (Bureau of Foreign and Domestic Commerce) records.
British Film Institute library: special collections, Basil Dean and Sidney Carroll.

2. Official papers (HMSO)

Report of the Committee on Cinematograph Films (1936), Cmd. 5320.
Minutes of Evidence to the Committee on Cinematograph Films (1936).
Proposals for Legislation on Cinematograph Films (1937), Cmd. 5529.
Tendencies to Monopoly in the Cinematograph Film Industry: Report of a Committee appointed by the Cinematograph Films Council (1944).
Recommendations of the Cinematograph Films Council for new legislation on Cinematograph Films (1947).
Report of the Film Studio Committee (1948).
Distribution and Exhibition of Cinematograph Films: Report of Committee of Enquiry (1949), Cmd. 7839.
Structure and Trading Practices of the Film Industry: Recommendations of the Cinematograph Films Council (1964), Cmnd. 2324.
Report on the Supply of Films for Exhibition in Cinemas (Monopolies Commission), (1966), HC 206, 1966–7.
Review of Films Legislation: Report of the Cinematograph Films Council (1968), Cmnd. 3584.
The Future of the British Film Industry: Report of the Prime Minister's Working Party (1976), Cmnd. 6372.
Proposals for the setting up of a British Film Authority: Report of the Interim Action Committee (1978), Cmnd. 7071.
The Financing of the British Film Industry: Second Report of the Interim Action Committee (1979), Cmnd. 7597.
Film Policy (1984), Cmnd. 9319.
Parliamentary Debates, 5th Series (Hansard).
NFFC Annual Reports.
CFC Annual Reports.

3 Secondary sources

Arts Enquiry, *The Factual Film* (Oxford University Press, 1947).
Ashley, Walter, *The Cinema and the Public* (Nicolson and Watson, 1934).

269

Association of Cine-Technicians, *Film Business is Big Business* (ACT, 1939).

Balcon, Michael, *Michael Balcon presents . . . a Lifetime of Films* (Hutchinson, 1969).

Balio, Tino (ed.), *The American Film Industry* (University of Wisconsin Press, 1976).

Balio, Tino, *United Artists, the Company Built by the Stars* (University of Wisconsin Press, 1976).

Betts, Ernest, *The Film Business: A History of British Cinema, 1896–1972* (Allen and Unwin, 1973).

Inside Pictures, with some reflections from the outside (Cresset Press, 1960).

Bond, Ralph, *Monopoly: the future of British films* (ACT, 1946).

Box, Muriel, *Odd Woman Out: an autobiography* (Frewin, 1974).

Brunel, Adrian, *Nice Work: the story of 30 years in British film production* (Forbes Robertson, 1949).

Commission on Educational and Cultural Films, *The Film in National Life* (Allen and Unwin, 1932).

Crow, Duncan, 'The Protected Industry', series of articles in *Sight and Sound*, December 1950 – April 1951, vol. 19, nos. 8–12.

Curran, James and Porter, Vincent (eds.), *British Cinema History* (Weidenfeld and Nicolson, 1983).

Davenport, Nicholas, *Memoirs of a City Radical* (Weidenfeld and Nicolson, 1974).

Dean, Basil, *The Mind's Eye: an autobiography, 1927–1972* (Hutchinson 1972).

Dickinson, Margaret and Hartog, Simon, interview with Sir Harold Wilson in *Screen*, vol. 22, no. 3, 1981.

Eves, Vicki, 'The structure of the British film industry' in *Screen*, vol. 2, no. 1, 1970.

Foot, Paul, *The Politics of Harold Wilson* (Penguin, 1968).

Golden, Nathan D., *Review of Foreign Film Markets, 1938* (US Dept. of Commerce, 1939).

Gruner, Anthony S., 'The Eady Scheme', *Daily Film Renter*, 30 December 1952.

Guback, T. H., *The International Film Industry* (Indiana, 1969).

Hardy, Forsyth, *John Grierson, A Documentary Biography* (Faber and Faber, 1979).

Korda, Michael, *Charmed Lives: A Family Romance* (Random House, 1979).

Kulik, Karol, *Alexander Korda, the man who could work miracles* (Allen and Unwin, 1975).

Low, Rachael, *The History of the British Film, 1918–29* (Allen and Unwin, 1971).

Documentary and Educational Films of the 1930s (Allen and Unwin, 1979).

MacCann, Richard Dyer, 'Subsidy for the Screen: Grierson and Group 3, 1951–55', *Sight and Sound*, vol. 46, no. 3, 1977.

Morgan, Guy, *Red Roses Every Night* (Quality Press, 1948).

Mullally, Frederick, *Films – an alternative to Rank* (Socialist Book Centre, 1946).

Political and Economic Planning, *The British Film Industry* (PEP, 1952)

'The British Film Industry, 1958', *Planning*, 24, no. 424, 23 June 1958.

Rotha, Paul, *Rotha on the Film* (Faber and Faber, 1958).

Rowson, Simon, 'The value of remittances abroad for cinematograph films', *Journal of the Royal Statistical Society*, 1934.

'The Future of the Films Act', paper to the CEA's Annual Conference, 1935 (BFI Library).

'A Statistical Survey of the cinema industry in Great Britain in 1934', *Journal of the Royal Statistical Society*, 1936.

Spraos, John, *The Decline of the Cinema: an Economist's Report* (Allen and Unwin, 1962).

Street, Sarah, 'The Hays Office and the Defence of the British Market in the 1930s', *Historical Journal of Film, Radio and Television*, vol. 5, no. 1, 1985.

Walker, Alexander, *Hollywood England: the British Film Industry in the 1960s* (Michael Joseph, 1974).

Wilcox, Herbert, *Twenty-five Thousand Sunsets* (Bodley Head, 1967).

Wood, Alan, *Mr. Rank* (Hodder and Stoughton, 1952).

Index

274

276